MW00514032

To John Hess with my best regards and best wishes October 22, 2001 Michael Kosztarab

Transylvanian Roots

The True Life Adventures of a Hungarian-American

by
Michael Kosztarab

with ethnographic illustrations by
Zoltán Albert

Pocahontas Press, Inc.
Blacksburg, Virginia

Transylvanian Roots: The True Life Adventures of a Hungarian-American
    by Michael Kosztarab
    with ethnographic illustrations by Zoltán Albert
    Cover art by Levente Csutak
Published in the United States of America by Pocahontas Press, Inc.,
    Blacksburg, Virginia
Printed and bound in the United States of America by
    McNaughton & Gunn, Saline, Michigan.

ISBN 0-936015-72-1 – softcover. ISBN 0-936015-75-6 – hardcover.
    First printing 1997

Library of Congress Cataloging-in Publication Data:

Kosztarab, Michael, 1927 –
    Transylvanian roots : The true life adventures of a Hungarian-American / by Michael Kosztarab : with ethnographic illustrations by Zoltán Albert.
        p.   cm.
    Includes bibliographical references and index.
    ISBN 0-936015-75-6 (alk. paper)
    1. Kosztarab, Michael, 1927–   . 2. Hungarian Americans -- Biography. I. Title.
    E184.H95K66   1997
    973'.00494511'0092--dc21
    [B]   97-36397
                                                                            CIP

Dedication

My reason for writing this book is the same now in 1997 as was Orbán's in 1863: "There are few places in Europe so poorly known to outsiders as Transylvania is. Within this land, the Switzerland of East Central Europe, how many people know about the existence of the Land of the Seklers *(Székelys)*? The reason for writing this book ..." I have also translated Orbán's (1863) heartfelt dedication to his six volumes on Transylvania, because I also believe in the same principles: "My soul and heart is filled with respect and fraternity toward all the nationalities living in this land, and with the hope of betterment I cast the veil of forgiveness and reconciliation on the mistakes of the past — but I have no power to silence the unbiased voice of history."

In the 1930s the poet Attila József, also of Transylvanian ancestry, expressed well the same feelings in the last four lines of his famous poem "At the Danube" (Translated by Gyorgyi Voros):

The battles our ancestors fought
memory resolves to peace;
at the last, to settle our common affairs
is our duty: and it is no small task.

The famous Romanian historian Nicolae Bălcescu writes in his "Istoria Romanilor," on page 312: "The problem in Transylvania was not, and is not, how the Romanians, the Hungarians, the Saxon-Germans or the Székelys must proceed in order that they alone rule this land and eliminate the others, but how to find ways among themselves toward the possibilities of harmony within the framework of a federative state, in which equal rights may be enjoyed by all individuals just as by all nations." (Published in Bucharest, 1902.)

So, I dedicate this book to all the people of Transylvania who learned throughout the centuries to live in peace and to respect each other, despite their different religions and ethnic backgrounds.

About the Cover —

Carved wooden gates, as pictured on the cover, are characteristic of Sekler (Székely) folk art. The central entryway is large enough for hay-filled wagons to pass through. Just below the wood-shingled roof are nesting holes for pigeons. Underneath is carved the greeting: "Blessing to those entering. Peace to those departing." Over the small door the builders would inscribe their names and the date of construction, much like the words found on the cornerstone of a public building.

Here, the artist has left his mark:

"Prepared by Levente Csutak, Braşov — 1981."

Contents

Other Books by Michael Kosztarab —

Scale Insects of Northeastern North America: Identification, Biology, and Distribution. Martinsville: Virginia Museum of Natural History. Special Publication No. 3. 650 pages.

Scale Insects of Central Europe. Academic Publishers (Hungary) and Junk Company, (Holland). 456 pages, 2 editions. With F. Kozár.

Systematics of the North American Insects and Arachnids: Status and Needs. Virginia Agricultural Experiment Station, Information Series 90–1. 247 pages. Edited with C. W. Schaefer.

Introduction and Acknowledgments

With this book the author tries to make up for promises carried for 40 years — that is, to tell family members and friends about his unusual life, interwoven with the fate of many Transylvanians, whom he considers among the most misunderstood and mistreated people of the world.

Transylvania may appear to be a fictional place to many readers, and usually ties in with Dracula stories in many minds. The author, a native of this enchanted land, through his own biographical sketch, familiarizes the reader with its unique multicultural people and their customs. Transylvania in many ways resembles Switzerland in that both have several cultures speaking three or four different languages. Few people know that, after the City of Geneva, the independent principality of Transylvania was the first to adopt a policy of religious tolerance, while later most of Europe was engaged in the 30-year religious wars. Thus, Transylvania became the easternmost bastion of Protestantism in Europe, with Calvinists, Lutherans, and Unitarians living together with Roman, Armenian, and Uniate Catholics, Jews, and Eastern Orthodox Christians. The author as a youngster received indoctrination in four of these religions.

Besides being informative, the book also includes some exciting stories. Such are the author's three escapes, one from the Nazis and two from the Communists. He was arrested under both dictatorships, and had to smuggle his 7-month-old daughter to the free world in a bundle of old clothes. His experiences in helping Jews to escape deportation to extermination camps, on a smaller scale, is somewhat similar to the story told in the book and film *Schindler's List*.

Because Transylvania is often recognized through stories about Dracula, that subject is also summarized here. And, a number of trips to foreign countries and across the United States while pursuing professional goals make the accounts more interesting.

Each chapter by itself tells a complete story, but for a better understanding of the events, the reader is advised to start from the beginning. The first two chapters may appear chronologically out of place, for they cover events that happened after those detailed in Chapter 10; the author chose to place what he felt to be the most exciting "chapters" of his life first, hoping the reader, having read these two escape stories, would want to learn more about life in the four areas of the world (Transylvania, Bucharest, Budapest, and the United States) that led to many unusual and often adventurous events.

Most of the characters described are still alive; when possible, with their permission, their real names are used. For an easy overview, family relationships are given in a family tree in the Addendum of this book. The author gives thanks to them all for the privilege to use their names in this book, and to the same persons who read parts of the manuscript and gave advice while it was being prepared. The line drawings were prepared by Zoltán Albert, and the drawing of Seklers' gate used on the cover was prepared by Levente Csutak. Both artists are from Braşov in Transylvania. The maps and photographs are, with two exceptions, from the author's personal collection. For readers who want to learn more about the history of Transylvania and its people, a "Cited References" list is provided. Searching for topics or persons of special interest is made easy with the "Index."

Special thanks are extended to the author's wife, Tili, who made pleasant the environment for writing the manuscript, to other relatives and friends who read and criticized pertinent sections of the manuscript, and to Siegfried Hill, who pre-edited and typed the first draft. Heartfelt thanks are due to Stephen Sisa, who provided consultation to the author on the brief "History of Transylvania" section, and to Gyorgyi Voros who corrected and edited the second draft and made numerous valuable suggestions. For the final editing and many improvements, the author is indebted to Mary Holliman, Lisa Johnson, and David Bruce Wallace of Pocahontas Press in Blacksburg, Virginia. The author takes sole responsibility for the final printed text.

Pronunciation (in <u>bold</u>) of Foreign Language Letters

— Often with Phonetic Symbols —

Hungarian

a	=	as in	s**a**w
á	=	as in	f**ar**, h**ear**t
cs	=	as in	**ch**icken, **ch**ief
e	=	as in	**e**l**e**m**e**nt
é	=	as in	gr**ea**t, m**ai**l
gy	=	as in	**du**ke
j	=	as in	e**y**e
ly	=	as in	**y**ear, **y**es
ny	=	as in	**n**ew
ö	=	as in	g**ir**l, h**er**
s	=	as in	**sh**are
sz	=	as in	**s**ound
ty	=	as in	**tu**ne
ü	=	as in	men**u**
zs	=	as in	mea**s**ure

Romanian

ă	=	as in	**ea**rth
c	=	as in	**k**ill
ce	=	as in	**ch**eck
ci	=	as in	**chee**se
ghe	=	as in	**ge**orge
ghi	=	as in	**gy**psy
î	=	as in	**ea**rth
j	=	as in	**j**ournal
ş	=	as in	**sh**oulder
ţ	=	as in	**ts**ar

Saxon/German

ä	=	as in	f**ai**r
j	=	as in	**y**ear, **y**es
ö	=	as in	g**ir**l, h**er**
sch	=	as in	**sh**oulder
ü	=	as in	men**u**
v	=	as in	**f**ox
z	=	as in	ro**s**e

1 — Escape to Freedom (1956)

The early morning sky over Budapest was dark with clouds. A misty fine rain was falling and washing the almost empty blood-stained streets. Only some Soviet soldiers, with gloomy faces, were slowly removing the cobblestones used for barricades against their troops and tanks by the freedom fighters just a few days earlier. It was the 18th of November 1956. The Hungarian nation was on general strike against the Soviet invaders and their puppet Hungarian government, which had been organized on Soviet soil and sent to "pacify" the Nation.

The mighty 800,000-member Communist Party (called the Hungarian Workers Party) had shrunk to just 30,000 members between October 25 and November 3. During those few days people, not fearing to express their true convictions, joined the many other parties that sprang up.

The country had been free for only ten days. The Hungarian Revolutionary Government waited for the United Nations to respond to its request to declare Hungary a neutral nation, and help negotiate the withdrawal of Soviet troops from Hungary. Unfortunately, U.N. recognition never reached the Hungarians. The major western powers were preoccupied with the Suez Canal crisis, and the Soviets were able to take advantage of the situation. Initially they gave the impression of willingness to free the Hungarians from Soviet domination; they even recalled some troops from Hungary. Unfortunately, Premier Khrushchev and the other Soviet leaders must have realized that allowing the Hungarian nation independence would precipitate a chain reaction among other satellite nations. At that time, there were popular movements against Soviet domination in East Berlin and Warsaw, and — according to Romanian radio reports — demonstrations had been started by ethnic Hungarians living there against Communism in Transylvania.

Khrushchev instructed his trusted trouble shooter, Ambassador Andropov, to organize in Budapest a series of plots that would bring Hungary back under tight Soviet control. First, Andropov invited the new Hungarian Chief of the Revolutionary Army, Colonel Maléter, to a Soviet military camp at Tököl, just outside Budapest, to sign a treaty for the peaceful removal of Soviet troops and their families from Hungary. Maléter went, but he and his staff were trapped, arrested by Serov, Chief of the Soviet Secret Service, and executed in 1958.

Next, during a 24-hour period, the Soviets moved new troops back into the country, especially to Budapest, where the main resistance was expected. At 4 a.m. Sunday morning, November 4, 1956, Soviet planes started dropping bombs over the city to crush the revolt, intimidate the population, and create panic. The bombs were followed by Soviet tanks which took over the city and destroyed many buildings where pockets of resistance existed.

Young students, some only 15 or 16 years old, and factory workers were fighting the invaders on the streets, from buildings, and from behind hastily built barricades of cobblestones. The freedom fighters had only small firearms and Molotov cocktails to use against the mighty tanks. Many of them died on the streets. Their futile fight slowed as they ran out of ammunition. The tanks reached the Danube River, where the picturesque Gothic Parliament building (Fig. 1) had provided refuge for members of the new free Hungarian government. The building was surrounded by Soviet troops by the afternoon of November 4th. From among the members of the Revolutionary government, István Bibo remained in the Parliament. He had just prepared a proclamation to the Nation,

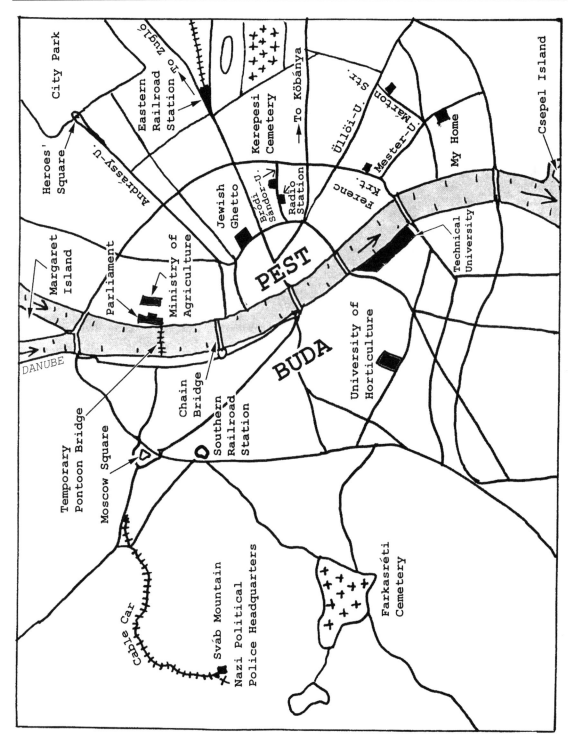

Figure 1. Section of Budapest where most events mentioned in the text took place.

and a radio message to U.S. President Eisenhower, when the Soviet soldiers entered the building.

Some Soviet soldiers, who got out of their tanks at the Parliament for their first sight of the Danube, asked if it was the Suez Canal. They had been told before deployment that they would be sent to the Suez Canal to secure it for Egypt against the imperialist western powers. Most of these new soldiers were from the far eastern provinces of the Soviet Union, and had been sent to replace the Ukrainian and Russian soldiers, who had lived in Hungary long enough to sympathize with the freedom fighters and provide guns for them.

The next ploy by Soviet Ambassador Andropov had been to lure the members of the Hungarian government out of the Yugoslavian Embassy, where they had sought political asylum. His office assured them all, including Prime Minister Imre Nagy, that they would be safe to leave the Embassy. The Hungarians boarded the buses provided for this move on November 22nd. Just a few blocks away, the buses were stopped by Russian tanks. All passengers were arrested, taken to Romania, and later many, including Nagy, were brought back to Hungary and executed in 1958. In a few years, Andropov was rewarded for "bringing peace to Hungary" by being named Premier of the USSR.

During the ten days of freedom, there had been no public transportation, so I had walked across town to my office three times. The streets were filled with debris from the fights. Many of the buses and streetcars that had been used for barricades were badly damaged. During my walks I saw dead Soviet soldiers and temporary burial grounds for the freedom fighters in public squares and parks. Destroyed automobiles and Soviet tanks were also a common sight. Citizens wandered among the wreckage, lining up for bread or other essentials. To help the freedom fighters and the city residents, some farming towns sent truckloads of vegetables and other staples which were being given away free at public squares.

While visiting at my University, I found a number of students armed with small firearms taking turns in guarding the entrances to our university buildings. They volunteered to keep away possible prowlers, who might damage or pillage our research equipment, laboratory facilities, or materials stored there. I was impressed by their concern, and when I expressed my admiration, I was invited to join them and take my turn to fill gaps in their guarding schedule. But I had to confess that I did not know how to use their guns if needed. So I was seated with a group and the students demonstrated to me the use of their small firearms. Because of the sudden re-invasion of Budapest by Soviet troops, I did not have to participate in the guarding duties. After the Communists returned to power, all the students and young faculty who participated as volunteers in guarding the University were accused of bearing arms against the Communists and the Soviet troops, and were dismissed from the University. Many were also arrested.

Despite the carnage, the Nation was in a state of euphoria after having waited 11 years for freedom. In their entire history the Hungarians had probably never been more united than at this time. People experienced a collective moral cleansing. Everyone volunteered to help those in greater need. Because many homes and apartments had been destroyed during the Revolution, many families were homeless. To help them, large wicker baskets were placed behind broken shop windows with signs asking for donations for the homeless. I have never seen such large piles of paper currency as those that accumulated by late afternoon each day before November 4th, when crews in trucks collected the donations. Everyone felt responsible for the needy, and no one thought of taking advantage of the unguarded money.

My entomologist's heart was broken one day, when walking on the streets of Pest in the rain, I ran into a group of fellow entomologists pulling and pushing a cart filled with insect boxes. They were salvaging parts of the precious, 100-year-old research collections that had been drenched when bombs and ensuing fire destroyed the roof and top floor of the museum.

I never forgave myself for not jumping in to help them, but my first obligation was to my family. We needed food, and our five-month-old daughter, Eva, needed milk. Milk had become a very rare and precious commodity, and only through farm connections were we able to purchase some. My office in Buda (Fig. 1) was about eight miles from my home in Pest, on the other side of the Danube. Because we had no public transportation, I had to walk. One good reason for walking there was to receive part of my month's salary in invaluable staple food, in short supply in the city. I had also received from my department head (Balás) the folder with my socio-political background that contained many notes from Communist Party trustees/agents. The Personnel Departments were raided during the few days of freedom, and their material distributed. Now I had a chance to read opinions from a number of people in my office and neighborhood.

Tili's parents had just arrived home from vacation when the activities resulting in the revolution started. On the evening of Monday, October 22, I participated in the meeting organized by the University students held at the Technical University (Fig. 1) just a few blocks from my working place. The students' demands — originally 13 points that were later expanded to 16 — were put together, and a peaceful demonstration march leading to the Polish Embassy was planned for the next day.

Although requested, no permission had yet been received from the police. The students insisted that we would have the march even without approval. Apparently the Mighty Party leadership could not make up their minds. But after realizing that they couldn't stop it, the ban was lifted by early afternoon on Tuesday, October 23. Thousands of students showed up on the square next to the Technical University. I joined them with other young faculty. We carried only the Hungarian flag while shouting such slogans as "Freedom for Hungary", but later, as the crowd warmed up, we included

"Down with the Soviet Occupation." Soon, our flags had a round hole in the center. Someone had suggested the removal of its Communist Emblem.

Our group walked north, along the western bank of the Danube, to reach the statue of General Bem, a Polish-born patriot of the 1848 Revolution. The crowd's enthusiasm and determination increased after the 16 points were read and Peter Veres, my idol and in 1956 the Writers' Union president, made a speech and read his Union's seven-point declaration. As the crowd proceeded to walk to the Parliament, I decided to go home and allay my family's worries. I was already overdue for my usual supper date, and my family might have been wondering about my whereabouts in the middle of the anti-government demonstrations. I had not realized that enroute I had used the last streetcar transportation for many weeks to come. At home I climbed to the attic and rolled out the family's Hungarian flag, and with much joy I displayed it from our flagpole. For days we were glued to the radio because no newspapers were printed during that time.

We learned from the radio, and later from eye-witnesses, that the demonstrating crowds reached the Budapest Radio Station (Fig. 1), demanding the reading of the students' 16 points. After refusal, the Secret Police (AVH) started shooting into the crowd. The students were soon supplied with small firearms by regular soldiers sent to reinforce the Radio Station.

So the Revolution started. Several book shops that carried Russian books were broken into and their contents burned on the street. The hated Stalin statue was broken into souvenir pieces. The next morning (Wednesday, October 24) the Russian troops with tanks moved into the center of the city and opened fire without provocation on unarmed civilians. So Hell broke loose on the streets. But the following day a number of Soviet soldiers with tanks made peace with the demonstrators and provided the crowd with transportation to the Parliament Square. Here they were shot at by the AVH and the Soviet tanks sympathetic to the AVH that were waiting there.

With his speech, Gerö, the hated Prime Minister, instead of calming, further inflamed the Nation. Finally, he was removed and Imre Nagy, on popular demand, took over the leadership; a cease-fire was signed on the 28th. After much destruction and thousands of dead, all fighting came to an end by the 30th of October. The Soviets repeatedly promised withdrawal of troops from Hungary, but instead they brought in more and only inside Budapest gave the impression that they were gone.

Nagy hurriedly put through a number of important actions. He and the Council of Ministers abolished the one-party system on October 30. On November 1, after realizing that more Soviet troops had entered Hungary and that the Soviet government had broken their agreement, Hungary withdrew from the Warsaw Treaty. Later, during the same afternoon, neutrality was declared for Hungary and the government asked the U.N. and major western powers to officially accept the changed status. Instead, Nagy was betrayed by some Communist members of his Cabinet, like Kádár, when it was broadcast late that evening (Nov. 1) that the Hungarian Socialist Workers Party had been formed. On November 6th, the same group formed a new counter government at Szolnok (actually it was believed that it was formed on Russian soil). So the Nation went on strike against Kádár's Puppet Government.

After November 10, through Radio Free Europe and Voice of America, we had become aware that there was no hope for an independent Hungary after the invasion by the Soviet troops. Also, I learned at work, at the University of Horticulture, that some of our colleagues and students had been picked up by the agents of the new illegal Kádár government, with help from Soviet troops. Many ended up in jails without a trial, or in concentration camps set up for the freedom fighters and sympathizers of the short-lived revolt.

Although I did not fight on the streets, my family had openly supported the Revolution. Therefore, we could also be incarcerated or, at best, both lose our jobs. Almost all intellectuals were employed by the mighty Communist government. Because our future in Hungary looked so bleak, Tili and I decided around November 15th to leave Hungary and start a new life in the West, as far as possible from the Soviet border. Unless you were a Party member, there was no possibility of future advances in your profession. Even college education was restricted to a select few, and the Party had the final word in admissions.

Losing a job meant that you would be "black-listed" and no other position as an intellectual would be available in the country for you. Apartments were also controlled by the government. We had to share the home of my wife's parents, with no hope of renting an apartment of our own.

If I stayed in Hungary and outlived the persecutions facing the sympathizers of the Revolution, to keep my job as a faculty member at the University, I would have to join the Communist Party. I had already been told by the University Party Leadership, before the Revolution, that it was expected from me to become a member of the Party. They used the argument that because of my good work performance, my social background as the son of a state railroad-shop worker, and my reputation as one who had resisted the Nazi occupation by helping Jews to escape from incarceration in the Ghetto, I was predestined to become a good Party member. What they did not tell me was that because there was no Party member in our Department of Entomology, and all Departments had to have at least one, they needed me to take the role in becoming the local contact, who often served as the trusted political agent for the Party. Such agents had to spy on the rest of the employees and provide reports to the Party on their political activities, thoughts, religious beliefs, even their friends.

This was the alternative choice left for me to be able to keep my job as a university faculty member. But I did not want this choice. I felt sorry for letting down my students by leaving. The students in my classes trusted me and liked my teaching methods. They had put up my name twice in three years for meritorious teaching awards, which I had received.

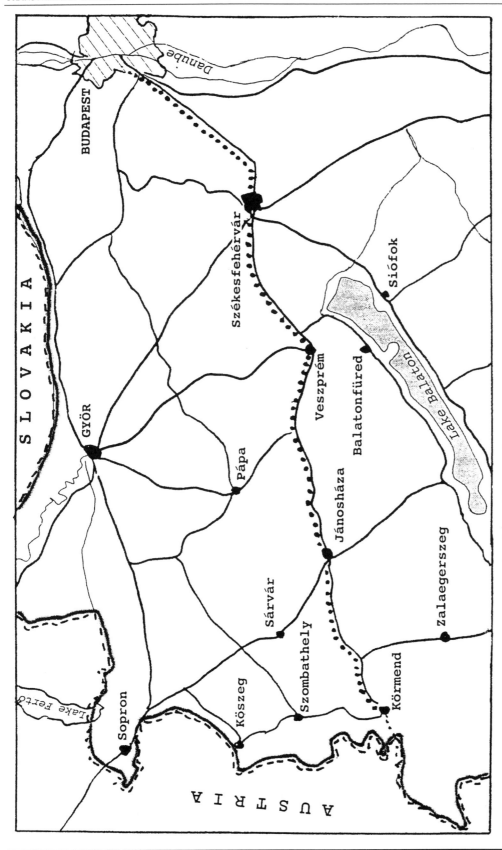

Figure 2. Western Hungary. The dotted line indicates our escape route to Körmend.

The other reason for leaving the country was that Tili and I heavily considered the future of our only child. As an adult would she face the same political harassment and uncertainties under a Communist system which we did? We both thought that she deserved a better future.

The news of our decision to leave the country caused heartache to our parents. They were concerned about the safety of their only granddaughter, 5-month-old Eva. They begged us not to risk her health on such a risky adventure. Because of the general strike, we would have neither medical services nor public transportation available to us. We expected to have to travel to the border, 250 kilometers away, in an open pick-up truck at the end of November.

It was an agonizing choice to make, and caused us some sleepless nights. To ease our minds, we discussed the alternatives between ourselves and also with Tili's parents. To avoid more heartache, I was afraid to tell my own mother, or anyone else except my father, about our plans. Should we risk Eva's health and relative safety by taking her on the road, with the many uncertainties facing us? What if we were arrested by the Soviets while trying to escape to Austria, and were taken with our baby daughter to jail, or worse, shipped to a Soviet prison camp? We would never forgive ourselves for risking her life with such an adventure. If we left her behind with Tili's parents, she would be kept in the same safe environment, with her grandparents who adored her and had helped to care for her for five months already. Her daily supply of milk was also assured by then. It was in the news that families who had been separated due to the events of the Revolution, would have help from the International Red Cross to be reunited. We did not realize at that time that the new Communist Government resisted reunification of the separated families for about five years if parents left for the West.

After much soul-searching, we agreed to leave little Eva in the care of my wife's parents until we could find a safe way for her to join us.

My wife's nephew, Laci, was able to secure a pick-up truck with a canvas-covered bed. He also obtained official travel papers for our destination, the western border town of Körmend, which bordered the only non-Communist country, Austria. One of my colleagues working in the Russian Language Department of our university typed a Russian language travel order on university stationery for me, to go to Körmend to pick up some equipment for the university. On a last-minute impulse, I stuffed two foreign letters into an inside pocket . These were the last letters I had received from two American entomologist colleagues. I thought that after we reached freedom, these letters might help with our immigration process, because we had no relatives in America to serve as required sponsors.

Tili and I boarded the back of the truck with some other refugees on the 19th of November. On the way we were repeatedly stopped by policemen checking all vehicles traveling west. They didn't question our documents, although we were dressed suspiciously for the short trip to Körmend. Also the size and contents of our luggage could have revealed our true intentions. We were relieved at each stop when the policeman accepted our stories. Actually, they were sympathetic and lenient towards refugees.

After several hours, we approached Körmend (Fig. 2), and I thought we could relax. But at that point, at a hidden curve in the road, we encountered some Soviet soldiers. They stepped out and stopped our truck, demanding passes and other documents from us. Apparently, my carefully prepared "official" Russian papers did not impress them. They must have realized from our luggage that we were heading to Austria. So they ordered all of us to board their own truck for further interrogation at their military headquarters in Körmend. Reluctantly, we boarded the back of their open truck, huddling together in the cold wind under the watchful eye of one soldier who sat in the back with us.

I realized that we would soon be carefully searched for weapons and incriminating documents. I got really scared when I remembered that I had the two American letters in my inside pocket, one even with the official seal of the U.S. government. Finding such a letter, even if they could not read English, would be sufficient evidence to incriminate me as a spy, and they might shoot me on the spot. So while the guard was carefully rolling his home-made cigarette, I tore the letter from Professor Gordon F. Ferris of Stanford University into tiny pieces and, covering my mouth, I chewed and swallowed every last piece.

Encouraged by having successfully dispensed with one letter, but not knowing how long our ride would last, I started to work on the second one. I also broke it into small scraps and had taken my first mouthful when I ran into a problem. I could not swallow the parchment-like U.S. government stationery that probably contained 50% rag, making it indigestible. So I removed the slimy paper scraps and put these back into my coat pocket. Just at that moment we arrived at the Soviet military headquarters.

I badly wanted to destroy the last crumpled scraps of paper before being searched. My opportunity came when we stepped down from the truck in front of a three-story building and I noticed that our truck made deep tracks in the muddy road. When our guard took his eyes off us and looked toward a new group of soldiers coming to replace him, I dropped the pieces of the letter in the muddy tracks behind the truck. Without bending down, I used my foot to cover the last scraps with mud.

My sense of relief did not last long! An officer came out of the building and walked straight to our group. With an angry red face he ordered me to retrieve what I had just buried in the mud. He must have been watching our group from behind the curtains of the window of his office. I had no choice, especially since a pistol was pointing at me, but to collect the muddy scraps of my letter received from Dr. Harold Morrison, scale insect specialist of the U.S. Department of Agriculture. If he had only used onion-skin paper, it would have been safely inside my stomach by then, instead of the sensation of butterflies. After seeing the pitiful-looking results of my digging, a handful of muddy paper scraps, the officer ordered us to be taken to the town police station so that the Hungarian police could figure out what I had been hiding from them. With Soviet guards in front and behind us, our group walked to the local police station.

The police station faced the street, with a gate and an entrance-way on the left. It had a large fenced-in courtyard with a small outhouse in the rear. We entered the courtyard and waited as a group for interrogation. The policeman who guarded us carried into the station my handful of mud-soaked evidence. I would have liked to sink into the ground instead of facing a likely beating and incarceration without trial.

While we were waiting, we noticed people using the outhouse at the end of the courtyard. It occurred to us that we might try to escape while pretending to use that toilet. So when the outhouse became empty, Tili and I approached it. But, instead of entering, we hid behind the small structure, where we noticed a hole in the tall wooden fence. It was just large enough for a person to squeeze through.

When the policeman guarding our group appeared to be preoccupied, Tili made the short dash in front of me and got through the hole. I followed close behind her, and tried to do the same. But because I had a bulging back-pack and a suitcase in my hand, I stumbled and made a loud noise with my heavy shoes. As I was straightening up, the guard shouted and ordered us to stop. He also called for help from inside the building to catch us. Instead of stopping, we ran into the neighbors' yard. Instead of running down the street through the gate, we chose to run down into the farm cellar (Fig. 3) through the open door just in front of us. With our hearts beating fast, we hid in the darkest corner, behind a wooden trough.

The policemen running after us asked the people living in the house, Mr. and Mrs. László Dékán, if they had seen us. They said they had and that we had gone down to the street. The policemen followed our empty tracks. Dékán and his wife must have seen us running into

*Figure 3. The Dékáns'
house, showing the
door to the cellar,
inviting us to hide.*

their cellar. But Dékán was a shoe-repairman in the town, and a Communist Party member, so the police would not question his word. We were always grateful for their help, especially since in those days, soon after the lost Revolution, it was a punishable offense to give help to refugees.

After dark, Mrs. Dékán came down and offered us upstairs home for the night. They also served us our first meal since morning. After learning about our determination to escape from Hungary, the Dékáns offered some useful advice. We were told that because the town streets are patrolled day and night, we should not carry all our belongings. They offered to mail whatever we left behind to our parents. Later we learned that they had kept that promise. Without a suitcase and backpack and with appropriate clothing, we could mix with the local folks. So the next day we doubled all the clothes we wore, and took extra socks in Tili's small shopping bag. Mrs. Dékán, who as a Jew had probably had similar experiences during the Nazi occupation, led us to the western end of the town that evening, by walking just 30 feet ahead of us. There she pointed to the trail that would take us to the next town, Horvátnádalja, where a young man was known to lead refugees to the Austrian border. We waved good-by and followed the trail.

Soon we found a large German shepherd that could have belonged to the police, sitting in the middle of our trail. Frightened, we walked in a long semicircle in the potato fields to avoid the dog. By the time we reached the first houses of the next village it was pitch dark. We debated about entering the first or the second house to ask for directions to our guide. Thank God we entered the second house, because we learned later that a trusted Communist policeman was living in the first. The local folks told us that a recently imposed regulation prohibited foot traffic after dark in the towns along the Austrian border.

After receiving directions, we walked close to the walls, ready to jump into dark doorways if anyone approached. We found at Horvátnádalja (Fig. 4) the house and our guide, Zoltán. He greeted us with some apprehension. He told us that the chance of escape had just worsened, because on that day, November 20, the Soviet troops had taken over patrolling the border because they did not trust the Hungarian soldiers. Therefore, he suggested that we wait until the following evening, so he could learn the new routine used by the Soviets during their patrol.

We were disappointed! We had already spent one night close to the border with the Dékáns, and now we would have to accept Zoltán's hospitality for one more night. We

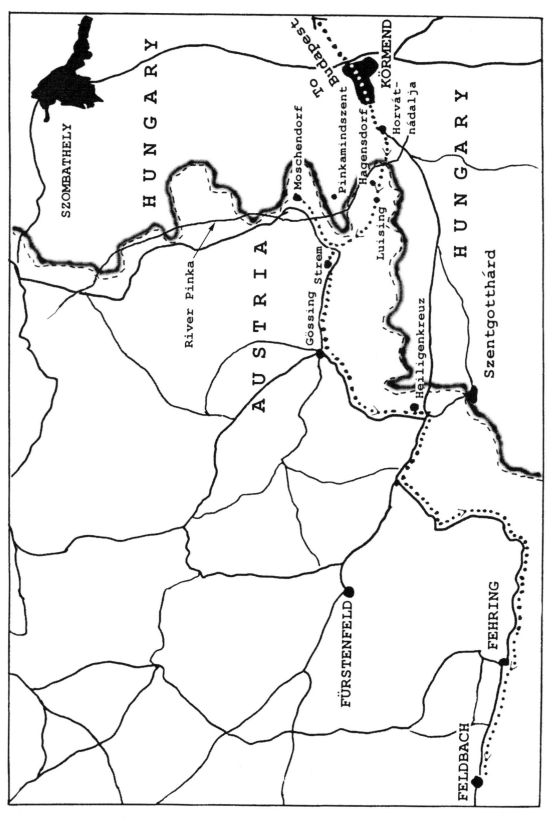

Figure 4. The section of the Hungarian-Austrian border across which we escaped.

were offered bread, milk, and salami. Soon Gábor, a trusted young friend of Zoltán's, arrived. Gábor, who was also helping people to the border, had a couple with him in the yard and was ready to take a chance that night. He said that he had already explored the routine used by the soldiers on patrol and was sure we would pull through. All this gave us back our lost confidence, especially when Zoltán agreed to accompany Gábor. The two guides walked about 60 meters ahead of us, and the four of us followed. Each time they reached a street corner, a bridge, or another crossing point, they checked first for possible patrols and, when satisfied, they waved for us to follow them. While in the open fields, we often had to flatten ourselves on the ground while the Soviets shot flares high into the night sky trying to locate refugees. Then, as the darkness took over again, we would quietly get up and follow our guides.

At one point, we were scared almost to death, because two strangers stood up from a ditch just in front of us. We thought this was the end of our journey, and we had been caught by patrols! It turned out they were also refugees, two young freedom fighters, but without local guides. After eavesdropping on us, they realized that we were also heading in the same direction. So they happily joined our group. Now, eight of us walked in single file on a narrow foot path. Soon we heard voices approaching, that later proved to be from two drunk fellows heading back from the border on bicycles. As many times before, we jumped into a long trench until the fellows disappeared. They probably had a toast of brandy after safely delivering their charges. I also carried a flask of brandy and our watches in my winter coat pocket. They were intended for bribing Soviet soldiers. Our wedding rings were also hidden inside the toes of my shoes for the same purpose, to trade for our freedom. We understood that such bargains often succeeded, especially if only one or two soldiers were involved.

Looking back later, we realized we never could have made it through these dramatic events with our five-month-old Eva. We would

not have risked her health and safety running away from the police station in Körmend or taking her to those cold open fields during the night. Also it would have been unthinkable to jump into the ditches with her every time some danger threatened. And what about her crying in the quiet night while walking in the town streets or on open fields toward the border? Not to mention the many other mishaps we were still facing.

After our long night's walk, we finally approached the ice-cold River Pinka (Fig. 4). According to our two guides, Austria was on the other bank. Realizing that we were so close to freedom invigorated us. We forgot how tired we were after the long walks between the two towns and through open fields. Unfortunately, our celebration did not last long! Suddenly we saw lights flashing on the other side of the river. This scared our guides, who thought these flashes were from Soviet border patrols. We did not know at the time that the light was provided by Austrian border patrols to help refugees find the border. So the two guides hurriedly bade good-bye, while I emptied my pockets, and handed over my last month's salary, 1,800 Forints, just enough to buy a bicycle. Zoltán had not asked for compensation for risking his neck for us, but I felt I should reward him. The guides hurriedly departed and left us sitting in the bushes on the river bank.

We were scared, so I suggested to our group to stay calm and keep quiet until the lights and commotion on the other side of the river disappeared. I was prepared for 2-3 hours of waiting, until the suspicious patrols returned to their station. But our two young freedom fighters did not have much patience, and soon after the lights faded away, one of the fellows searched for a suitable crossing point in the river. Soon, he was wading across, and we reluctantly followed him, holding our belongings high, while crossing the waist-high icy river.

There were no patrols this time on the other side. We shook off some of the water, but soon my pants legs hardened from the frozen water, and I was walking in a pair of "stove pipes" that were very noisy when they rubbed against

Figure 5. The stone Border Marker, indicating the border between Hungary and Austria, that needed to be found during the night.

each other. At one point I sat down and changed my soaked and cold socks with dry ones from Tili's bag. That provided some relief. We also decided that it was time to warm ourselves with the brandy carried for bribing Soviet patrols. We felt confident now that the worst was over, that we must have reached Austria and were probably safe. Unfortunately, it was a very dark moonless night and we had no compass for orientation and were afraid of getting lost and unintentionally returning to Hungary. The border in this area had a sack-like bulge (Fig. 4) of Austrian territory that was surrounded by Hungary on both south and north, and we had entered the sack from the east. Therefore, if we were not heading straight westward, we could accidentally re-enter Hungary.

As we were hesitating about our next step, near a small creek, another group of refugees showed up on the other side. They were convinced that our group was still in Hungary, while they were already in Austria. It was a funny feeling to listen to the arguments over the creek. Then I suggested we settle the dispute by finding a border-marking stone. We started looking in all directions, on both sides of the creek, for a border marker (Fig. 5). After a time our group found one. We happily surrounded it, and under the cover of several winter coats,

one of us lit a match to see the markings on the flat top of the stone. There were the letters we were all anxiously looking for — an "Ö" (Österreich, or Austria) pointing toward our side of the creek and an "M" (Magyarország, or Hungary) pointing to the other side of the creek (Fig. 5). Satisfied, our compatriots from the other side of the creek came over to join our group.

After walking a little further, we found a small bench made from a tree log, and a path that ended at the bench. Along the path we discovered some Austrian cigarette wrappers and empty match boxes. These increased our confidence that we were following the path used by the Austrian border patrols. Eventually, we came to the end of the forest where we could see, beyond an open field, the silhouette of the first town against the sky. The church was on high ground and its characteristic steeple style assured us that this was an Austrian town. As we approached the town of Luising (Fig. 4), we happily discovered two lighted windows in what turned out to be a school building, which then became our destination. Hurrying to this place, we found a lighted classroom heated with a large Dutch glazed-tile stove, and several townspeople assisting other newly arrived Hungarian refugees. After midnight on the 21st of November, we finally had made it

Figure 6. Some of the Refugee Shelter volunteers in Deutschkreuz, Austria, 25 years later.

to freedom! A great joy warmed our hearts. We dried our wet clothes in front of the stove while sipping hot drinks and eating delicious home-baked chocolate-filled buns.

I often raise the question: was it the work of Destiny or just pure luck, that the most significant events in my life have occurred on the 21st day of the month? It must have started with my birth date of 7-7-1927; where multiplying the three times 7 in my birth date equals 21. I started a better new life on 21st of October (1940) when as a teenager I crossed to Hungary from Romania; I successfully passed my hardest and most important college exam in Botany (that only about half of my 240 classmates ever passed) on December 21, 1948; I married Tili on the 21st of October 1953; our only child, Eva, was born on the 21st of June 1956; and I escaped to freedom, and a new life started, on the 21st of November 1956.

About 25 years later, I went back to visit some of the towns along the Austrian-Hungarian border. It was a nostalgic trip, but I also wanted to express my personal thanks to people for their help and hospitality in 1956–57. Luckily, I met a group of elderly folks sitting on a bench in their churchyard in Deutschkreuz on a Sunday afternoon (Fig. 6). All were in their 60s and 70s, and each had some memories to share from that time. They were some of the people who had spent long nights helping the cold, wet, and hungry refugees from Hungary. Because I slept in their local shelter for five nights during January 1957 while trying to rescue my baby daughter from Hungary, I probably enjoyed their hospitality longer than other refugees. These folks put out their hearts for us at the time when we needed it most. We had just become homeless, jobless, displaced persons. Many of us had left behind our closest relatives, had only the one shirt we were wearing, and spoke little, if any, of the language of the country that welcomed us.

I hope historians will remember and recognize these Austrian friends. If someday I become a rich man, I shall erect a monument properly honoring our helping angels in Burgenland at the Austrian-Hungarian border.

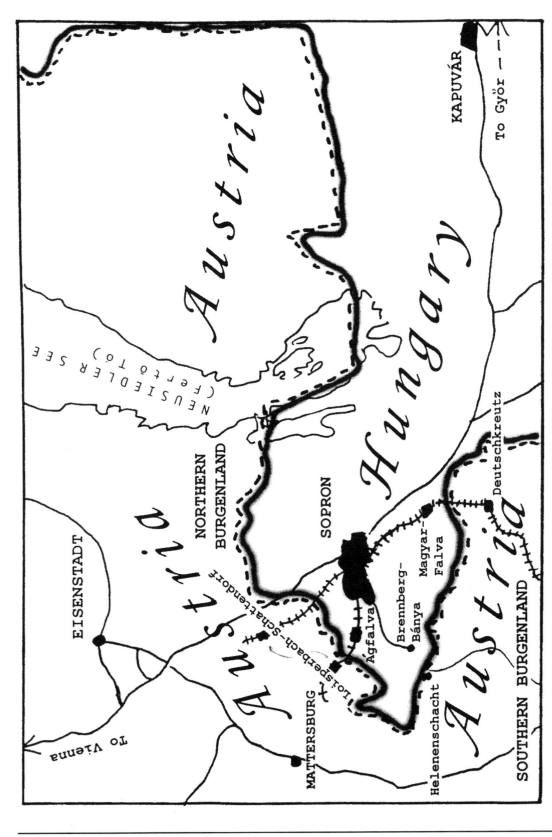

Figure 7. The bulging border section around Sopron, marking the route of my ten railroad trips while smuggling baby Eva out of Hungary.

2 — Smuggling Our Package-Baby (1957)

The bus came early. It was still dark at around 6 a.m. These special buses took a route along the Hungarian-Austrian border each morning to pick up newly arrived refugees from Hungary. There were some nights in November 1956 when as many as 5,000 new refugees crossed the border, creating an enormous challenge for the unprepared Austrian authorities.

We were taken to Hagensdorf (Fig. 4) where the closest temporary shelter was set up. The building was a large community hall, with piles of straw scattered on the wood floor for beds. Families took sections of the floor space along the walls and in the corners. There were about 40 of us. We were told that the arrangement was very temporary and only until there was room at the over-crowded refugee camps. After breakfast, Tili and I went to the local post office to send a telegram to inform Tili's parents in Budapest that we had arrived safely in Austria. Not having money, I begged the clerk to accept my ball-point pen instead of money. With an understanding smile for my offer and probably for my Hungarian accent, the clerk sent the telegram without accepting any payment. It was an advantage for us that we had studied German before our escape to Austria.

After a noisy night in the crowded hall, we decided to leave early next morning. We hitchhiked to Strem (Fig. 4), a large town with an abbey. The abbey was already filled with a group of refugees, now waiting for transportation to a camp. We lined up to board the first bus and sat in the left corner of the long back seat.

During the ride snow started covering the road. Our bus had no snow chains and suddenly skidded and turned over at a curb. Tili was seated near the window, and the four persons from the same seat fell on top of her.

She, the only one injured, cried out from the great pain she felt in her hip. I felt desperate, not being able to help her. Soon a local physician stopped, took her to his office, and called the ambulance after he realized that her injury was serious. We were taken to the closest hospital in Feldbach, Steiermark (Fig. 4). After her x-rays were examined at the hospital, she was told that she had a fractured hip and that the treatment would require six weeks in the hospital.

Frustrated but resigned, I went to the Welfare Department in the Town Hall to ask for housing and a job during the time Tili would be in the Feldbach General Hospital. The office sent me to the Schwarz family, one of the local families that volunteered to assist refugees. My hosts had also been refugees from Yugoslavia. Because of their German name, Tito's government had forced them to escape to Austria in 1945. Here they made a living as hog-raising farmers. In the three weeks I stayed with them, I ate enough pork sausages, ham, and bacon to last me a lifetime. I had a room of my own and on my bed a large goose feather comforter to sweat under, to cleanse myself of past and future sins. I always suffer under goose feather covers that are too warm, but common in that part of Europe.

I started looking for a job because we had no money. We needed some for essentials, but also to finance my trip back to Hungary to get our six-month-old Eva. After visiting a number of local businesses, I found temporary employment with the Suppan Construction Company as an unskilled laborer. They assigned me to help mix mortar and transport it and the bricks as they were needed. We were enlarging a pretzel factory. The factory workers noticed my unprotected hands moving piles of bricks. They

Figure 8. Tall fence around Camp Roeder near Salzburg, where Hungarian refugees were kept during 1956-57.

knew better than me that the skin on my fingers would not last long. So they donated work gloves to me. Also each Friday they gave me a big bag of pretzels and occasional small gifts to share with Tili in the hospital.

It was a miserable way to start a new life in the "free world." We had landed penniless in a strange town with only the clothes we were wearing. Tili was hospitalized for six weeks; I, a university assistant professor, became the brick-layer's helper during this frigid December; our only child Eva and our parents were separated from us for an unknown length of time while we were facing the uncertain future of homeless refugees. Somehow, we lived through the many sobbing sleepless nights in Austria. It really helped with our psychological readjustment that the local people in the eastern part of Austria, who themselves had experienced several years of Soviet occupation, were very sympathetic and helpful to us. They did their best to make our lives easier, as shown by our many other fortunate experiences with them.

One Saturday, I hitchhiked to the city of Graz, the district seat, to apply for emigration to the United States. I was told to get ready soon because we would be taken to Salzburg before Christmas for further processing for immigration at the Camp Roeder Refugee Camp. U.S. Vice President Nixon had visited the overcrowded camps in Austria, and President Eisenhower had given permission for 5,000 Hungarian refugees to emigrate to the USA.

To get closer to Tili's hospital and to my job, I moved into the center of the town, to the Neuholds' house. They were among the families who volunteered to temporarily house Hungarian refugees. They owned and operated a shoe and hat shop, and still had the shoe shop in 1994. At dinner we drank hard apple cider that was kept in large wooden barrels in their cellar. All these Austrian customs and thriving capitalist enterprises were new to me.

Like most of the other 200,000 Hungarian refugees, we escaped to the West with just the clothes we were wearing. A local "clothes bank" had been set up by volunteers in the town and stocked with clothes and other essentials donated by welfare organizations from Austria and other countries. From this "bank" we obtained extra clothing and two old suitcases. We badly needed suitcases because, as it turned out after our escape, we had to change shelters 13 times in six months. The last time I went to the clothes bank, I told the volunteer that all I really needed was a belt to hold up my trousers. He looked me over and said, "I'm sorry, we don't keep belts in stock — but take mine, I can get a new one soon." Then he unbuckled his belt and handed it to me. I swallowed my pride as my eyes filled with tears for this expression of human kindness.

Figure 9. The tall watchtower of the Hungarian border guards, near Loisperbach, Austria.

The day before Christmas we were taken to a big empty hall in downtown Graz for "processing" before boarding a train to the Salzburg refugee camp. Tili was taken to the hall by ambulance. In a corner I tied a string to the walls and hung sheets from it to provide privacy during our miserable night there. The next day we boarded the train and reached Salzburg by late afternoon. Tili was again taken by ambulance to the Salzburg Community Hospital, while the rest of us, "able-bodied," ended up in Camp Roeder, a former U.S. military camp, now converted to house refugees (Fig. 8). I shared a room in a wooden barrack with three other "single" men. We had time to kill while waiting for further processing by officials of the western countries to which we intended to emigrate.

Soon after our arrival, we were lined up for delousing with DDT dust that was puffed into our opened clothes. I smelled like DDT for weeks after this adventure, but had no body lice or fleas — common pests in crowded camps. Because fleas can transmit plague and lice transmit typhus, it was important to prevent epidemics. We now use other chemicals besides the notorious DDT to protect us from parasitic insects.

I took the bus from the camp to visit Tili in the hospital every day. We often discussed the chances for getting our baby out of Hungary. Eva was on our minds constantly, and we both missed her very much. We also realized that we might have to wait months — or even years — until the Communist authorities, still full of vengeance against those who escaped to the West, would permit the Red Cross to arrange family reunions.

One day, Tili met a friend of hers, the father of a refugee family, who was able to get a package of their clothes out of Hungary by passing it through the window of an Austrian train that crossed daily from Northern Burgenland to Southern Burgenland in Austria, through a small corner of Hungarian territory (Fig. 7). We both realized simultaneously that this might be a way to get Eva out of Hungary. Maybe she could be hidden in a bundle of clothes and someone could pass the bundle to me while I stood in the window of the Austrian train during the short stops in Hungary. We decided that while Tili was recuperating in the hospital, I would go to the Hungarian border to explore the possibility of smuggling Eva out of Hungary.

Since our escape, the Austrian border had been fortified with more frequent patrols and watch dogs, stronger barbed-wire fences , and guards stationed in the tall watch towers (Fig. 9). Only residents of towns bordering Austria could enter the 30-km wide border area. Outsiders needed police permits to enter this restricted zone. Consequently, even if I were successful in crossing the border and getting Eva in Budapest, I would not be able to get out of Hungary with her. All vehicles and trains were inspected before entering the border zone. Tili and I concluded that we needed someone who resided in the border zone, whom we could trust with our baby's life and who had dependable nerves for the ordeal of smuggling. Tili knew a family from the border town of Sopron, where the "package" could change hands in the railroad station. She wrote a letter to the Besskos asking for their assistance. Besides she wrote a second one to her parents asking them

Figure 10. The railroad station that served as my daily starting point to Sopron, Hungary.

to release Eva to a member of the Bessko family.

The next day I took the letters and about 1,200 Austrian Shillings, with a portion converted to Hungarian Forints, which I had earned as a mason's handyman, to the Austrian border station Loisperbach-Shattendorf (Figs. 7, 10). From this railroad station I could see the border about 300 meters away. During the train's brief stop at the border crossing, two Hungarian border patrols stepped up to the last steps of the train with their machine guns on their shoulders. They guarded both sides of the train while it crossed the 12-km long stretch of Hungarian land, so that nobody could enter the train. This extra precaution would make our plan even riskier. I noticed that the farthest point from these guards was the first train window, just behind the locomotive.

Now I had to find a safe way to deliver my letter to the Besskos, 8 km across the border. In those days all letters coming from the west were inspected by the Hungarian Communist officials, so we could not rely on the postal system. Therefore, I needed to find someone who lived in Austria close to the Hungarian border, and who had local connections on the other side across the border. I learned that a retired miner, Mr. Julius Stubna, lived near the border with his wife; I knew their entomologist son, who worked in Hungary. So I hitch-hiked

to their place, near Helenenschacht (Fig. 7). I found them at their home, which bordered the outer barbed-wire fence set up by the Hungarian border guards. From their back fence began the wide no-man's land strip (Fig. 11) that was carefully raked so that any footprints could be easily detected. During my visit, I told the Stubnas that, as an entomologist and a friend of their son, I felt I knew them well enough to ask them for a favor. Then, I explained my plan. I asked them to suggest a safe way for me to send my two letters to the Besskos in Sopron where their son was also working. After hearing more details, they refused to help. They were probably worried that I might be a Communist agent and their assistance could endanger their son's future in Hungary, because it was still a punishable offense to assist refugees.

The Stubnas must have noticed my obvious disappointment, and kindly offered me an excellent supper and shelter for the night. The next morning, Mr. Stubna confided that he might be able to help me. He told me that during the Hungarian Revolution he had befriended a trusty border guard who still came out with his comrade every afternoon to patrol the border section adjoining his backyard. Mr. Stubna thought that this soldier might be willing to deliver my letters to a trusted forest ranger, Mr. András Hedl, who lived along the way to his quarters. The forest ranger could

Figure 11. The no-man's-land strip behind the Stubna's house, with two barbed-wire fences, across which I tossed my three letters. Note the raked strip.

then deliver my letters to the Besskos. I agreed to try this plan. I quickly wrote a third letter asking the forest ranger for his assistance. I enclosed enough Hungarian money to pay for a two-way bus ride to Sopron.

Next we had to figure out how to deliver the letters to the soldier across the 40-meter-wide raked no-man's land with two barbed-wire fences (Fig.11). The soldiers could get into trouble if fresh footprints appeared. After some thought, we cut down a large straight oak branch to use as a lance. We split one end of the branch, and inserted the large envelope containing the three letters into the wedge and tied it with a string. By the time the border patrols showed up and we obtained their consent, I practiced a few times and then I was ready to toss the "lance" across the border strip. It worked! The soldiers, on their return walk, delivered my precious messages. Luckily for us, they never realized that they were helping to

smuggle a baby across the very border that they were supposed to be guarding against such events.

I later learned that the forest ranger's wife took the first bus to deliver my letters. She rang the Besskos' doorbell and when she heard footsteps coming towards the door, she quickly pushed my envelope in the mail slot in their door and left before she could be seen.

Up until now, everyone had cooperated beautifully with our plans. They knowingly risked being jailed for helping us. But when the Besskos read my letter requesting their assistance, they thought I must be a lunatic. I asked that one of their family members use my enclosed money for a train ride to Budapest to show Tili's letter to her parents, disguise Eva in a bundle of clothes and bring her to the Sopron railroad station. I would be waiting for her in the train to be passed to me through the first compartment window behind the locomotive. I also asked the Besskos to meet my train that evening to signal their willingness to cooperate by waving a handkerchief in their left hand. I would do the same from my window so that we would recognize each other, since we had never met before. After receiving their signal, I would take the train each evening until the baby was delivered.

Although the Besskos dismissed my request as unrealistic, their 17-year old son, Csaba, and 19-year old son, Attila, were willing to try it. The older Besskos reluctantly agreed to allow them. So the two boys came out to the station that evening to meet me from a distance. I was ecstatic when I saw them standing on the station platform with their handkerchiefs waving in their left hands. The next day only Csaba showed up. I pulled down my window, and asked the nearest guard to let me greet my friend in the station. The guard did not answer me, but walked a little further away. That gave me the courage to shout a greeting to Csaba and ask him about his family. He responded by saying that his brother, Attila, was now in Budapest. The good news warmed my heart.

I continued my two trips daily through Sopron and started spending the nights in

Figure 12. The Refugee Shelter in Deutsch-kreutz, Austria, where I slept five nights during the "baby smuggling" operation. Note the stork nest on the chimney.

Deutschkreutz (Fig. 7), the closest Austrian town, just 8 km south of Sopron. A refugee shelter (Fig. 12) was still being maintained there by volunteers. After breakfast I took the same train north through Hungary, and stopped in the first Austrian town, Loisperbach (Fig. 10). There I stayed until late afternoon in a small restaurant close to the railroad station. While eating lunch I listened to western jukebox music for the first time in my life. The restaurant customers kept the music going almost constantly with their coins. There were no jukeboxes in Hungary where I came from.

In this restaurant and bar I had a chance to meet a number of people and trade stories. Some of the other customers were also looking for opportunities to help their close rela-

tives leave Hungary. I was the only one waiting for a baby.

One of the people I met was a "professional" smuggler, a man about 50 years old, who apparently crossed the border almost every night. He claimed to live nearby. Every time I met him he was under the influence of apricot brandy, and offered to get Eva out of Hungary for a negotiable fee in Shillings. I wrote Tili about this possibility, in case all else failed, although I was uncomfortable with him.

Then, I befriended the conductor and locomotive engineer of my train. After they learned about my problem, they offered their help. The conductor suggested that the young man leave Eva in a covered wicker basket (Moses-style), on the platform between the railroad tracks and he would get off the train to bring it into my compartment. The locomotive engineer also volunteered to create extra steam during this activity to cover up my car, so the guards would not be able to see what was going on under my window. I felt good after all this encouragement and cooperation offered by these strangers. It was refreshing to be able to write good news in my daily postcard messages to Tili after all the earlier difficulties.

On my ninth trip across Hungary, I pulled down my window while stopping in Sopron and saw Attila in the shadow of the two railroad station buildings. He held a canary yellow blanket covering a bundle in his arms. I got really excited, when I recognized that blanket. It was the only kind available in our socialist shops for babies. Although we had not liked the color at the time, it was a welcome sight now. It identified our precious cargo.

Attila had just arrived by train from Budapest and, after his mother fed Eva and changed diapers in the rail station, he wanted to show me from a safe distance that Eva was already in Sopron with them. While waving to him, I suddenly realized that there were no extra guards this time, and the two usual guards were already standing on the last steps of the train. The station master came out of his office as usual to signal for the train to leave. As he walked near my window on his way toward the locomotive, I shouted to him, begging him to wait for me to get my baby from the station platform. He slowed down and looked up at me with a shocked face. He must have thought I was crazy. His hesitation encouraged Attila to run across four rail tracks to my window and toss the bundle up to me, while the already "indoctrinated" locomotive engineer hastily started the train. Everything happened so fast that there was no time for the engineer to employ the promised steam cover. Attila ran back and out of the station, while I placed the precious cargo on the bench beside me.

With trembling fingers, I opened the bundle to find a smiling face looking at me. Eva had no idea yet that she had just crossed the Rubicon to freedom! Still shaking from the excitement, with moist eyes, I realized the risk wasn't over yet. We still had one more stop in Hungary at the Magyarfalva station (Fig. 7), before we would reach the Austrian border. I was convinced that the guards, who must have seen the incident, would demand that I return the bundle. So I rushed Eva to another compartment where some local Austrian women were sitting, and begged them to hold the baby until we arrived to Deutschkreuz, the first Austrian town. They didn't know what to think of my hurried request in my heavily accented German, but I didn't have time to make myself clear. So, I just left Eva on the bench, and ran back to the window in my own compartment.

Then I stuffed my winter coat into the same yellow blanket, making a new but similar bundle. If cornered by the border guards, I would let them have the bundle, claiming that I had received some old clothes. We soon stopped at Magyarfalva, but no guards came, and at the border stop our guards left the train. So we rolled into Austria. As soon as the tall watch towers of the Hungarian border guards were out of sight, I ran back for Eva. This time the women around her were very apologetic for not cooperating sooner and were delighted with my ever-smiling baby. Now, with my calmed nerves, I was better able to explain the adventure we had just gone through. They cheered for our success.

I left the train in Deutschkreutz. Because the local refugee shelter couldn't accommodate babies, I stayed with a former Hungarian refugee family, who had a baby close to Eva's age. Here we had supper, slept, and left early the next morning, taking the same train that I had already been on nine times. While stopping in Sopron, I looked out of the window by habit and was astonished to see Attila and Csaba. They were standing on the platform holding a small package. Because of Eva's hasty and unplanned escape the night before, they had left out the extra clothes and birth certificate Eva's grandmother had provided. But this time the extra guards were out in full force, surrounding my train. So I waved good-by to the boys, motioning that, with Eva, I had all I needed. I watched as the boys were stopped and questioned by the police. Luckily they were soon released with a stern warning, and told not to come back to the railroad station when a foreign train was in. Later, when Attila also escaped to Austria, he mailed Eva's birth certificate to us.

In Vienna I had to transfer to an express train for Salzburg. Once on the train I realized that I was unprepared for Eva's needs. It was time to feed her and she needed a new diaper. I found milk at the train's snack bar and used pieces of my pajamas shirt for a diaper. Somehow we managed until reaching Tili's hospital in Salzburg that evening.

With a throbbing heart, I entered the big hospital room where Tili lay in bed, with several other patients in the same room. With my precious bundle in hand, I greeted Tili. She was astonished to see us so soon. It seemed a miracle, because out of ten trips, only on the ninth, when Eva was in the station, were there no extra guards on the station platform. With tears in our eyes, we were finally reunited.

(To be continued in Chapter 11)

Postscript: Forty years later Eva and her family, Tili, and I visited the now modernized Sopron railroad station (Fig. 97) to show my two grandsons the place where these exciting events happened.

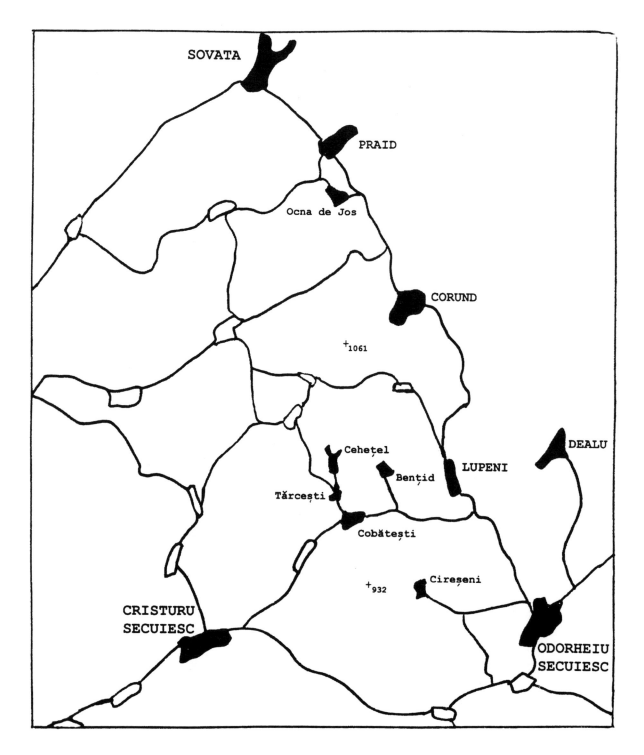

*Figure 13. Map section for eastern Transylvania, showing Cehețel —
"the Albert's Cradle" — with part of the county of Odorhei.*

3 — It All Started in Transylvania (1930–)

In my text the first-time mentioned localities, besides the present Romanian name, will have the earlier Hungarian and/or German-Saxon names in parentheses. But later only the Romanian names are given.

After my birth in Bucharest, while my mother was still in the hospital with me, a fortune-telling gypsy woman sat down at her bedside and told mother about the future of her son. My mother was so pleased about the good news foretold of the future of her 5-day-old son that she gave the fortune teller 10 leis, twice what she usually got from other customers. When I was old enough, mother repeatedly told me the "prognosis." The gypsy had said that I would be very fortunate in my life, and that I would travel to America. After checking the top of my hairy head, the fortune teller discovered two cowlicks. She told my mother that these were the sure signs that I would have two wives. So, when I met Tili, I told her only about the first part of the "prognosis." After I got to America, my mother still firmly believed the gypsy's prognosis and told Tili the rest of the prediction. Thank God Tili did not believe in fortune-teller stories.

Both of my parents were Transylvanian Hungarians, but from different regions. My mother, Berta Albert, was a Sekler (székely), from the town of Cehețel (Csehétfalva) in the County of Odorhei (Udvarhely)(Fig. 13), while my father, also Michael, was a Chango (csángó) from the town of Tărlungeni (Tatrang) in the County of Brașov (Brasso)(Fig. 14). At birth, they were Hungarians, but after the 1920 Paris (Trianon) Treaty their homeplaces became part of Romania and they automatically became Romanian citizens. Because of the hardships faced by the Hungarian ethnic farmers in Transylvania, my parents left their homes and found jobs in the fast-developing Romanian capital of Bucharest. This is where I was born in 1927. My mother was 19 years old and my father 27.

Both of my parents became half-orphaned early in life. My mother was only six in 1914 when her father, János Albert, died at Kosice (Kassa) — now Slovakia — from dysentery complicated by malnutrition while serving as a soldier in the army of the Austrian-Hungarian monarchy. So grandmother Teréz had to struggle for years to raise three war orphans on a minimal income. Her youngest, Ilona, the fourth orphan, was adopted by a childless relative in the village.

My father's mother, Anna Molnár, died in 1908 when he was 8 years old. His father, János Kosztarab, remarried and, from there on, because of his father's new marriage and siblings from that union, my father was temporarily taken care of by his mother's relatives in the village. Life was never easy for such children, where one parent had died early and the family was poor. Therefore, father finished only six grades of schooling and started working for his room and board at age 12, first in his home town, later for a small monthly wage for Saxon farmers in the nearby villages. This is where he learned some Saxon-German. At age 18 he was invited to join his Uncle George Váncsa's enterprise in Bucharest. Váncsa had two fancy horse-drawn carriages and four horses which he hired out to taxi people around before "horseless carriages" took over that business. There my father had to learn Romanian.

Soon my father realized that he could get a better pay from restauranteurs preparing and frying their mititeis, small sausages of ground meat, a favorite dish in Bucharest. At age 21,

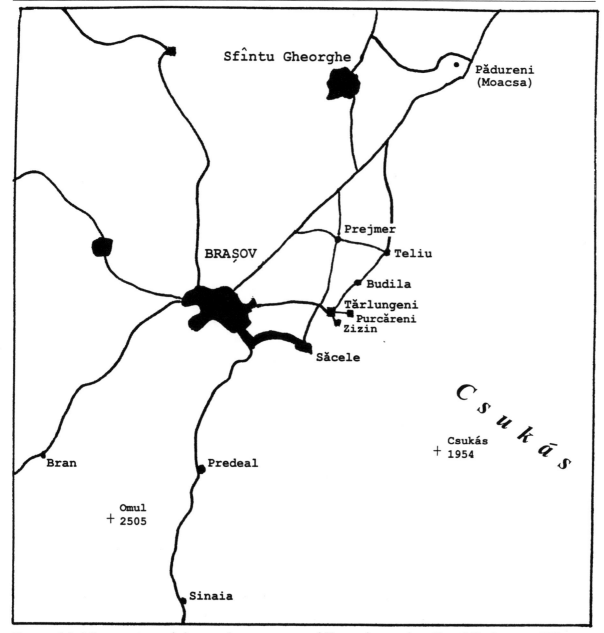

Figure 14. Map section of the southeast corner of Transylvania (see Fig. 15) showing Tǎrlungeni, "The Kosztarabs' cradle", and surrounding towns and areas mentioned in the text.

he was drafted by the military into the Gendarmery for a 3-year-long service.

He told me about some of his experiences in the Romanian Gendarmery. Two of these may sound unbelievable to Westerners. He was often assigned as assistant to a Romanian sergeant, his superior in the Service, while patrolling the streets in Bucharest. When the sergeant needed to supplement his meager in-come, he would often stop well-dressed tourists on the sidewalks and demand the presentation of their personal identification certificate. Many did not carry this document with them. So he threatened them with arrest and a trip to the Prefecture. After some hassling, the person usually realized that he could avoid the arrest if he paid baksheesh to the sergeant. By then, my father had already been instructed to step aside and look the other way while the "transaction" took place. Unfortunately the baksheesh system, introduced during the Ottoman Occupation, still persisted when I lived there in the 1930s.

In the Prefecture, my father discovered that the Shef (Chief) often sat behind a desk with a deep desk drawer that could be pulled from both the front and back of the desk. Citizens who were arrested, often on drummed-up charges, or those seeking a business permit, were seated in front of the desk with the deep drawer, while the Shef was seated on the other side of the 2-way drawer. After listening to the person's plea or request, the Shef usually spoke of how difficult and time-consuming it would be to take care of the matter, and pushed the empty drawer against the citizen's stomach, implying that the Shef would act in his favor if he would place some bills in the empty drawer. When done, the Shef would pull the drawer to his side, inspect the amount, and if satisfied, act on the case. If he considered the money insufficient, he would present more excuses until new bills were placed in the drawer to finally satisfy the Shef. Later, when my father was in business for himself as a house-painter, he never had a business license, but paid the license fee directly to the official in charge, and thus was not bothered by tax-collectors.

After the military service, my father needed two more years to recuperate financially while learning housepainting, a trade that became his profession. At age 26 he married my mother.

My mother was raised in poverty with two younger brothers: Sándor (Alexander) and Zsiga (Sigismund). Her widowed mother Teréz (Theresa) received a minimal war-widow pension, 300 leis, or about US$60, every three months from the Romanian government. She also earned some wages while working as a seasonal farm laborer and a sharecropper. She raised vegetables and fruits in her garden to meet the needs of the family. To ease the burden on grandmother, from age 12 to 14 my mother went to work in the household of a Saxon family at Sighişoara (Segesvár)(Fig. 15).

The latter, a childless family, wanted to adopt my mother, but grandmother would not allow this, and rather took mother, at ages 15–16, to Cluj (Kolozsvár)(Fig. 15) to work for a Jewish family.

My mother liked the place and was very happy to be able to attend weekly performances of the Hungarian Theatre in that city. Grandmother showed up again and took mother at age 16 to Bucharest (Fig. 15) where she found a job with a Jewish family named Gross. She was treated well as were the rest of the Hungarian personnel serving the large household. Apparently well-to-do Jewish families preferred to hire Hungarian girls, and treated them as family members; they were called daughters, "Fata Mea." Therefore, many Hungarian girls from Transylvania preferred to work for Jewish families. They found them more humane and generous than other rich families. For example, the daily ration at the Gross family was 1/2 kilogram of meat per servant with their other food. Besides room and board, they also paid 1,000 leis per month for the cook. They often allowed husbands to move into the house when one of the women servants married.

In a typical household, there were one or two maids and a cook, all Hungarian, while the governess for the children was German and the chauffeur was usually Romanian. Sunday afternoons were free, but the personnel were required to return home by dark, probably to shelter their young girls from bad affairs. Some bordellos were openly searching for young Hungarian girls to set up in their business. Therefore, the Reformed (Calvinist) Church had a program, with the aid of nuns called "Diakons", to provide temporary shelter and find suitable jobs for young girls before the agents of the bordellos contacted them.

It was customary among the Transylvanian Hungarian farming families to send each son for a few years to a city to learn a profession. They also sent their daughters for a few years to a city or larger town, to learn a trade while working as a maid for a family, often dressmaking, sewing, or how to run a household. Often the high taxes on farming played a role

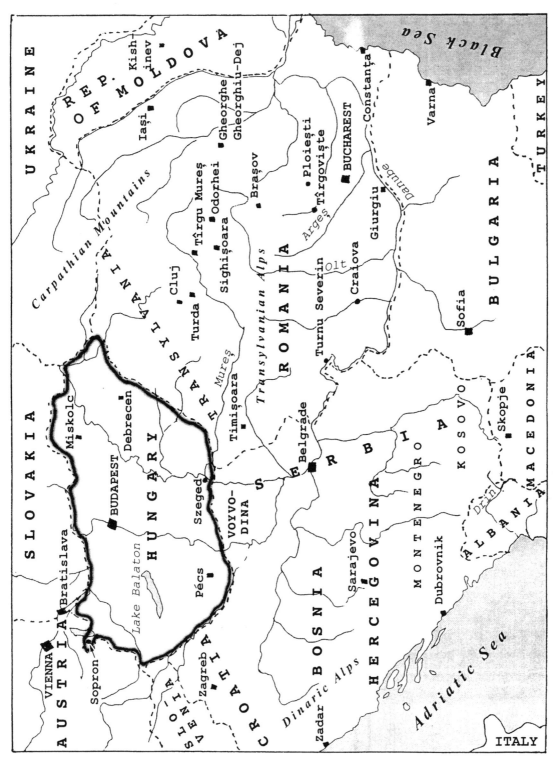

Figure 15. Map with parts of east Central Europe and the northern Balkans (1996).

in such decisions, as did the need to gather a dowry for the future brides.

This was the environment in Bucharest that my mother entered at age 16. Soon, my father discovered her while visiting his Aunt Anna. They found they had a lot in common and made plans to get married. They did so in 1926, and I was born the next year. My father was pleased to have me, his first born, a boy, so I was named in honor of his uncle, also Michael, my paternal grandfather's youngest brother, who not long before had accidentally been shot in a crossfire between political factions fighting in the streets of Bucharest.

Because there was no Hungarian Lutheran Church in Bucharest, I was baptized as a Lutheran in the Hungarian Reformed Church on Ştirbei Voda Street, just behind the Royal Palace (Fig.17). The officiating minister, as I came to know him later, was an ascetic-looking person, Sándor Nagy. His associate Kányádi's younger son, Tibor, was my classmate and friend for four years in the Calvinist school.

The global economic depression reached Bucharest, and soon my father lost his investments in a bakery product distribution business. Many of his customers would not pay their debts for products received and services rendered by my father because the Romanian government had passed a law that outstanding loans and unpaid bills were to be forgiven.

Due to the economic uncertainty, my parents decided, when I was 9 months old, to take me to my widowed grandmother who lived alone in her town, Cehețel. It was a very painful decision to make, especially for my mother, to leave me with my grandmother for an uncertain length of time. She had many sleepless and tearful nights for the five years we were apart. Usually only once a year could my parents afford to see me. My mother also decided, as did many other Depression-Era Hungarian mothers, that one child was enough. That is why Tili and I were raised as single children.

My grandmother was very pleased with her new joyful responsibility of raising me, her first-born grandchild. She was in her early forties when I was taken to her as a nine-month-old baby. She was compensated for keeping me with 500 leis per month, about 20% of my father's monthly salary (2,600 lei) when he worked as the caretaker for a four-story apartment building on 17 Maria Rosetti Street.

Grandmother Teréz came from a Roman-Catholic family in Dealu (Oroszhegy)(Fig. 13). She married my grandfather, János Albert, and they lived in an entirely Unitarian community. She had a two-room house (Fig. 32) with a separate summer kitchen with an oven (Fig. 33) for baking bread. The basement walls and the foundations of her typical Sekler house were made of large field stones. The walls were plastered logs, white-washed in a light bluish color. The roof was covered with red tiles, but was without a chimney (Fig. 16), because the attic served as a general-purpose smokehouse; the smoke from the cooking and heating fire collected in the attic and gradually dissipated through the cracks under the red tiles. As an entomologist, I later realized why my grandmother's and other Sekler houses did not have much insect infestation in the stored beans and grain, or among the hanging bacon slabs and sausages kept in the attic: the constant smoke must have repelled pest insects.

In the back, several outbuildings marked the edge of the yard (Fig. 18). To the left was the

Figure 16. Sekler house without a chimney.

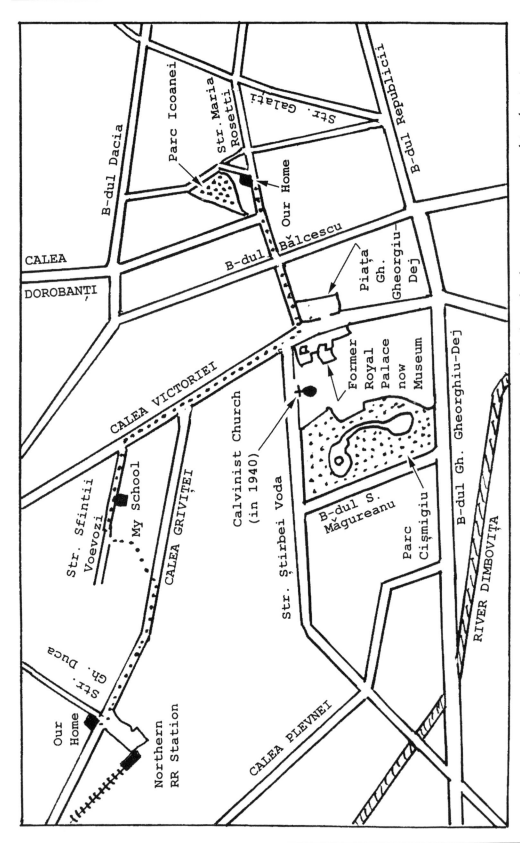

Figure 17. Section of Bucharest, showing our residences, my school, and other sites mentioned in the text.

cow barn and to the right was the sheep or swine barn along with the chicken coop. To the latter an outdoor toilet was attached. Between the barns was the hay shed with a large hay loft extending over the cow and sheep barns, with room for carriages, wagons, and farm machinery. Behind the barns was a large garden. Vegetables were grown on the right side and included cabbage, lettuce, sorrel, onions, garlic, peas, pole beans, potatoes, sunchokes (Jerusalem artichokes), carrots, and parsnips. As ever-hungry children, my playmates and I often pulled up some carrots or sunchoke tubers, washed them in the creek, and ate them. A small orchard occupied the left side of the garden; in it grew walnuts, apples, pears, and plums. We had no peaches, apricots, or grapes because it was too cold in the mountains for these fruits.

In the middle of the farm yard, between the barn and the house, was a large red mulberry tree that provided sweet fruits for chicken, ducks, and geese, also for children. When many mulberries were available, some ended up in crocks for fermenting and brandy making.

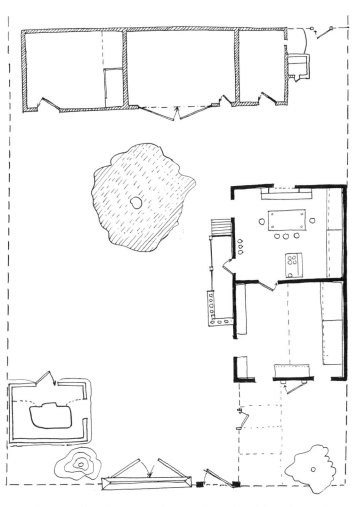

Figure 18. Layout of Grandmother Teréz's yard, considered a typical Sekler "homestead."

Almost every Sekler household had a flower garden in front that could be enjoyed both from the house and from the street by people passing by. Grandma preferred those flowers that had a good smell and that could be cut for bouquets to be taken into the house or to church on Sunday. She had an old rose bush with large red flowers, perennial carnations, tall phlox, and a bed of perennial herbs, including mints. The latter provided the base for her favorite mint liqueur. She also made caraway seed liqueur by slightly roasting the seeds, crushing and soaking them for 4 to 6 weeks in 95% alcohol with dried orange peels saved from the previous Christmas. She often had no money, but still sent me to the town's Jewish grocer, Mr. Ghiladi (whose son Miksa was a good friend of Uncle Zsiga), with a basketful of fresh eggs to be traded for a bottle of alcohol for her homemade sweet liqueurs. Her standard recipe called for three basic ingredients, each one-third of the final product. She used 2 cups of 95% grain alcohol already flavored with the extracts of fresh mint or caraway seed with orange peel. The flavored alcohol was drained from the added ingredients, poured into a 6- or 7- cup bottle, to which she added a cooled syrup made from 2 cups of sugar heated in two cups of water. She served this in small glasses to friends visiting us. After I was 3 or 4 years old, I also got a sip which usually made me choke, but most times I bravely asked for more. Fresh fruit such as sour cherries or dried apricots were also soaked and extracted by my mother in Bucharest and made into a tasty liqueur.

Some of the fruits from our orchard were dried over a slow fire in wicker trays (Fig. 20) for use during the winter. From plums we made a thick preserve to last until next fall. The "English" walnuts from our small orchard were supplemented by filberts that we gathered from the edge of the Common's Forest. A small, tasty green apple (Batul) kept well during most of the winter when mixed in straw on shelves in our root cellar. We stored here the root vegetables, including potatoes, to last for 9 months. We also prepared enough sauerkraut in a wooden barrel to last through the winter. The tasty sauerkraut juice was gradually drained and served as a drink to go with baked potatoes. This provided full evening meals during the winter. We drew our drinking water from a neighbor's well and carried it in wooden buckets (Fig. 19).

At least once a day we ate cornmush, soft or hard, as a bread substitute. Cornmush with layered sheep cheese is still one of my favorite Transylvanian "soul foods." (My Cornmush Casserole Recipe is given in the Addendum.) Bread was baked once weekly. Usually, on Friday grandmother got up very early to start the dough with a cup of starter saved from the last week's dough. To rise, the dough was kept warm in a wooden tub in the bed, well covered

Figure 19. Wooden bucket for drinking water.

with feather bedding, and usually it was kept in my bed at my feet while I was still sleeping. Grandma added mashed potatoes to the dough to keep the 4 or 5 loaves of baked bread fresh for one week. The leftover dough she scraped off from the long wooden tub and molded into a "pigeon" to be baked as a weekly treat for me.

One day, with my playmate Palko (Paul), I raced to

Figure 20. Fruit dryer in the back of our fruit orchard.

see who could eat handfuls of mulberries the fastest. Without realizing it, I also picked up a bee that stung the inside of my throat before meeting its fate in my stomach. My throat got so swollen that it almost closed my esophagus. I lost my ability to swallow food or liquids for a day or two. The closest physician was 12 kilometers away, if he was home. Without telephone lines yet, I just had to manage with cold compresses and some sweetened milk until my throat opened well enough for food intake. I learned then to check my food more closely before swallowing it.

I enjoyed fishing with my playmates by diverting the small creek in front of our house and draining some pools until we could catch fish with our hands. After cleaning and salting, I fried these little (4-6 inches long) fish over grandmother's wood stove. They really smelled up the place, but Grandma let me enjoy my new hobby. Later, as a teenager, I learned to catch fish in the shallow river with an eating fork. There, I slowly lifted the flat rocks and pierced the hiding fish with my fork.

By late summer, our village smelled from the drying hemp ("marijuana") stems. These were laid against the fences to dry. Hemp cultivation was common in the Transylvanian villages. The fully grown stems were harvested. The seeds were separated and dried and then fed to the chickens. We must have had many "happy" chickens in Transylvania. Such seeds

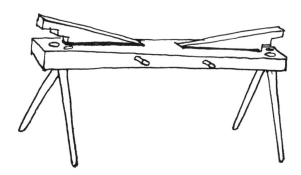

Figure 21. Wooden hemp-stem chopper.

are still sold in pet shops in Europe for caged birds. The green stems were bundled and soaked in shallow ponds under heavy rocks until the fiber came loose from the stem. Then the stems were dried and chopped with wooden hemp-stem choppers (Fig. 21) so that the fibers came loose. The fibers were used in thread-making for ropes, burlap sacks, and other clothlike materials. The leftover dry stems became an ideal kindling to start a fire in the stoves. We never had a thought that the hemp leaves were good for anything else.

There is an ancient and unique industry with folk-art designs in some Sekler communities. Here the natives remove the new growth of a variety of shelf mushroom, *Fomes fomentarius*, that grows on the trunks of large beech, birch, poplar, and willow trees. They soak, boil, and hammer the material into flat sheets. After these are dry, they are moistened slightly and placed on spherical molds to form men's caps, stretching the sheets as needed. The brown caps have the appearance of being made from chamois leather. Ladies' purses and artistically designed table runners are also made from the same material.

In late fall old trees were marked in the town's Commons Forest for felling by villagers. Each family received a quota of trees to be felled for fuel for the entire year, or for extra income when some of it was sold in the nearby city's firewood markets. Some poor families immediately purchased from the proceeds of such sales shoes and warm clothing for their children before the winter came.

No one in the community we lived in had property insurance coverage, and the houses, because of the lack of chimneys, sometimes caught fire. After such accidents, the entire town pitched in to rebuild the lost household. They called such activities "Kaláka". As in the barn-raising traditions of American farmers, each family sent some able-bodied persons to help. Some worked on logs, others on the stones or other construction materials, while the women prepared the special meals for the participants and helped with the youngsters to plaster the walls with an adobe mixture of clay and chaff; cow dung was sometimes added as an adhesive.

Other community actions included the local road repairs and maintenance. We had no medical insurance or Social Security from the government, but nobody starved or had to beg for donations in the village. Children of single mothers were often adopted by relatives or by childless couples in the town. When war refugees arrived in town, they were given temporary shelter, meals, and share-cropping options to be able to support themselves until some permanent arrangements could be found.

On laundry days, Grandma used her home-made soap. The clothes were heated in a large soapwater-filled cauldron and taken to the creek-side for washing by pounding them with a wooden pounder or dolly beater (Fig. 22).

Figure 22. Wooden pounder or dolly beater used by Sekler women when doing laundry along the river banks.

Our village was located along a small creek in a narrow valley, surrounded by hilly agricultural land that was bordered by a spruce forest on one mountainside and beech forests on the other three sides. The cultivated land was divided into three sections and rotated each year. Apparently, each family owned some parcels in each of the three areas. One third of the land was used for potatoes and corn or other crops that in those days required hoeing by hand, while another third was planted with small grains (wheat, rye, barley, and oats). The third area was left fallow and used as pasture for that year. The latter land was used for potatoes and corn the next year, while the small grain areas were allowed to lie fallow and were used for grazing. The aged horse and cow manure was spread on the fields before these were plowed for corn and potatoes.

I joined my farming relatives, to take the weekly share of bread, smoked meats, and other food to the shepherd family who looked after the entire community's sheep. At the same time we picked up our eight sheep's worth share of fresh sheep cheese. Before returning to the village, my uncle Áron presented a bottle of home-made brandy to the shepherd. The latter smiled, and allowed Áron to place the low moveable fence sections (karam) around his fields so that his land would benefit from some extra sheep manure when the sheep were enclosed at night.

Besides the shepherd family, another family was in charge of herding the pigs daily to pasture, a third was doing the same with the milking cows, and in the spring a fourth family herded the calves and steers to the high community mountain pastures where they remained until the end of September. The latter family also received weekly visitors from the village, the owners of some of the animals under their care. They carried to the "cowboys" their weekly allotment of bread, sheep cheese, bacon, etc. This ancient collaborative system worked very well when I was a child and lived in the area.

In late fall, when the field work ended, the menfolk fetched firewood, sawed it into pieces, split it, and stacked it up under a porch or roof, or against the side of the house, for drying. Many farmers enjoyed wood carving and the making of wooden farm tools during the long winter. One project that for some lasted through two or three winters was the artistic design, planning, preparation, carving, and painting of a set of fancy, wooden farm gates (Fig. 23) that would last for 2 to 3 generations. For some villagers it became a *magnum opus* and much effort went into it. Another carving project involved the preparation of memorial poles called kopjafa (kopyahfah). They are ornately carved thick wooden poles, somewhat similar to Native American Totem poles. Traditionally a kopjafa is a grave marker, which through its intricate pattern (Fig. 24) could be a narrative of one's life story. The pattern for the top will tell the sex of the dead and, for the deceased woman, the number of notches carved tells how many children she had.

Figure 23. A carved wooden Sekler farm gate.

Figure 24. The corner of a cemetery with carved memorial poles, called Kopjafa (Kopyahfah), used as grave markers.

Also during the fall, after the corn harvest, families invited neighbors and friends for an evening filled with fun, while doing some useful chores. Women, seated in a circle and often singing together, spun threads from wool, flax, or hemp (Fig. 25), to be used in weaving cloth, towels, sheets, etc., as my grandmother did on her loom (Fig. 26) during the long winter months. Each time one of the unmarried girls accidentally (or intentionally) dropped her spinner (Fig. 25) to the floor, one of the boys waiting close-by would jump to pick it up for her, returning it only after getting a kiss, while everyone laughed. So it was a great occasion for the youth to socialize, while older women were exchanging the latest gossip.

The menfolk, seated around a large pile of corn, told jokes as they husked it or scraped the kernels from the cobs into large wicker baskets. Such "fun with chores" evenings lasted late into the night, especially when home-made brandy with biscuits (pogácsa) or "Stovepipe cake" (Kürtös kalács) — a specialty of the Seklers — was served to the participants.

Community dances were organized on Saturday nights, usually in the town conference hall, next to the pub. Everyone was invited, usually without an entry fee. The pub-keeper paid for the musicians using his profits from the beverages sold. The orchestra was composed of local citizens, and on rare occasions a Gypsy band was hired. The orchestra's traditional instruments included one or two violins, a bass fiddle, clarinet, and zymbalon (dulcimer). Parents usually brought with them their unmarried daughters for their first dances, also to meet some "prospective suitors". Tshardash (Csárdás) was the favorite dance of the couples.

On Sunday morning, the street in front of each house was sprinkled with water to cut down on the dust and swept clean with wicker brooms. Many unmarried girls prepared a small flower bouquet for their favorite boy, to be attached to their hat while going to church. They also provided them with an embroidered, personalized handkerchief to decorate their breast pockets on special occasions, including church services. In the church, the men sat on one aisle, while the women sat on another, with the young unmarried girls standing in a group in front. Young boys, like me, sat in the balcony next to the organist and closely watched how one of the teenagers operated the organ bellows with his feet. The Unitarian church with its white-washed walls looked very simple and Puritan, but the young minister gave such excellent and moving sermons that we never paid attention to the walls. After service, the folks would mingle for a while in front of the church. Widows often took their flower bouquets to the close-by cemetery. Many church buildings had a large garden that also served as a cemetery,

and the entire complex was enclosed by thick masonry walls with only one entrance. Such arrangements were handy for making the church into an easily defensible fortress (Fig. 27) to serve as a safe haven for the people of the town in case of attack by invading Turks or others.

No plate was passed around for contributions in the church. The married minister received from the community a house, some cropland and a garden to raise his own food, as well as a yearly allotment of grain, sheep cheese, and other offerings from the families.

During the wheat-threshing time, the threshing machine was moved from household to household almost daily, by a team of six oxen. Wood was used for the steam engine, to which was belted a large flywheel that ran the threshing unit. Usually a crew of 20 to 30 people, including teenagers, assisted with the threshing. It was a mutual help arrangement between several (8–12) families to help each other with the threshing chore. Each person, including women and children, had their work assigned. I was always assigned to the removal and storage of the chaff, and to carry the cold water jug around to the workers. The special meals prepared for the workers usually included two meats, chicken and pork. Only after work, at the evening meal, was the brandy passed around. After I was 10 years old, during my

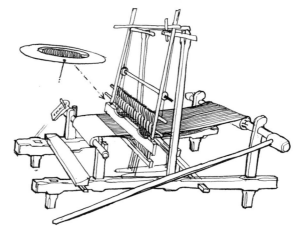

Figure 25. Chango girl threading wool, flax, or hemp from the farm.

Figure 26. Loom that Grandmother used during the winters to weave cloth, towels, and sheets for the family.

Figure 27. Unitarian fortress church that provided safety for the community during attack by the Turks, Crimean Tatars, and other invaders of Transylvania.

free summers I joined Grandma, who had many invitations, and was happy to participate in such events because besides working with friends, we enjoyed the special meals.

Occasionally during the summers, Uncle Zsiga from Bucharest visited grandmother and brought with him fresh tomatoes, green peppers, eggplant, and lemons, which were not available in our village. Uncle Zsiga, being only 14 years older than me, was close to me. I liked him, even when he played some jokes on me. He showed me how to plant willow trees on the creek bank and how to trap wild birds by using a large sifter or old dish washing tub with bait under it and a rope tied to a stick propping it up.

I was always looking forward with much excitement and anticipation to Christmas while I was with Grandma and later as a youngster during our visits with her. My parents came from Bucharest and brought Grandma and me some special gifts, food items, and candies. Smoked ham with cabbage was prepared, along

with the traditional "Stovepipe cake", walnut and poppyseed rolls, my favorites even today. My parents also brought oranges and tangerines, not seen by us for a year. Grandma made sure that the orange peel was saved and dried for her liqueur-making recipe (given earlier).

Only after I was four years old did I learn that the Christmas tree decorations were homemade and all were edible. These included popcorn strung on thread. It made several swirls around the tree branches. Walnuts were wrapped in colored aluminum foil. We saved all year long for this occasion the wrappers from candies we consumed. For hangers, sharpened matchsticks (now we use half a toothpick) were pressed into the end of the walnuts to serve as a stem for a loop of thread. Small pretzels were baked and also attached with a thread loop. Small red apples were also hung from sharpened matchstick stems. Some special Christmas candies (called *szalon cukor*) wrapped in colorful aluminum foil were also hung from the tree. I learned in my early years that I could

28

unwrap this candy, eat it, and wrap back the empty foil so that Grandma or my parents would not realize until the taking down of the tree that all such candies had disappeared and only the wrapping was left on the tree. We used only spruce trees, which were plentiful and free from the nearby Commons Forest. Wax candles and sparkles were also attached and lit under close parental supervision to avoid a fire.

Until I was four, my tree was prepared in secret and brought from our front room by a person, usually Uncle Zsiga, who was wrapped from head to toe in a white bed sheet to give the appearance of an angel, but it really looked like a ghost bringing my Christmas tree. It worked for three years. I believed the story until the Christmas that Uncle Zsiga, while bringing in the decorated tree from the front room, stumbled over the door threshold and loosened the sheet, thus revealing his shoes and trousers. So, I screamed with excitement, "Look! He is Uncle Zsiga!" The folks laughed, and from then on I also helped with the preparation of the Christmas tree.

In 1995 one such Transylvanian Christmas tree, without wax candles and sparkles, was prepared by a group of students from Hungary, Tili, and myself for a Red Cross Display and Competition of International Christmas Trees. It was well received by visitors and won the First Prize in Montgomery County, Virginia.

The winter brought much snow to the mountainous area we lived in. Horse-drawn wooden sleighs came into use in the village. They made it easier for horses to pull loads of firewood or lumber. The cold weather made possible the butchering of the hogs that were being fattened up to provide, until next sum-

mer, without the benefit of refrigeration, the slabs of salted bacon and ham used in the preparation of our meals and the sausages and ham that we smoked and stored in the attic.

For us children, the hog butchering was a day of excitements. Usually, a relative or friend experienced in butchering the hog and preparing the meat and sausages was invited to help. It was still dark when the pig was slaughtered. Its blood was collected in a large bowl and stirred to avoid coagulation. It was used to make blood sausage. After the innards were removed, the pig was placed on flaming straw to burn off the hair. After it was scalded and the skin scraped clean, the loitering children got their usual treat. The strawfire-roasted earlobes and tail were divided among us to chew with much delight.

The cleaned carcass was carried into the house and placed on a large table for further processing, while some women washed, cleaned, and salted the intestines at the manure pile so these could be used as casings for the sausage preparation. Others were cutting and grinding the meat chunks and chopping onions and garlic to mix into the sausage meat along with salt, black pepper, and red paprika. Empty plates were lined up on the table, on which was placed for each family of relatives, friends, and neighbors, enough samples of sausages, liver- and bloodwurst, and special cuts of meat to make a meal for the family. The recipients reciprocated when they butchered their own hogs. This way the season of eating fresh meat was extended for all the villagers. Not having a butcher shop in most villages, and with no refrigeration available, this custom proved to be very practical. Our other fresh meat sources were live chickens. Each time we visited relatives in the villages during the summers, after the usual greetings, someone from the host family disappeared. That person got some corn kernels to lure, and a sharp knife. He chased down and cornered in the backyard some chickens or a large hen to be used immediately in preparing a meal for us.

Because of my Transylvanian upbringing and living in such isolated mountain communities as just described, I learned early in life to become self-sufficient as is true for other people around the world who live in isolation, especially in the mountains. In addition, we were poor and had to get by on food that we raised, on wood that we fetched from the community forest for fuel, and on cloth made of fibers from things we grew, such as hemp, flax, and wool from our sheep.

So, when I appear thrifty, the reader should consider the customs of the times and the surroundings where I lived. We were also isolated from outside markets by World War II. No coffee, tea, seafood, citrus and other tropical fruits, or spices were imported. For a coffee substitute, a mixture of roasted and ground barley and chicory root was often used. This was surely caffeine free! For tea, we picked and dried the young shoots and leaves of blackberry and raspberry, and also used rosehips. The latter, because of its high vitamin C content, served as a citrus fruit supplement during the winter months. Seafood seldom reached us, and only in the form of canned tuna and sardines, but my family never could afford this luxury in the 1930s. For a winter "vitamin" source, although I never heard this word in Transylvania as a child, we stored home-grown apples, carrots, and sauerkraut.

We never worried about prematurely fallen fruits that were usually ripe but infested with moth larvae (like coddling moth) — the reason for their early drop. Such wormy fruits were picked up daily and mixed into the fruit mush in a large ceramic or wooden crock, to be fermented and used for distilling brandy during late fall. Removing daily the fallen fruits from the ground could have been the reason that we did not have to spray the fruit trees against pest insects. The worms were collected with the fruits before they had a chance to crawl back into the tree to damage it further, pupate, and overwinter there. We never noticed a difference between the brandy made from healthy or wormy fruits!

But we noticed a difference in quality, when our plum trees for plum brandy making were infested with Plum *Lecanium* or Brown Scale

insects. These insects produce much liquid excrement, which is known as the sugar-rich honeydew. Honeydew drips over the foliage and serves as growth media for sooty mold, a fungus that covers the leaf surface with black mycelia. The black coating interferes with the photosynthesis in the leaves, enhanced by the sun when it can reach the leaf surface to induce sugar production in the fruits. Less sugar in the plums resulted in less flavor and alcohol content in the brandy. Some folks think this was the reason for me to choose scale insects for a lifetime study.

29

In most villages of Transylvania, as in my paternal grandfather's village of Tărlungeni, we had one or more brandy distilleries owned by local farmers. The villagers, with fermented mush, signed up to use the equipment for one or more nights. As a child, I watched one night, with amazement, how the fire was kept going under the distiller, how the cooling water was replenished periodically, and how the final product was dripping in the bottles. The periodic tasting for "quality control" produced high-spirited and singing caretakers that usually woke up grandma (my father's stepmother), who wanted to make sure that she was present toward the completion of the task. She counted the bottles and set aside from every 10, one bottle for the owner of the distillery for the use of the equipment, and one to be delivered to the local police chief, as liquor tax. I don't think that the latter bottles reached the tax collectors of the country. Such distilling was legal, as long as the brandy was not sold but kept for family use. Even in 1996 this practice was alive, except that now two bottles from every ten are kept by the owner of the distillery. Grandma made sure that all the leftover bottles were hurriedly removed and hidden from the men-folk in strategic locations around the house known only to her. I learned that Uncle Zsiga would search for these bottles for days and, after emptying their contents, would refill them with water to avoid early discovery and the usual scolding that followed.

Grandma fetched bottles only for special family events and holidays, and to serve to the hard-working crews at harvest and threshing times. I remember once when she poured out some brandy for my grandfather, because we went out at 5 a.m. to cut firewood in the forest on a cold, late-fall morning. Grandfather, as usual, let me have a sip from his glass when I volunteered to join him. We really needed "inner warming" for the task ahead of us.

I fetched our drinking water from nearby springs, a duty entrusted to me when out in the fields. For lunch, each of us carried a 2-inch-thick large slice of farm bread, one large onion, and a cube about 4x4 inches of salt-cured bacon on the skin. At noon, we made a small fire and cut and sharpened two hazelnut twigs. On a twig we slid one half of the onion, the opened-up bacon, and the other onion half with the onion halves facing and holding tight the sandwiched-in bacon. We roasted the onion halves with the bacon, often turning the stick and dripping the bacon fat over our bread. We salted the roasted onion and ate it as a relish with the sliced bacon and with the "enriched" bread. Those days cholesterol problems were unknown to us. But, I learned later in life that people living in the cold northern climates or in high mountains eat more fatty food and drink more alcoholic beverages than most others in the south.

Figure 30. Figures 28, 29, and 30 are samples of water and milk jugs made in potteries in Corund.

After we filled the horse-drawn farm cart "to the brim" with firewood, we secured the load with chains; on steep slopes we had to tie 2 or 3 wheels with chains to avoid rolling too fast down the steep road bed. I realized soon why we had such small horses. With their shorter legs they were better adapted to such a terrain. In our case, they even got on their knees to hold back the heavily loaded cart while grandfather and I were, for counter-weight, hanging down from the branches and trunks sticking out at the back. I learned soon that we could warm ourselves four times with the same load of firewood. First, when we felled and processed the trees for transportation; during transportation out of the gullies and home on such treacherous roads; when we cut the logs with hand saws and then split and stacked them under some shelter for the winter; and finally when we heated our home with them. In Transylvania, I had seen only wood used for fuel; when I was taken to Bucharest, I learned that the tall, modern buildings were heated with oil.

My paternal grandfather, János Kosztarab, had a series of tragic misfortunes in his family life. His first great love was a Sekler girl — a Miss Csia — in Braşov, but because of his mother's (Anna Pajor's) prejudice against girls from wealthy families, who might not be able to take the hardships of working in the farm fields, and her "low opinion" of the Seklers, he was not allowed to marry her, even after she expected a child from Grandfather. The embittered young lady gave birth to a baby boy, János Csia, but after that her own well-to-do Sekler family disinherited her for the "shame brought on her family." She showed up with the baby in her arms at my great-grandmother's doorstep and called her out, telling her: "Because you did not allow your

Figure 31. My Chango grandmother's 100-year-old dowry chest, still in use in Tărlungeni.

son to marry me, here is his baby boy, and you have to raise him now!" With that, she left the baby on Great Grandmother's stoop. János was raised in the family.

To satisfy his mother's demand, Grandfather married a local Chango girl. His first wife, Anna Molnár, my grandmother, died early, leaving behind two orphans, my 8-year-old father and his sister Anna, 6 years old. My grandmother Anna's dowry chest (Fig. 31) was saved for me by relatives, as was her ornate Chango belt that was used for generations for special occasions (confirmations, weddings, etc).

After his first wife's death, Grandfather remarried a young local widow, who bore him a boy and a girl. He had much joy in the youngsters and used to take them in his wagon to some out-of-town and farming activities. He did so when he took some grain to a water-wheel-powered mill in the next town. The children were 3 and 5 years old and slept on hay in the back of the wagon while, from the front, he handled the two oxen that pulled the wagon. On the way home, he decided to take a short-cut and cross at the shallows the broad local river, a tributary of the Olt. Apparently, the heavy rains in the close by high mountains produced a sudden flash flood that turned over the wagon just as they reached the middle of the river and the oxen stepped in a deep water hole. The oxen got loose and waded to the river bank, but the flood took the two sleeping

children and they drowned. I don't think that the children's mother ever forgave Grandfather for this accident. The resentment was still there, even after many years, when I spent a summer with them.

Grandfather owned a few acres of farmland and some pastures far and high in the mountains. While with him one summer, he took me up to his pasture at Döblen on the slopes of Mt. Csukás (Fig. 14), to make hay. We carried food to last for a week, and tied a cow to the end of the cart for a milk source, because we had to stay long enough to cure the fresh hay before bringing it back to the town with us. For protection from rain, we built a temporary shelter from freshly cut tree branches; it served as our sleeping quarters during the nights. Fresh hay compensated for mattresses. We cooked our meals on an open campfire. Our most common meals included potato soup, scrambled eggs with a lot of fried onions, and corn mush. After the evening meal, I placed some potatoes in the still hot ashes, covered with hot embers, and enjoyed the baked hot potatoes with cold milk for "dessert." While there, I turned the hay over with a large wooden pitchfork to speed the drying, fetched spring water, collected wild mushrooms to eat, and filled three gallon-sized jars with fresh raspberries to be processed at home into preserves. I had to be careful while picking the berries because the local brown bears also liked the

Figure 32. Interior of a typical general-use room in a Sekler house.

raspberries. I was told if a bear approached me, to play dead and lie motionless on the ground. The bears normally don't touch "dead bodies." I didn't think I could manage that type of self-protection; I would rather run for my life. You can't count on climbing a tree, as we did when chased by wolves or dogs. Bears are good tree climbers. Thank goodness, I was lucky and no bears came to munch berries when I was in the berry patch. — But one early morning, after getting out of our shelter, Grandfather noticed near our fire-pit a fairly fresh pile of bear dung, still steaming in the early morning cold air. Our visitor must have been looking for leftover food. Luckily, we kept the food inside the shelter. — As a city boy, I was relieved after we finally stacked high the wagon with dry hay and drove home where I could sleep indoors again and in a bed. The leftover hay was stored for later use in a haystack held upright by a strong and tall wooden stake in its center.

My paternal great-grandmother Anna Pajor, after not allowing my grandfather to marry his first love, Miss Csia, a Sekler girl, must have had a fit when her other two children, András, and Ilona, married the two children of a Sekler family, the Demeters, in Pădureni (Besenyö) (Fig. 14). — The matron tried to rule with an iron hand over Aunt Ilona's family, who lived with her after she became a widow. They would be the heirs of her estate. But she did not want her farm to be divided among too many grandchildren. So after three grandchildren were born, she demanded from Uncle Ferenc Demeter that he start sleeping in the hayloft during the summer and in the outside, or "summer", kitchen during the winter. After the "bed separation", two more grandchildren were born.

My maternal grandmother Teréz had only two old books in her home: the Roman-Catholic prayer book and a Unitarian hymnal, both printed in the mid-1800s. The first had some pictures of Saints and of major biblical events, but was not very interesting for a youngster. The second had some hand-written notes on our family tree, started by my great-grandfather, Joseph Albert. It also contained a few pressed dry flower heads with faded petals. Grandmother used to take both books and me to the Unitarian Church services on Sundays. There she sang from the Unitarian hymnal and prayed from the Catholic prayer book. She had a wonderful voice and loved to sing. I was indoctrinated until age 6 in both of these religions: Sundays in the Unitarian Church and in her home, where I learned the Catholic prayers. My mother, raised in this Unitarian town, received such religious indoctrination in school, although she was supposed to have followed grandmother's religion.

My grandmother's two religious books were the only inheritance my mother received after grandmother's death in 1939. As the only child, I also inherited these family treasures from my mother.

As a child, I envied those playmates of mine in the village whose parents owned more than the prayer and hymnal books. Whenever I stayed with such playmates in their homes, I paged through their illustrated books and especially picture magazines. Such possessions usually included old farmer's calendars and a popular monthly magazine (*Tolnai Világlapja*) passed down from relatives living in the cities.

Being a single child, I had many lonely hours while under the care of my widowed grandmother. Browsing through neighbors' books and magazines filled my lonely hours, but also opened an unseen new world beyond the borders of our village. To own books became my obsession as a teenager, and has stayed with me throughout my life.

My first three books were presented to me by the Calvinist Elementary School in Bucharest as prizes for my "scholastic" achievements. My father gave me a Hungarian translation of the book on the Microbe Hunters by Paul de Kruif

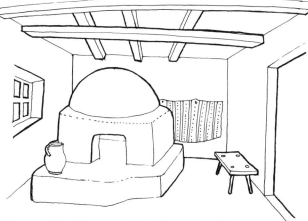

Figure 33. Summer kitchen with large oven for baking bread.

(1926) that I still treasure. The exciting stories about the French Pasteur, the German Koch, the American Theobald Smith, and the Hungarian Semmelweis and other explorers of science, made lasting impressions on me. I wanted to become a research scientist like they were. This book was followed by an Encyclopedia volume, written in Hungarian (*Uj Idök Lexikonja*). A Romanian neighbor, Gheorghe, who worked for the government, came across the book and gave it to me as a gift. His younger brother, Nicu, was a student at the Technical University and often helped me with solving my school homework math problems. Their unmarried sister, Maria, introduced me to some vegetable gardening skills. Together we planted the onion and garlic settings and the pole beans in the backyard garden when I stayed for a year in the suburbs of Bucharest at Dunavit 70, with Aunt Anna and Uncle András. Maria taught me how to stack the corners of our firewood pile so it would not collapse later. Such memorable good relationships with our native Romanian neighbors made it easy to forget that I was born and raised as an ethnic Hungarian in that country, except when later politicians stirred up chauvinistic feelings against the minorities.

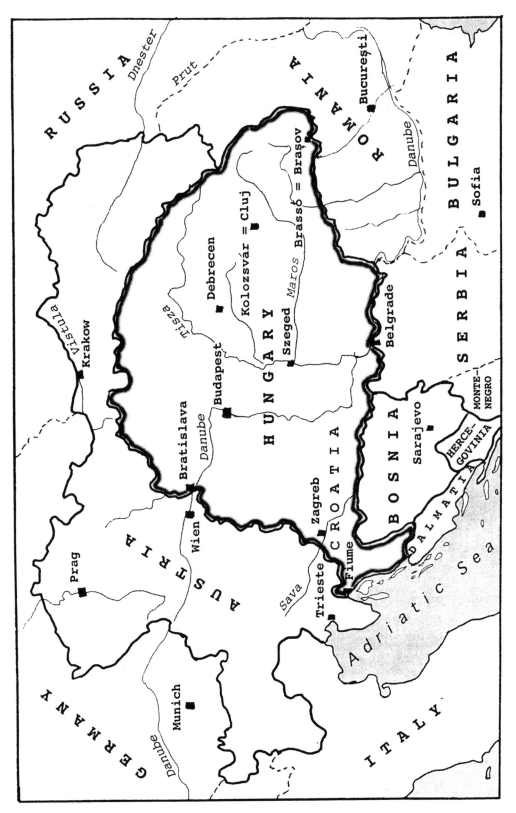

Figure 34. Hungary before 1918.

4 — A Brief History of Transylvania: Its People and Their Religions

Transylvania means "the land beyond the forest" in Latin. The name has been used since the Middle Ages, designating the easternmost province of the Hungarian Kingdom. Transylvania's Hungarian name, Erdély, means the same as in Latin and served as the basis for its later Latin name. The Romanian name, Ardeal, appears to be a Romanian transliteration of the Hungarian name. The Saxon-Germans living there refer to Transylvania as Siebenbürgen, meaning "the land of seven fortresses" that was depicted in the Coat of Arms of Transylvania (Fig. 35). In the latter, the eagle, or "Turul bird", symbolizes the Hungarians, the sun and moon the Seklers, and the 7 fortresses the Saxons of Transylvania. The reader will often find two or three different names that were given through the centuries to the same Transylvanian town by its inhabitants. I will use the current Romanian name, but the first time I mention it, I will place the Hungarian name and the Saxon-German names, when applicable, in parentheses. For example, the city considered for centuries the capital of Transylvania is called today Cluj-Napoca (Fig.34). Napoca was recently added to the name to emphasize its possession by the Romans. The names in parentheses, Kolozsvàr, Klausenburg, designate its earlier Hungarian and Saxon-German names.

The area is about the size of Portugal (40,000 square miles) and served for centuries as a bridge between four cultures: the Slavic, German, Latin, and Byzantine. It is the place where Roman Catholicism, Northern Protestanism, and Eastern Orthodoxism met and where religious tolerance was proclaimed by this independent country for the first time

Figure 35. Transylvania's coat of arms.

in the world (1564) and thus provided refuge for a variety of religious groups.

Transylvania (Fig. 36) is similar to Switzerland, but is also different in many ways. They are similar in that each is a land-locked mountainous region of Europe inhabited by three or four different cultures, speaking three or four different languages, and belonging to several religious denominations. The Swiss of Geneva and the Transylvanians (Fig. 37) were the first in Europe, and probably in the whole world, to declare a general freedom of religions. The Diet of Transylvania at Turda (Torda) passed a proclamation in 1564 that became law in 1568. This religious freedom was one reason that a variety of immigrants settled in Transylvania, as later in the United States, where religious freedom was established by law in Virginia in

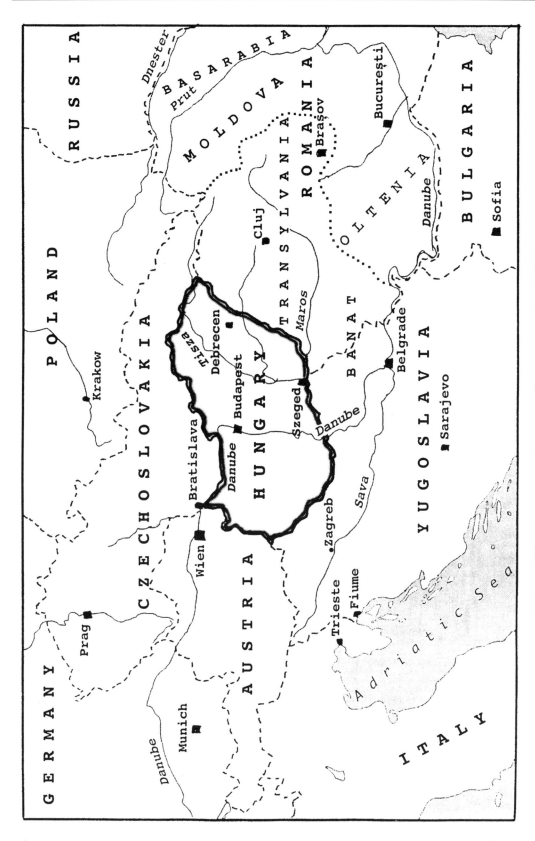

Figure 36. Hungary and surrounding areas after 1920.

Figure 37. The Wall of Reformation in Geneva, citing Stephen Bocskay, the Prince of Transylvania, in recognition of his practice of religious freedom for all.

1785, and later became the First Amendment to the U.S. Constitution.

The four religions recognized at the Transylvanian Diet in 1564 were the Calvinists, Lutherans, Roman Catholics, and Unitarians. Although the Eastern Orthodox were not mentioned in the Law, they enjoyed free practice of religion. Also, the newly immigrated Anabaptist craftsmen and Jewish merchants received similar privileges from Prince Gábor Bethlen, as the Armenian Catholics did later.

Transylvania differs from Switzerland, however, in several ways:

Whereas in Switzerland the different ethnic and religious groups settled in separate areas (Cantons) of the country, in Transylvania, except for the earlier entirely Sekler and Saxon communities, all the communities are mixed-ethnic communities. Unfortunately, this latter fact served as the basis for outsiders to stir up ethnic discordance.

While Switzerland was spared from most foreign invasions, the Transylvanians were affected by several. Because Switzerland's neutrality and independence had already been recognized for over a century, it could avoid participation in both World Wars of the 20th century. The Transylvanians enjoyed independence only between 1541 and 1690, while the Turks ruled Central Hungary, isolating Transylvania from the Hapsburg Emperors. In addition, the Transylvanians were affected by the 1848 Revolution, the two World Wars, and the Soviet domination of East Central and Eastern Europe for 45 years in the middle of the 20th century.

The area of Transylvania was recognized as Dacia by the Romans, who held it for 165 years. They took the land from Dacia's chieftain Decebalus in 106 A.D. and evacuated it in 271 A.D. Soon the Goths occupied it, to be pushed out by the Huns, who held the land between 367 and 453 A.D. until the Gepids and later the Avars took over and stayed for three centuries. After the breakup of the Avar Empire, the Bulgarians held Transylvania for about 90 years, to be defeated by the Hungarians, who settled in the area around 900 A.D. and held it for 1000 years, until 1918 (Fig. 34).

The Hungarians, coming from the East under the leadership of Chieftain Árpád, entered the Carpathian Basin in 896 A.D., and the tribes of Gyula and Kende occupied Transylvania. They found there only small communities of peaceful people. They strengthened the southern and eastern frontiers against the pressure from the Petchenegs, who controlled the adjoining area east of the Carpathian Mountains and south of the Transylvanian Alps, that later became the land of the Vlachs (Romania).

After 100 years in the Carpathian Basin the Hungarians accepted Western Christianity in the form of Roman-Catholicism under István the First (Saint Stephen). Today, the approximately 2.5 million Hungarian-speaking Transylvanians (the official Romanian Census of 1977 gave 1,671,000 only) are divided into three major groups:

(1) **Magyars**. These people are the majority (more than 1 million), who live in the villages and large cities of central and western Transylvania. There is new evidence that the ancient homeland of the Hungarians (Magyars) was in the South Caucasian Mountains, along the River Kura, where they intermingled racially, linguistically, and culturally with the Sumerians. One evidence for this surmise is the cuneiform writing practiced through the milennia by their brothers, the Seklers, which must have originated in Sumeria.

(2) **Szèkelys** (Seklers)(Fig.38). These people are considered the oldest inhabitants of Transylvania. When the Magyars conquered the Carpathian Basin, they found there the Seklers, presumably the descendants of the Avars, though some believe that the Seklers are actually descendants of Attila's Huns: the group that remained there after the majority of Huns returned to the East. These people live mainly in eastern Transylvania, a region that was for a short time after WWII part of the Autonomous Hungarian Province with an 80% Hungarian population and that was replaced in 1968 with the new county names of Covasna, Harghita, and Mureş. The number of Seklers on this land was officially estimated to be more than 600,000, but many were not included in the Romanian Census as Hungarians, especially those who were forced to live in other parts of Romania (e.g., Bucharest) or who were married to non-Hungarians.

(3) **Csángó-Hungarians** (Chango). These people emigrated from Sekler lands to southeastern Transylvania into the Ţara Bărcei (Barcaság) and formed eleven communities around and in Braşov, including my father's town of Tărlungeni (Tatrang)(Fig. 14). Their presence was documented in the mid-15th cen-

tury. Other Changos have crossed the Eastern Carpathians to Moldova since the Middle Ages, especially after the brutal Siculeni (Mádéfalva) massacre by Hapsburg troops in 1764. There is archaeological evidence that some Changos were already living in Moldova starting from the 10th century (Kiss, 1988). Their present numbers were estimated to be approximately 150,000 in the Province of Moldova (Bálint, 1993), but the Government Census registered them as Romanians. The Changos near Braşov were estimated to number around 25,000 in 1930 (Binder, 1994).

The varied religions and the other peoples of Transylvania will be further discussed below, but an excellent summary with more detailed information on the history of the ethnic minority churches in Transylvania was printed by Romániai Magyar Szó, in 1992.

The influence of the Reformation in Transylvania started with Saxon merchants who returned from the Leipzig Fair of 1519 in Germany. They brought with them the first Lutheran literature. Protestanism spread rapidly with the printing of some sections of, and later the entire, Bible in the native tongues of the Saxons and Hungarians. After the lost Battle of Mohács in 1526, the Turks occupied the south-central parts of Hungary. The western and northern border areas were under the Hapsburg Kings with Roman-Catholic dominance, while the Transylvanians, after being cut off from outside dominance, elected János Szapolyai, the Viceroy of Transylvania, as their new King.

While the Transylvanian Saxons became Lutherans, only nine Hungarian villages near Braşov, under the influence of the Saxons in nearby Braşov became Lutherans, including my ancestors on my father's side in the village of Tărlungeni. The rest of the Hungarian-speaking population, including the Seklers, who were recognized in the Hungarian Constitution as a "separate nation", chose a variety of religions. In some large villages the residents often established two or three different churches, while in smaller communities like that of my mother's ancestors, people of the entire village belonged to one church, Unitarian, Calvinist, or Roman-Catholic. The residents lived in peace together, respecting each other's choice of religious affiliation. In the case of inter-faith marriages, it became an unwritten custom among Transylvanian Hungarians that the boys followed their father's religion while the girls followed their mother's. I believe even the Pope in Rome must have closed one eye to this custom, to keep his flock in Transylvania happy.

This was the basis for my indoctrination in four religions. My widowed grandmother Theresa Nagy came from a Catholic town, Dealu, to live in Cehețel, a Unitarian village. She taught me my first Roman-Catholic prayers, but on Sundays we attended Unitarian services, the only ones available in town. Unitarians believe only in a one-person God; Christ is to be followed rather than worshipped. Thus, they do not believe in the doctrine of the Holy Trinity. Because of the unique tradition of religious freedom, the Unitarian religion emerged from Transylvania. Its founder Ferenc Dávid was born in Cluj and started preaching Unitarianism from the end of 1565. He was supported by King Szapolyai, who himself converted to Unitarianism in 1568. An excellent up-to-date summary on the fate of the mistreated Unitarians in Transylvania was compiled by Gellérd (1996).

In Bucharest, I was enrolled for six years in the only bilingual school, the Calvinist (Reformed) Church-affiliated elementary school, where I learned many of their hymns and was often taken to their church services. Because of my father's religion, I received religious instruction for 8 years in Lutheranism. So, with all these religious indoctrinations, as an adult I became an ecumenical Roman Catholic.

The first German-speaking Saxons arrived in Transylvania around 1150-1160 A.D. The group called Flanders came from the western side of the Rhein River and settled on sparsely-inhabited land owned by the Hungarian king in Transylvania. They built prosperous cities at the crossing routes over the Carpathian Mountains, at Brașov (Kronstadt) and Sibiu (Hermanstadt), also at Bistrița (Bistritz). The

King used the new settlers to defend the country's southeastern borders from the often-invading Petchenegs and Cumans. A new group came from the Mosel River area, Luxembourg and Saxony, to northern Transylvania and to the southeast during the 12th and the beginning of the 13th century.

German-speaking immigrant groups brought new ideas and skills to Transylvania. They built new cities and fortresses, and modernized agriculture, sylviculture, mining, craftsmanship, and trade. They organized the defense of the border areas. Most of their

Figure 38. A Sekler man in traditional outfit (boots and white woolen trousers).

churches were built as fortresses against the invading foreign armies (Fig. 39), as did the Calvinist Hungarians in that area (Fig. 40).

Another large group who spoke a German dialect were the Swabians. After the retreat of the Turks from the Banat (Bánság), and the later Crimean Tatar incursion (sent by the Turks) through Transylvania in 1717, the depopulated area was re-colonized by Swabian settlers, Serbs, and Vlachs (Romanians). The Swabians, who came from southern Germany between 1718-1766, were Roman-Catholics; thus most of them were easily assimilated into the Hungarian culture. Their skills in agriculture had a benevolent influence on the economy of the Banat. By 1920, when Romania annexed from Hungary the regions of Banat and Transylvania, about 350,000 Swabians were living there. Unfortunately, the Romanian Land Reforms had devastating consequences on their communities. The minority nationalities — Saxons, Swabians, and Hungarians — lost most of their

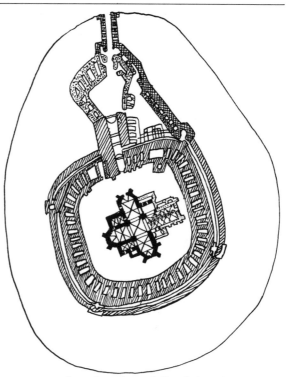

Figure 39. Saxon Lutheran Fortress Church in Prejmer near Braşov.

land to the benefit of the majority nationality, the Romanians.

The Saxons took leadership positions among the German-speaking groups and acquired some privileges for themselves from the King, including self-government, in exchange for taxes and military service. Their numbers increased to 800,000 by World War II. Their deportation to forced labor camps in the former Soviet Union after 1944, where many died from malnutrition and contagious diseases, and the major emigration to West Germany, reduced their numbers to 330,000 by 1977. At present their number is less than 150,000.

The remaining Transylvanian Saxons, held as hostages by Ceauşescu's government, were allowed to emigrate to West Germany only after a ransom was paid by relatives or the West German government. My cousin Zoltán married a Saxon girl, and I helped them escape to West Germany through Hungary and Austria in 1986. Later, Zoltán was forced to deposit 12,000 Deutschmarks with Romanian officials in exchange for his wife's parents' freedom to leave Transylvania for West Germany. Fortunately, because of Ceauşescu's fall, their deposited sum was returned. The emigrations still

continue after the downfall of the Ceauşescu regime.

Jews settled in Transylvania in large numbers, starting from the late 18th century; most came from Poland and its surrounding areas. The largest numbers found new homes in the counties of Maramures (Máramaros), Satu Mare (Szatmár), and Bihor (Bihar). By 1920 there were 171,443 Jews in Transylvania. Most of them were engaged in commerce, but a sizable group of intellectuals associated themselves with the Hungarian ethnic minority and contributed much to Transylvanian Hungarian literature and other arts between 1920 and 1940. Most of those who survived the persecutions during World War II left Romania, including Transylvania. I know only of the freckle-faced Rozsika, — daughter of Ghiladi, our town of Ceheţel's grocer — and the only red-haired girl in town, who succeeded in emigrating to Israel. My Uncle Zsiga, while living in Ceheţel, provided shelter for Rozsika and a young Jewish girl so they could escape deportation by the Nazis.

The official mentality of the Romanian government toward the Jews was revealed by their Premier Ion Bratianu:

Once and for all, I have come to say [to Colonel House, President Wilson's chief aide] that these people may go to Palestine, or to Hell for all I care, but I shall not let them settle down in my country, devouring locusts that they are! (As cited by Sisa 1990, p. 235; from Stephen Bonsal's *Suitors and Suppliants*.)

Armenian Catholics, being Christians, escaped persecution by the Muslim Turks by coming in large groups to Transylvania via Greece and Vlachia. Although some had been present since the Middle Ages, the largest groups arrived between 1654 and 1672. They settled in Sekler's land, around Gheorgheni (Gyergyószentmiklos), and at Gerla (Szamosújvár), Dumbraveni (Erzsébetváros), where they became wealthy merchants, thus adding to the principality's multi-ethnic flavor. Although many assimilated into the Hungarian population, their numbers still reached 12,000 by the turn of the 19th century. Gypsies, who call themselves Romas, arrived during the Turkish wars; they are discussed at my Fourth trip, in the section "Transylvania Revisited".

Romanian historians date their claim to Transylvania since Decebalus' time. As I was told by my Romanian history teacher, the Dacs intermarried with those Roman soldiers who did not leave Dacia during the Roman evacuation ordered by Emperor Aurelian. So a new nation of Vlachs resulted from these marriages and by the intermingling of the Roman settlers and native Dacians. The original Dacians changed their name to Vlachs and since 1867 to Romanian, to emphasize their Roman heritage. The many words of Latin origin (31%) in the Romanian language are supposed to serve as proof for this theory.

Seton-Watson (1963), in his detailed study on the Romanians, cited the above-described theory of Daco-Roman origin from the Romanian historians Iorga and Parvan. He pre-

Figure 40. *Calvinist Fortress Church at Văleni (Magyarvalko).*

sented both the latter's theories and those of some other historians who challenge it. He noted

the unique obscurity of Romanian history, if he [the historian] is here reminded that we are reduced to the merest speculation and conjecture with regard to the contemporaries of Henry III of England and King Louis of France.

Seton-Watson was referring here to the lack of scientific information on the origins of the Daco-Romans or Vlachs, the highly claimed ancestors of the present Romanians, between 271 and the Hungarian conquest in 896 A.D. The reader finds in Seton-Watson's book, besides an extensive bibliography on printed studies on Romania, four chapters dealing exclusively with Transylvania.

Another group of linguists and historians discovered many similarities and word roots in the Romanian language, linking it to Albanian* and Slavic (DuNay, 1977). These scientists claim

---

* I myself benefited from the linguistic relationship between Romanian and Albanian, when I was instructing students from Albania at our University in Budapest

that the original Vlachs came from northern Albania (Stadtmüller, 1980). They gradually moved northward from that region into their present territories (Fig. 15). Being mostly shepherds and living in the high mountains with their flocks of sheep and goats, they survived through the centuries, while other tribes living in the valleys were exterminated by the invading barbarians. Because many of these shepherds were working for Roman landlords, they picked up Latin words. But the highest percentage (45.7%) of Romanian words are of Slavic origin, especially those used for sheep herding. So they must have had contact with and intermarried with members of local Slavic tribes already scattered across the Balkan Peninsula. Proof for the latter version of the origin of the Romanians is found today not only in the language, but also in the fact that the large communities living on isolated mountain tops and elsewhere all over the Balkan Peninsula speak Romanian dialects. One of the largest communities, the Istro-Rumanians, is located on the coast of present-day Croatia, around Zadar (Fig. 15), along the Adriatic Sea. These people speak a dialect of the Romanian language, as do the large groups across the Balkans who speak the Arumanian dialects (DuNay, 1977; Rosetti, 1968). Having given both theories on the origin of the Romanian Nation, I leave it to the discretion of the reader to make a judgment on the subject. For further reading on this topic, a bibliography is given both at the end of this chapter and at the end of the book.

The first authentic document officially mentioning Vlachs in Transylvania (Sibiu) is from 1210 A.D. Their small settlement was limited to the Royal Estate of Székes, by a 1293 Royal decree. Due both to mass voluntary and to government-sponsored immigration of a portion of the Vlach population to Transylvania, more than twice as many Romanians live in Transylvania today than are Hungarians. For example, the population of Cluj increased from

121,753 in 1948 to 214,812 by 1974 (Pascu, 1974).

The Vlach population in Transylvania shunned the movement of the Reformation and adhered to the Byzantine or Eastern Orthodox Church. Their churches (Fig. 41) are colorfully ornamented. Some historians believe that the name Romanian was actually based on their religious affiliation, given to them by the Turks, who dominated parts of the Balkans for 300–400 years. Today, the Turks still call the Greeks and other members of the Byzantine Church, rumlars (Romans).

There were a number of attempts to convert the Transylvanian Vlach population. Toward this goal a Romanian language catechism was printed in Sibiu in 1544, and the Romanian convert Coresi translated and printed four gospels in Braşov during 1560 and 1561; the rest of the New Testament was printed in 1563. All these efforts failed to convert the Vlachs to Protestanism or Roman-Catholicism.

Only the Magyar (Hungarian), Sekler, and Saxon populations were obligated to serve in the defense of the country, not the Vlachs. This is one reason that, while the populations of the former three decreased due to many wars, the latter increased. More Vlachs filled the depopulated villages of the former three nationalities.

To establish equality for the Vlach population with the already-accepted four religions in Transylvania, the "Union with Rome" was accepted at their Synod of 1700. Therefore, 200,000 Transylvanian Orthodox Vlachs became Romanian Rite Catholics or "Uniate Catholics" and thus received a more favorable status from the Austrian Catholic Government than did those who remained in the Orthodox Church (Tautu, 1967). They were authorized to elect their own bishop-metropolitan and keep their Vlach vernacular as the liturgical language. Their situation somewhat improved by 1761, when Empress Maria Theresa appointed an autonomous Vlach Orthodox bishop for Transylvania, but still the Orthodox Vlachs were considered aliens in the Empire, according to Stroup (1983). Embittered Vlach peasants —

---

in the early 1950s. Often I found Romanian words that these students would understand when they had problems with their still-limited Hungarian vocabulary.

under the leadership of Horea, Cloşca, and Crişan — revolted in 1784 and massacred first members of the administration, nobility, and prosperous town dwellers; later they even turned against the non-Orthodox clergy and Hungarian peasants. Their initial demands included political equality, land reform, and equal taxation. Later, these moderate demands were greatly expanded, moving Emperor Joseph to employ military action to crush the rebellion.

The Vlach national consciousness and the foundations for their Daco-Roman origin emerged from the writings of Uniate Catholic priests Micu-Klein, Sincai, and others educated in Rome. They found in their language many similarities to the Latin spoken by the Romans. So they concluded that they were the direct descendants of the Romans who lived in Dacia, and therefore were the oldest inhabitants of the area. This, they felt, gave them the right to rule over the "late-comer" Hungarians and Saxons. Based on their finding, they turned to Emperor Leopold the Second for recognition of their equality among the nationalities of the Austrian Empire. Although the Romans occupied Dacia (the "Homeland" of today's Romanians) for only 165–170 years, the theory of Daco-Roman origin was successfully disseminated internationally, especially by Professor Iorga, and adopted by some Western historians. Historians pointed out that many other nationalities in Europe were occupied by the Romans for longer periods than the Dacs, but none of these claim Roman ancestry. Even in Britannia, which was occupied by the Romans for almost 400 years, Latin did not become the language of the country. The mystery surrounding the myth-making process and the nationalism of Romanians is discussed in detail by Kövári (1979).

The Vlachs — recognized for the first time in the Greek chronicles in 976 A.D. as primitive herdsmen living near today's Albanian bor-

Figure 41. An ornamented Romanian Eastern Orthodox church in Transylvania.

der who later moved northward into their presently occupied teritories — changed their name to Romanian, after the Principalities of Vlachia (Muntenia today) and Moldova were united in 1878. They also changed their Eastern Orthodox liturgical language from Slavic (Cyrillic) to the Roman alphabet.

In 1920, the Paris (Trianon) Peace Treaty broke up the 1100-year-old Hungary (Fig. 36) and awarded the Province of Transylvania, with 2 million Hungarians in it, to Romania. The unjust treatment of the Hungarians has since been publicized and challenged by a number of Western politicians and historians. In 1940 the Arbitration of Vienna requested by both Hungary and Romania returned to Hungary the northern and eastern parts of Transylvania with predominantly Hungarian populations. This partial solution lasted only for four years, when the Romanian Government, keeping with their long tradition, changed sides in WWII and went over to the Soviets in exchange for the parts of Transylvania previously returned to Hungary.

My family, with two million other native Transylvanian Hungarians, became victims of the power struggle between the Axis Powers and the Soviet and Western Alliance. Although the Paris (Trianon) Peace Treaty included instructions for the protection of the ethnic minorities, these instructions were completely disregarded by Romania, as described by Zathureczky (1967), Illyés (1982), and other historians. The official attitude toward the 2 million ethnic Hungarians was to eliminate them as soon as possible through economic strangulation, discrimination, job reallocations, and other means. This sentiment was expressed by the Romanian Premier Ion Bratianu to Dudley Heathcote, a reporter for the *Saturday Review* in 1937:

> I can assure you that, if you return to Cluj (Kolozsvár) or Oradea (Nagyvárad) on a visit in ten years' time, you will not find the Hungarian minorities who are living there today.

In my experience, while living among three nationalities in Transylvania and with Romanians in Bucharest, the people in mixed-culture communities can get along well as long as the politicians and religious leaders are not inciting the population against the minority religious or ethnic groups in order to divert attention from their country's economic and political problems. Unfortunately, as long as the Eastern Orthodox faith is recognized as the State Religion in Romania and Serbia, with privileges from their governments, it is easy for the ruling politicians to obtain the support of the clergy for their actions. When in a country a single religion is supported by the government (and there are still many such countries throughout the world), the otherwise neutral population can be incited to atrocities and pogroms against ethnic groups or against the members of another religion through the school systems and the media controlled by the government, and also through the clergy during religious services. I strongly believe that if people wanted to stop such wars happening in the future as occurred in the former Yugoslavia, the Philippines, on the Indian Subcontinent, and elsewhere, official "state" religions should be abolished. Throughout the history of mankind, more wars have started for religious differences than for any other reason. This situation will continue as long as people are made to believe in a frequently mentioned religious doctrine that "we are God's *only* chosen people, and everyone else is inferior to us." It is an obvious discrimination that when the present Romanian government returned the property of the Orthodox church nationalized earlier by the Communist government, it declined to do the same with the 1500-plus school buildings, libraries, and other property owned by the churches of the Hungarian ethnic minority.

Because of the Romanian Government-condoned atrocities against the ethnic minority (*e.g.*, at Tîrgu Mureş [Marosvásárhely] as recently as 1990), many Transylvanians would like to see their homeland become independent. Barring that, they would support a Federal Government providing equality and autonomy for all ethnic groups. Is it too much to ask for the 21st Century? These solutions were proposed by the Romanian historian Nicolae Bălcescu in 1902, as given in the Dedication to this book.

For further reading on the history of Transylvania, I am listing some literature in the Cited References: For English-speaking readers, I recommend Seton-Watson (1963), Zathureczky (1967), Löte (1980), Halmos (1982), Illyes (1982), Cadzow, Ludanyi and Elteto (1983), Sisa (1990), and Kazár (1993). An extensive bibliography on Hungarians in Romania and Transylvania was printed by the United States Library of Congress (Bako and Solyom-Fekete, 1969). For those who read Hungarian, much detail is found in the six-volumes by Orbán (1863–73); and in the 3 volumes by Makkai and Mócsi Vol I; Szász Vol II; Makkai and Szász, Vol. III (1987); also in Sisa (1993).

5 — In Search of the Truth About Dracula

Figure 42. Dracula, as depicted in Transylvania.

I am not a historian. My reason for writing on this subject is that, whenever I am introduced as a Transylvanian, people ask for the truth about Dracula. My qualifications as an authority on Dracula are that both of my parents were Transylvanian; I was born in the Romanian capital of Bucharest; as a youngster I spent six years in Transylvania and eight in Bucharest and I attended a bilingual school in Bucharest for six years where the true story of Dracula was told by our knowledgeable Romanian history teacher. I have revisited Transylvania several times, including the Bran Castle, as recently as 1996 and have heard many folk tales while in Romania, but I have also read studies by historians on Dracula. Now, I share the facts and speculations with those who are interested in the subject but have no time to read the available lengthy studies and books on Dracula. Those who want more in-

formation should read the two books by Florescu and McNally (1972, 1973).

Some German historians, probably through the influence of their Saxon brothers who lived in Transylvania for centuries and were mistreated by Dracula for often working against him, transformed the historical Dracula into a blood-thirsty vampire, starting with a series of six publications in Germany between 1480 and 1500 (Panaitescu, 1991). But only Bram Stoker's novel *Dracula*, printed in London during 1897, received much popular attention. These books were soon followed by innumerable accounts in different languages; eventually about 200 films on Dracula were produced. Many of these films depicted Count Dracula as a person who came back from the dead ("Undead") and had large pointed bat-like ears, large protruding canine teeth, a pointed nose, sharply defined cheeks, and blood-shot eyes.

Dracula (Fig. 42), or Vlad Ţepeş (The Impaler) was born in 1430 or 1431 in Sighişoara, Transylvania (Fig. 15) as the son of Vlad II, Dracul (The Devil), who was the Prince of Vlachia between 1436-1447. The name "Dracul" (meaning "the devil" in Romanian) stuck to the family because the father had received the order of the Dragon from the Hungarian King Sigismund for his bravery in fighting the Turks. The ending of "la" in Dracula's name is a diminutive term in the Romanian language meaning "the son of Dracul".

Dracula and his younger brother, Radu the Handsome, were given to the Turkish Sultan as hostages by their father in 1444, to guarantee his loyalty and peace with the Sultan. While his brother must have had admirers in the Sultan's harem who gave him the "handsome" surname, Dracula observed how the Ottoman empire was held together by the Turks. To achieve their goals they practiced intrigue, double-dealing, intimidation, torture, and mass killing. Dracula learned all these techniques while in Constantinople, directly from the Turks, with whom he would have to deal later as enemies of Vlachia.

He proved to be a good student because when he attained power as Prince of Vlachia, he practiced the Turks' methods. After returning to Vlachia, he became a vassal prince of the Hungarian King. His principality Vlachia was sandwiched between the Ottoman Empire and the Hungarian Kingdom. The latter two were fighting for domination of the area. Transylvania was part of Hungary at that time but became an independent Principality for a short period between 1541 and 1690.

Dracula (Fig. 42) ruled three times; his first reign lasted for a short time during 1448. By then, the Turks already dominated the Balkans, excepting Albania. He had his second and longest reign between 1456 and 1462 while successfully keeping the Turks away from Vlachia. Because of his success in resisting the Turks, Vlachia did not suffer the same fate as the Kingdoms of Serbia and Bulgaria, which became provinces of the Ottoman Empire. For these reasons, he was considered a great statesman and a national hero by his countrymen.

In 1462, the Turks were prepared to occupy Vlachia. Unfortunately, that year Dracula was imprisoned by King Matthias of Hungary for royal insubordination. He was released only in 1474, but in 1475 was given military command by his former captor, King Matthias, to fight against the Turks. His third and last short reign in Vlachia lasted through November and December of 1476, and ended in December when he was killed in battle against the invading Turks at the fortification he had built near the present capital of Bucharest. His decapitated corpse was buried at the island Monastery of Snagov on Lake Snagov, close to Bucharest. His head was sent to the Sultan as proof that the menace to the Turks from Dracula was gone. Because of his brave fights against the Turks, ending in a hero's death, he

will always be remembered as one of the great statesmen of the Romanians.

The question that needs to be answered is: how did a national hero attain such a gruesome reputation? Even in my childhood, my misbehaving Romanian playmates in Bucharest were intimidated by their parents with Dracula. I often heard such threats as: "Jon, if you don't behave, Dracula will come for you tonight!" Also "Dute la Dracu!" (Go to the Devil!) was commonly said to chastise my playmates.

To understand Dracula's strange behavior and the attrocities he committed, we have to see them through the looking glass of his time and the medieval customs of the region he lived in. He did not invent the cruel torture and killing method of impaling his prisoners. Those methods were already in use before him by the Tatars and Turks.

Boyars (rich land owners) of Vlachia often changed their alliances according to their self-interest. Sometimes they allied themselves with Hungarian Kings, other times with the Turks against Dracula. Dracula sought revenge; for Easter Day in 1459 he invited some 500 boyars to a feast at a lakeside near the capital Tîrgovişte (Fig. 15). After the feast, the boyars were massacred by being impaled on sharpened wooden stakes. This scene was immortalized by the Romanian painter Teodor Aman.

While Dracula hated the boyars for their power and lack of subordination, he was just to the oppressed peasantry. He often gave the belongings of disloyal boyars to the peasantry, acting like Robin Hood. His army was made up of small landholders and freemen, rather than boyars. He instilled such a fear in his fighting men that when some were captured by the Turks, they confessed that they feared death by execution at the hands of the Turks less than they feared Dracula, who was known to impale his own soldiers who had sustained back wounds, under suspicion that they had retreated after a lost battle. He is thought to have killed about 100,000 Vlachians while in power, about 20% of the population.

After Dracula refused the Sultan's demand for a tribute of 10,000 ducats and 500 youths, the Sultan decided in 1461 to entrap Dracula and get rid of him for good. With Dracula out of the way he felt he could conquer Vlachia without a fight. He sent two envoys, Hamza Pasha and a Greek intermediary, to the port of Giurgiu (Fig. 15) on the Danube. It was the Sultan's intent to lure Dracula there on the pretense of discussing ways of improving relations between the two countries, and then ambush him. Dracula, knowing well the Turks, sensed the ambush, but pretended to accept the invitation. He hid his own cavalry in the nearby forest and, with a surprise attack, captured the two envoys and their soldiers. The captured Turks were led in chains to a field near the Vlachian capital, Tîrgoviște, and all were impaled and left in the fields to intimidate his enemies. After six months, during the summer of 1462, the Turkish Sultan ordered the termination of his campaign to subdue Dracula.

One of Dracula's Turkish campaigns was highly praised by my history teachers. It was the campaign along the Danube River that immortalized him as a real Christian Crusader. After the fortress Giurgiu — built on the Danube River by Dracula's grandfather — was burned down, he requested assistance from the Pope and Christian Kings in the area to initiate a new Crusade against the Turks. He could already count on his 10,000 to 20,000 Vlachian fighters. To impress King Matthias of Hungary and gain support for his request for military aid, Dracula sent, along with the dispatch reporting the re-capture of Giurgiu, 23,809 Turkish heads, ears, and noses. He got an unexpected response: no assistance was promised by Matthias to destroy the Turkish presence along the Danube River. So, Dracula continued his offensives alone both on the Danube River and on land toward the Black Sea, liberating much land and many Bulgarians from the Turkish yoke.

To finally capture Vlachia and open the way to conquering Hungary, Sultan Mohammed the Conquerer assembled a new invasion force. It was made up of the largest army of those times, with about 250,000 men to be sent in two forces. One came up on the sea, the other on land from Bulgaria. The two forces were to be united at Tîrgoviște. Dracula had only about 31,000 men but, by applying partisan tactics and by scorching the land while retreating, he succeeded in slowing down the invasion forces. One night Dracula dared to invade the Turkish Main Camp with fast cavalry , hoping to reach the Sultan's tent and kill him. The tactic resulted in many casualties and much confusion in the Turkish camp, but Dracula's men had to retreat before being captured themselves by the Turks. So the Sultan's two armies joined and approached the outskirts of Tîrgoviște. Here, at the sight of the many Turks impaled half a year earlier, the Sultan lost his "appetite" for further conquest. Apparently the other reason for the withdrawal was a breakout of the plague among his men that started taking its toll just as the armies reached Tîrgoviște. Dracula himself had retreated to his castle on the upper Argeş River (Fig. 15) and later moved across the Carpathians to Transylvania.

Dracula often retreated from Vlachia across the Southern Carpathian Mountains or Transylvanian Alps into Transylvania, where he felt more secure, especially among supporters such as John Hunyadi, the Governor of Transylvania, and some of the Hungarian Kings with whom he had a mutual self-interest in keeping the Turks out of the area. During 1451 through 1456 he sought asylum in the Southern Transylvanian city of Sibiu close to the Vlachian border. It gave historians many headaches to understand Dracula's thinking when, four years after he left Sibiu — the city that gave him shelter — he raided it, torturing, impaling, and killing thousands of his former neighbors. This is probably why Matthias, King of Hungary, son of John Hunyadi, instead of giving safe asylum to Dracula when cornered by the Turks, rather arrested him at Făgăraş (Fogaras) and sent him bound in chains to the Hungarian capital of Buda. At Buda, and later north of Buda in the Fortress of Visegrad, Dracula spent 12 years imprisoned, until 1474.

His first wife was already dead in 1462, probably of suicide by jumping off the tower of their castle before the Turks arrived. When he

Figure 43. Part of Dracula's Bran Castle, with its many towers.

It has several floors, many small rooms, and an intricate secret escape route system with narrow passageways; some starting inside a fireplace, another one inside a water well in the courtyard (Fig. 44), where the soldiers descended on a rope to reach their escape tunnels. The castle had no toilets available to visitors; the closest was down the hill from the castle in the parking area. I hope no visitor comes with diarrhea. Most of the old furniture was removed for repairs; some of the walls and rooms were also under repair. Apparently the dry rot fungus, *Merulius lacrymans,* affected the wood floors and ceilings. The few pieces of wooden furniture on display were nicely carved and the ceiling beams were colorfully painted. An English-speaking guide showed the foreign visitors around. Most of her talk centered around the Romanian Queen Maria, who spent many years there.

Figure 44. Waterwell in the courtyard of Bran Castle. An escape tunnel starts from the side of the well bottom.

later re-married, he took King Matthias' sister, but to do this he had to renounce his Orthodox faith and join the Roman Catholic Church. His marriage and conversion must have helped in his liberation in 1474, the entrusting to him of a military command by King Matthias in 1475, and his appointment to his third and final reign as Prince of Vlachia during 1476.

On one or more of Dracula's retreats to Transylvania, he spent some time near Braşov, in the Bran Castle. So in the fall of 1996 I visited the Bran Castle, considered one of the infamous castles of Dracula's time. As a foreign visitor, I paid four times the entry fee that locals normally pay. The castle (Fig. 43), with its many small and large towers, is seated high on a mountaintop, about 30 kilometers southwest of Braşov. It is located right above the old 1919 border between Romania and Hungary.

Dracula abhorred the Saxons of Transylvania for opposing him and even sheltering his rival to the Vlachian throne, Vladislav Dan. The latter, after being imprisoned at Făgăraş Castle in Transylvania, was ordered by Dracula to dig his own grave before being decapitated.

Many Saxon villages and the suburbs of Braşov (Fig. 14) were burned down by Dracula during his raids into Transylvania. Contemporary German writers, probably using reports by surviving Saxon villagers, wrote about such raids in the following manner:

> After capturing many people at Bod (Botfalu, Benndorf), near Braşov, and taking the prisoners to Vlachia, they all were impaled, including women and children.

My own Hungarian ancestors living in the nearby town of Tărlungeni survived the raids by hiding in caves in the high mountain of Csukás (Fig. 14). They were lucky that time. But later, one of my forefathers, János Koszta, was captured by the Turks. When he miraculously returned from captivity, the villagers added his second surname, Rab, meaning prisoner of war. Thus our family name changed to Koszta Rab, and later to Kosztarab for easier handling by the Romanian officials.

Another horrendous atrocity by Dracula included a group of about 400 young persons who were studying the Vlachian (Romanian) language in a house. For unknown reasons, on orders from Dracula they were locked in and the house burned down around them.

There were just too many gruesome and horrifying atrocities committed by Dracula during his lifetime. Some of these were described in detail in the early German literature, and others were documented by Bonfinius, King Matthias' official Court Historian, so I am not going to repeat those stories here.

Where did the stories on his taste for human blood start? I have heard one reasonable version which I could accept and will share it here. It was the custom of the times that rich landowners had the right (*Jus Prima Noctis*) to spend their first honeymoon night with young brides from the villages under their con-

Figure 45. Blood-thirsty bats are often depicted in Dracula stories.

trol. Dracula, as a Prince and thus owning much land with many villages, could have used this privilege. Some of the attractive brides never returned home from his castle. With these women he could have established harems like the ones he had seen at the Sultan's Palace while being kept as a hostage himself. So it was easy for the highly superstitious simple folks to start stories about him, that he could be "draining and drinking their blood to attain eternal youth." Some psychologist concluded that Dracula might have been a person with repressed sexual desires that explain his unusual behavior.

The rest of the Dracula stories seen on films or read in books could be the result of wild imaginations, without scientific proof. The association of blood-thirsty bats (Fig. 45) with Dracula is unfounded. As a zoologist, I know that the bats in Europe as in North America are our friends; they feed mostly on insects, often on night-flying moths whose caterpillars denude our vegetable gardens. Some feed on fruits, but these also help pollinate plants and disperse plant seeds. Only very rarely is one bat found infected with rabies, and we try to avoid them. They will bite only in self-defense, if mishandled.

The vampire bats that feed on the blood of livestock are known only in the tropical Americas. These bats are only inches long and just over one ounce (30-34 grams) in weight, with reddish-brown fur and with specially enlarged and bladelike upper incisors and canine teeth (Fig. 46) to pierce a sleeping animal's skin. They inject an anesthetic and anticoagulant saliva that numbs the wound, but also retards blood clotting. Each night they are able to ingest about half their body weight in blood, thus weakening the livestock but seldom killing them. Some

Figure 46. Enlarged teeth of a vampire bat, used to pierce sleeping animals' skin.

become more dangerous with the transmission of rabies and other diseases. Vampire bats only occasionally feed on humans.

The special powers of garlic have had a long tradition in Romanian folklore, and still persisted in the 1930s when I was a youngster living in Romania.Garlic was used in that part of the world for centuries as a medicine for all kinds of illnesses. In modern scientific medi-cine it has also proved its usefulness to man-kind. In the Dracula horror stories, to avoid vampires from reaching you, it was not enough to lock yourself inside a room for the night. Because a vampire could enter rooms through keyholes and chimneys, it was recommended to rub fresh garlic into the keyholes and chim-neys before dark. For added safety, even locked doors and windows, as well as farm animals, should be rubbed with garlic. I often witnessed in Romanian families who had moved from the villages to Bucharest, the custom of placing fresh garlic sections in a cloth bag and attach-ing the bag with a string to the neck of new-born babies to keep the devil (or vampires) and diseases away from the baby. I believe that it must have worked because fewer visitors kissed the babies with such stinking garlic; thus these babies avoided catching many diseases trans-mitted by kissing relatives and friends.

6 — As an Ethnic Minority in Bucharest (1933–40)

At age six my parents brought me to Bucharest (Figs. 15, 17) where they had a one-and-a-half room apartment with a kitchen. There, they were able to keep me under more comfortable conditions than my grandmother could in the small Transylvanian mountain village. Although I missed the spacious garden with fruit trees to climb, I soon readjusted to the new asphalt-covered environment, especially after I found some empty building lots and Romanian playmates.

The boys were older than I was. They spoke no Hungarian, and I did not know one word of Romanian when we met for the first time. I was the oddball in the group, and being the youngest, I was placed at the bottom of the pecking order — the one to freely play jokes on and have a good laugh on. Those days we used a lot of sign language. The first words they taught me in Romanian were the four-letter words, but they never told me their true meaning. They also had much fun in making me repeat these with my Hungarian accent.

One day they gave me a note and a coin to purchase something from the Greek grocer around the corner. I showed the note and the money to the grocer. He had a good laugh and pulled my hair. The note said: "Pull my hair for two leis."

They took advantage of me, and often kicked me for fun. Soon I learned how to defend myself against my harassing playmates. I curled my left leg behind my attacker and pushed the fellow over my leg so that he fell backwards to the ground. After jumping on the culprit, I beat him with my knuckles. Usually a third, older fellow had to step in to free my hostage from further beating.

I must have moved up on the pecking order quickly, because soon I was accepted by the kids on my street. Sometimes, they took me to their nearby church, just to show me how much prettier their Eastern Orthodox Church (Fig. 41) was than the bare Protestant one I had to attend. Surely, these had many golden icons on the walls, and beautiful candle holders with hundreds of wax candles burning in them. The people were kissing icons and during the service the air was full of the smell of burning incense and wax candles. With some priests (popa) singing in each corner, they reminded me of an opera performance.

In the rectory basement, a sour soup (ciorba) base was fermented in large casks from crushed grain and sold to the housewives as "borş." I was often asked to purchase such juice for my Romanian neighbors; it was also used as a substitute for vinegar.

It must have been a dream for the girls to become an Orthodox priest's wife those days. The priest normally had the largest family in the neighborhood. He had some young servant girls from the nearby villages assisting his wife with the housekeeping. The extra income from the selling of soup base must have been welcomed. In addition, it was customary to go around during some holidays, to parishioner's households and bless their property by sprinkling holy water while producing incense fumes from censers carried by an assistant.

Although my godfather was a Lutheran, his house was often visited for blessing and solicitation by the local Orthodox popa (priest). Godfather was rich, but a penny-pincher. He got tired of such solicitations, so one day when the popa was approaching his household, he ran up the ladder to his hay loft to hide there until the popa left his empty house. The popa, after searching in vain, still blessed the house. Soon after that, he climbed the ladder to the hay loft, while loudly praying and giving the impression that he was ready to bless the stored hay in the loft, until he discovered my godfather. Surely, he was successful in making his solicitation again.

My godfather was my father's relative. Because he was the richest in the extended family, many relatives selected him for the honor to be the godfather to their children, probably hoping for special gifts for his godchildren. He owned three rental properties with 12 apartments. In addition, he kept four beautiful horses to taxi passengers in his city carriages. Few taxis ran on the street yet. He also lured my father, as a 20-year-old bachelor, to Bucharest because he needed a "cheap relative" who, for room and board plus a little pocket money, would look after his horses and do chores around his houses in the Tei District, where many Hungarian ethnics lived. But, despite his wealth, my godfather never gave a gift on birthdays or Christmas to his godchildren.

His wife, Aunt Lujza, was cut from the same tree. Once, when visiting them, we were invited to stay for a late-afternoon dinner. Our soup was warmed up with the sun's heat on pavement stones in front of their kitchen. Usually it was only lukewarm with a lot of unthawed pork-fat floating on the top. He had the nerve to jokingly encourage me to eat more bread slices, probably to save on the meat, by telling me: "Eat well, Mişhu, don't starve like at home."

He wanted to save the tuition money required in the bilingual Church-affiliated school that I also attended. So he took his children out after 2-3 years and enrolled them in the free municipal Elementary school taught in the Romanian language. Because of the school transfer, his children failed; they later completed, with some difficulties, only the required 7th-grade elementary education. After halfway through their penny-pinching life, the Communist Government confiscated their life savings in the three rental properties. Not one relative felt sorry for them.

While my parents lived in Bucharest, many relatives arriving from Transylvania visited and stayed with us for days or weeks, especially when our apartment was just across from the main railroad station on Calea Griviţei (Fig. 17) where most arrived.

It was the custom in Bucharest to treat visitors, besides the Turkish coffee, with a very sweet strawberry preserve (called *dulceaţa*) made from equal amounts of sugar and whole strawberries. It came in handy during the hot summer to serve it on a small plate with a tall glass of cold water. Transylvanian relatives, especially from my father's side, showed up unexpectedly at any time of day. They usually brought for us as a gift some home-made smoked ham and sausages and a lot of apples from their trees. My mother bravely adjusted to the unannounced visitors.

My father paid the annual required 300 leis for registration and 1500 leis for tuition in the bilingual Church-affiliated Elementary school for six years. The school was a 45-minute walk from my home. Only in frigid weather did I get money to take the streetcar to school. Otherwise, I walked across the center of town, often stopping for window shopping around the Royal Palace or at stores on Calea Victoriei. One of the food stores close to the Royal Palace displayed fresh seafood from the Black Sea. I spent hours in front of the filled trays. We could never afford it. My appetite for seafood was built at that time, but I had to save my desire until I reached the United States.

During one of my walks home after school, I took a new wide road home to explore new areas of Bucharest. Here the sidewalk allowed room for the planting of trees. Each tree had a circular area of soil at the base with some tall ornamental plants with beautiful large leaves. The plants were also full of large colorful seeds enclosed in a green husk. I admired the plants and could not resist the temptation to eat some of the colorful seeds. Soon after my arrival home, I got really sick and threw up, thank God! Because I still had a few seeds in my pocket, the plants were identified as castor beans with very poisonous seeds. I learned the hard way not to eat products of unknown plants in the future.

It was a school requirement that on Sundays the students attend one of the Sunday schools depending on their faith and go to church services after. Our presence in the Sunday school class was marked in a small booklet with a date stamp. After a time, some of us learned that we could take off into the city after our presence was already entered into our attendance booklet. So we skipped the crowded church service and loitered in the city. The Calvinists and Roman Catholics had their own church building to go to, the Lutherans had their service in the "public hall" of our school, and the Unitarians met in a classroom. The Transylvanian Saxons held their services in German in a large Lutheran church next to their own school building. I was attending each week the religious classes offered by the Hungarian Lutherans at our school.

The first Hungarian school had been established in Bucharest by 1815, but Hungarians had been living there for almost 400 years. During the 16th century, priests of a Roman Catholic Mission settled there. Also Hussars of the Bercsényí Kuruc Army found refuge in Bucharest by mid-18th century. The 1930 Census listed 23,910 Hungarians, but their number rapidly increased thereafter (Beke, 1980).

Our school was called the Elementary School of the Reformed Church and was located at 50 Sfinţi Voevozi Street between the large main roads of Calea Griviţei and Calea Victoriei (Fig. 17). On one side of the school yard, the girl's play yard adjoined a long two-story building that served as the dormitory for Hungarian university students studying in Bucharest. On the other side of the low wire fence was the boy's play yard with a small building for the school caretaker's family. The latter, during the 10 o'clock break, sold us boiled milk in cups and rolls spread with butter. Some large linden trees provided shade, but each spring these were stripped of their flowers by students for linden flower tea-making at home. The tea was known for its medicinal powers.

From the third grade on we were introduced to some hand-craft making: first to small bas-ket making from raffia, then jigsaw-veneer work, next book binding; at age 12 we were taken to a cabinet shop where we learned how to make small household items from wood — candle holders, stools, coat hangers, and even small wood carvings. Our teachers were from Transylvania, where wood is widely utilized in everyday work. At the end of the school year ceremony our handiwork was displayed and students received awards for their quality work and their good grades. Usually the awards were books. I still have some of these, and one book for which I prepared the binding.

In our bilingual school, we had a jovial elderly Romanian teacher for instruction in Romanian History and Constitution. It created an awkward situation for our Romanian history teacher, when he gave us the official textbook history on our Hungarian ancestors. He told us of the barbarian Hungarian invaders of Europe, who placed their raw horse meat under their saddles to tenderize it while galloping across Europe. At the same time, we had to learn about the brave history of the Romanians and how many times they defeated their enemies, including the Hungarians. Our teacher tried hard to convert us into good Romanian patriots. He made us learn some Romanian patriotic stories and poems. One of those poems I found so beautiful and inspiring that I can still recite some of it. It is entitled "The Last Request", written by Coşbuc (latest printing, 1974). It is about a dying Romanian soldier in a Turkish prison, who is saying goodbye to his comrade returning home. As a last request, he asks him on his arrival home to kiss for him the ground of their fatherland.

One of the State Ministries next to our school received a great deal of foreign correspondence. Often after school my schoolmates and I would scrounge in their daily discarded paper waste. We removed the stamps from the envelopes and thus started our free stamp collections. I believe this hobby proved to be an educational experience for most of us. While trading and organizing our stamp collections, we learned much about art, history, and especially world geography. Later I expanded into collecting coins; without purchasing any, just saving from circulation and by trading.

We learned about the invasion of Abyssinia (now Ethiopia) by Mussolini's Italian troops through lengthy newspaper articles with pictures of the half-naked Abyssinians fighting with lances against the Italian armor. The Abyssinian King, "the Negus," was too proud to surrender in the face of imminent defeat. Rather, he went to Geneva and, in an eloquent speech, asked the League of Nations to stop the Italian invaders of his country. Unfortunately, his request was met without effective response. My schoolmates took the side of the Italians, "the Cultured Country that will bring modernization to those backward Abyssinians." I was alone with my stand for the Abyssinians and in condemning the invasion. So, for a while I was nicknamed "Negus" in my school.

The Calvinist (Reformed) Church was the largest among the churches for Hungarian-speaking people in Bucharest. They had an attractive old church, just behind the Royal Palace, where I was baptized as a Lutheran, after my father. This church inherited some land on which to build a several-story apartment house for extra income for the Parish. My mother's brother, Sándor, was working as a reinforced-concrete worker on the construction crew where he was cutting and tying steel rods with wire to be placed into wooden forms for poured concrete. Uncle Sándor told me that they could recycle the used, bent, rusty nails if someone pulled these out from the concrete form boards after the concrete hardened. So, I made a deal with the foreman to pull out the nails, straighten them, and return them for 5 leis per kilogram. I spent some sunny, hot days in a shady spot, pulling out the nails and straightening them. Thus I made some money to see my favorite movie matinees on Saturday afternoons. I think I saw King Kong 4 or 5 times and most of the Tarzan films.

Another source of my pocket money was from making lead soldiers. I purchased sections of old lead pipes from the junk yards. My classmate Pishti (Steve) Toth and I melted down the lead pipes to be poured into a metal mold for lead soldiers. The next day we peddled these in the school and in our neighborhood.

Twice my father took jobs as caretaker of 4- and 6-story new apartment houses. He controlled the central heating units that burned on heating oil, called *pacura*. He made his Turkish coffee instantly by having a small coffee pot on a long steel handle that he could insert over the flames of the heating chamber. In one building we had two elevators, in another one, four. The servants and deliverymen had to use the back stairways and elevators. Some folks visiting in our building had never used an elevator before and were afraid to use it alone. So, I was often asked to help out as a "lift boy." I usually received as tip a few coins (baksheesh) for my services. When there was no room for me in the elevator, I pushed the right buttons, closed the doors behind me, and let the elevator take my passengers alone to wherever they wanted to land. But, with my fast legs, I learned to race up or down in time to open the doors for my passengers on arrival. I think such races must have helped to build strong heart and leg muscles.

Our school helped to organize May Day celebrations for the Hungarian nationals living in Bucharest. Each year during 1933 to 1940, we had a big crowd there. It was good that not all the 100,000 Hungarians showed up to those events. The population of Bucharest was 600,000 and was considered to include the second-largest population of Hungarians after Budapest, the Hungarian capital. Ethnic Hungarians were attracted to the fast-developing Romanian capital that provided job opportunities, especially in building construction. Many Hungarian nationals had training in construction work. Some of my uncles were masons, concrete specialists, carpenters; my father – a house painter. The average construction worker earned 100 leis per day.

My father paid me 20 leis (US$5) when I helped him on weekends with house painting jobs. I still have in my nose the smell of the old-time poor quality paints (the reason I now avoid painting around my house). A wheat roll cost 1 leu and a 1 kilogram loaf of bread cost 5 leis. Some days, as hungry kids, we showed up at the local grocer and got for a half leu (50 banis) a thick slice of bread and, if we were "well off" that day, for another 50 banis the grocer would pour some sugar crystals or mustard over our bread slice.

While at the May Day celebrations in the Andronache Forest, I climbed with joy the oak trees that dominated the forest. After the asphalt-covered city playgrounds, it was much fun to be out in the woods. Soon after we got home from the forest, I started scratching my arms and legs, and soon a red rash covered most of my body. The physician prescribed only talcum powder to put on my skin to ease the pain, and ordered me to stop scratching. Usually it lasted several weeks after each May Day festival that we attended. I learned later as a budding entomologist that while climbing the trees in shorts, my skin picked up the poison-filled prickly hairs of caterpillars, including the Gypsy and Brown-tailed Moths. So, I avoided these insects in my later years, even as an entomologist.

One Christmas, my father gave me something I had always wanted. He purchased a used bicycle at the flea market, but after he painted it, it looked like new. So he surprised me with this for Christmas. I hardly could wait for the snow to melt to try out this new vehicle. My father ran with me for a few kilometers while holding the back of my seat so I wouldn't fall, until I learned to handle it. Some of my playmates on the street envied me for my bike. They often borrowed it, but I didn't want to lend it often enough. Therefore, I soon found myself running into steel thumbtacks laid out in my bicycle's path. I had too many blow-outs in the inner tubes for my father to fix. So, he got from my godfather some used solid-rubber "tubes" from his horse carriages and affixed these to my bicycle wheels. Without inner tubes, from there on I was able to pick up all the tacks laid out in my path. But my "lower abdomen" suffered from the hard rides each time I hit a bump.

Another Christmas, my father surprised me with my first homemade sled. He made and painted it in his basement shop, so I would not know about it ahead of time. The sled was a great hit with my playmates. We used it over small hills, but the real thrill came when we learned to loosely attach the pulling string to the back bumper of a bus or streetcar. Thus we had a long, free, but dangerous ride on the snow-covered streets. Some bus drivers and streetcar conductors gave us a hard time after discovering our riding method. We still enjoyed the free rides for some weeks one winter, but had to suddenly end our joyrides when, in a curve, one sled runner got into one streetcar track going in one direction, while the other runner got caught in another track going in another direction; thus splitting my sled in two. It was a scary experience. We ended up on the snowy pavement in the middle of a busy intersection. We were extremely lucky that no car was close behind to flatten us. I can't recommend such joyrides to my grandsons.

My mother's younger brother, Zsiga (Sigismund) moved to Bucharest where he worked as a freelance photographer. Because he did not have children yet and I had no older brother, with only 14 years difference between us, we were very close and got along very well, even after he married my father's first cousin, Aunt Vilma. I consider their two children, Zoltán and Lencsi, "twice my cousins."

Uncle Zsiga was probably the first photographer in Bucharest to produce color photographs of couples strolling on Sundays in the Cismigiu Public Park (Fig. 17). His camera, a large square box with a black cloth attached to the back, was set on a strong wooden tripod in the middle of walkway crossings, surrounded by beautiful flower beds. He was available to take pictures of strolling couples. They often were soldiers on Sunday leave with their sweethearts. After taking the shots with a flowerbed background, he asked for 30 to 60 minutes to develop and hand color the black-and-white print with a transparent color-fast ink. His pictures were unique and much sought after. When I was 12 years old he started hiring me to assist him in his new "Corso photography work." He took shots of young couples in their Sunday best while they were strolling on the "Sunday Corso", now Bulevardul Gheorghiu-Dej (Fig. 17). He gave them a signal to get their attention and their consent, before taking the candid shots. I handed the couples a card with an invitation to them to drop in the nearby photo shop on Monday and view the small contact prints, and to order prints if they liked them. My card gave the address of the shop, also the serial numbers of the film and the shot. Because very few young couples owned cameras in Bucharest those days, it was a unique new business. Uncle Zsiga paid me 10 leis (US$2.50) for an afternoon of Corso work, but paid me 50 leis (US$12) for a similar undertaking at a New Year's Eve party at a famous restaurant.

Aunt Vilma, my father's first cousin, lived next door from our building. She worked as a chambermaid to the millionaire family Reshowsky. I was told that Reshowsky was President of the Reşiţa Mining and Steel Company and was probably part owner also, and had a chauffeured Ford automobile. Aunt Vilma was a constant companion and assistant to the Reshowsky's only daughter of the same age. They lived in a large mansion surrounded by a sizeable garden. The four-story apartment house we lived in, with my father serving as general caretaker for it, was next to their mansion and was owned by the Reshowskys. I was the only young boy around, so the women at the Reshowsky's "adopted" me. They envied my dimples and pinched my cheeks each time I visited, and treated me with chocolate candies. For Christmas I received many toys and boxes of candies from the folks who knew me well. I helped them year-long as the boy always ready to run to the grocer or vegetable man with their orders.

On New Year's Day, it was customary in Bucharest for children to go around as well-wishers, called Colinda, with an artificial flower bouquet on a small stick and to shake the bouquet over the shoulder of adults while wishing them a "Happy and Prosperous New Year" through the recital of a traditional poem. Thus greeted, the adults were prepared to treat the well-wishers with candy and coins, like at Halloween in the United States. When I was 7 years old, I also started going around to our acquaintances to wish them "Happy New Year" and "bless" them with my flowers. Most people responded with candies, but at the rich Reshowsky family, one time they gave me a silver 100 lei coin, which was the largest coin I had ever owned. Full of surprise, I took it with much joy. But I remembered that such silver coins, due to counterfeiting, were tested on the market by being thrown against the cement floor to see if they chimed like silver. So, I threw this coin to the floor, testing its sound, and then, satisfied as to its authenticity, with a smiled thanks to the Reshowskys, who had their biggest laugh for New Year's Day. I have learned since from Hungarian gypsy horse traders not to look a gift horse in the mouth to check its age, especially while the donor is still around.

Most of my memories about my parents are from the times we lived in Bucharest. Therefore, I shall give some more details about them. My father was blessed with a cheerful attitude toward life. He liked to sing or whistle when working the monotonous chores of a housepainter, also to tell funny stories and jokes when with company. He liked to sit down after work in a pub with friends and wash down with a few beers the smell of the paint he used all day. He had a big heart and easily lent money to friends and acquaintances when asked. In the pub, he often paid the bills for the entire table company and generously tipped the waiters and Gypsy musicians. According to my mother, the main reason she had to take jobs was because father could not hold money long enough.

My father was a real handyman who would try to fix everything. So, he had many calls for helping out others. To save money, he fixed the holes in the soles of my shoes, cut my hair, and prepared delicious meals when needed. He was a patriotic Hungarian and was offended when the price set for my getting a High School education was to renounce his religion and change his family name to Romanian. He chose

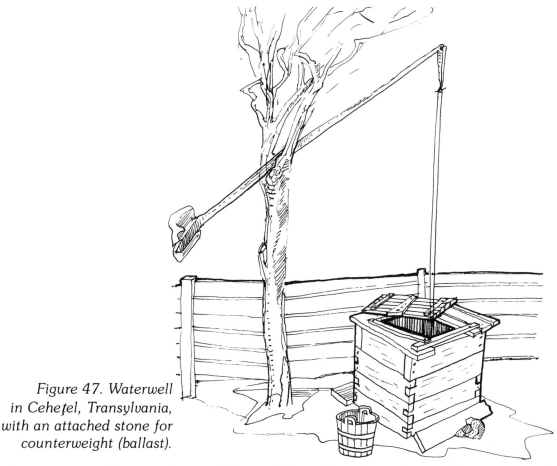

Figure 47. Waterwell in Cehețel, Transylvania, with an attached stone for counterweight (ballast).

instead to start a new life as a refugee in Hungary to see to it that I had a better future than he had. He had high hopes for his only son and wanted me to receive a good education. He often pointed out as an example some Jews, who were selling shoestrings, flint, and saccharin on the city sidewalks to send their children to University. He purchased a violin for me, soon to find out that I had not inherited his or my mother's musical talents. Then he got me old issues of the *Tolnai Világlapja*, a popular picture magazine, and the Hungarian version of the book *Microbe Hunters* by deKruif (1926), probably for inspiration and further education.

He was called to military service again at age 39. By offering to paint for free some military barracks, he soon was out of the service. I helped him with the barracks. He used an old backpack grape sprayer to put an even coat of whitewash on the ceilings and upper parts of the walls, thus cutting down on the use of the brush. To save on descending and ascending his ladder, he learned to "walk" the ladder to new locations while hanging on top with one hand and holding the paint bucket with the other. The smelly paint, often full of lead, must have affected his health. He was unable to give up smoking cigarettes and died from liver cancer at age 59.

My mother had to supplement my father's meager and often uncertain income as a house painter. Therefore, for a while she took washing and ironing jobs for wealthy tenants in our apartment buildings. Because of her special knowledge and skills in fixing a variety of international cuisines such as French, Hungarian, Jewish, Romanian, and Saxon, she took positions as cook for households of wealthy families in Bucharest. So, as a youngster, I benefited from eating her unique meals. She had a strong love for me, but never expressed it openly; this reticence is a Sekler custom.

She liked to sing while working, and had a beautiful voice, like her mother. She always found something to do. We never had a vacation, except for Christmas when visiting my grandma. The only entertainment she enjoyed was to go with my father to some Hungarian-language theatrical performances in Bucharest. She must have gotten used to the many moves we made, once every two to three years, while in Bucharest.

After my father passed away in Budapest, she re-married and I had the joy of sending my mother a duty-free wedding gift parcel from the United States. The personnel in the Post Office had their fun when reading on the form that it was a wedding gift for my mother.

I took my mother to a private nursing home at age 83, after she was widowed a second time and was unable to properly handle her household. She always looked forward to my once or twice yearly visits after she could no longer travel to us. While she lived alone, my cousin István Csere and a professional nurse, Klári Szigeti, looked after her on my behalf. She passed away at age 86 after slipping on a wet floor in the nursing home and catching pneumonia in the hospital.

Until age 11, I was a skinny, pale-faced boy from not eating well, but I did get much physical exercise. My parents showed me to a physician, who prescribed spoonfuls of cod liver oil that I hated to gobble down each day. It was made more digestible after I started taking spoonfuls of honey before and after the cod liver oil.

At age 12, for a year I was housed in the home of my father's uncle, András, with his wife, Aunt Anna. They were close to retirement and had never had children. Uncle András worked in the large Gagel bakery and brought home every day two large loaves of fresh, often still warm, bread. One loaf was given to our neighbor. Aunt Anna started the supper with a small glass of brandy, and I was also given a good sip. Apparently, the smell of the freshly baked bread, with the brandy, gave me a good appetite for their meals that I have never since lost. My physical condition improved without taking any more cod liver oil.

During the summer of 1940, as a 13-year-old, I worked for a bathroom tile-laying crew on a 6-story apartment building under construction. I was paid 40 leis per day, less than half of the workmens' pay. I mixed and carried up the flights a fine cement mix. This was poured and smoothed on the bath floors before I laid the small colorful tiles over it in a certain artistic design. The crew around me was composed of Hungarian nationals; Pál Kovács was from my mother's village. The contractor-foreman for our job was a Swabian from the province of Banat. The latter, one day, gave me the first face slaps I'd ever had from a stranger, for not following closely his instructions. I hated him for this and for his "Über Mensch" attitude toward ethnic minorities.

Because the German Army's victorious military advances in Western Europe were already in the everyday news coverages, some people with German backgrounds started treating the rest of us in Romania as second-rate citizens. Many of the local Jews in Bucharest were frightened by news from Germany. One weekend, we painted with my father an apartment occupied by a Jewish tailor family. The tailor told my father after reading in the newspaper Hitler's latest speeches, "Look what a housepainter can do in Germany." Hitler was called a housepainter, like my father was, by the local Jews. Most of the Bucharest Jews would not have dreamed at that time that the German troops would soon have access to our area. I sympathized with the Jews after I lived in the Jewish neighborhood and realized that they were treated even worse than ethnic Hungarians.

About 350,000 Jews were exterminated in Romania without pressure from the Germans. Many of them were killed before the Nazi Ironguard took power. There were about 900,000 Jews in the 1920s in Romania, but now there are only about 20,000 left who dare to openly call themselves Jews. The book by

Matatias Carp, *Black Book on the Sufferings of the Romanian Jews* (Bucharest, 1946), gives a detailed account of the attrocities, but the three volumes of this book were confiscated from Romanian libraries, while others "disappeared" from major libraries in the West (Ara-Kovács ,1990).

Because it had been in the news for some time now that Hungary had laid claim to part of Transylvania, nationalist politicians were inciting the otherwise friendly Romanian population to take their anger out on us. More than two million Transylvanian Hungarians had been forced to live under the Romanian government since 1920. So we were frightened to speak Hungarian in public. Some friends of mine were ordered to leave the streetcar in Bucharest for speaking among themselves in Hungarian. In their usual condemnation, these natives said: "If you eat Romanian bread, speak Romanian only!" I don't think this was applied to the German-speaking Swabians and Saxons in Romania.

My father in 1939 wanted to transfer me to a Municipal Middle School on our street (Maria Rosetti), so that I could be better prepared in the Romanian language for further studies in a High School. There was no bilingual High School for the 100,000 Hungarians living in Bucharest. So I had to prepare myself to attend the Romanian language High School. At registration time, my father and I were met by the Principal of the Middle School. He refused to register me unless my parents and I agreed to change our religion to the official State Religion, Eastern Orthodox, and our family name to a Romanian-sounding one. He suggested Costeanu or Costescu. We refused.

We left the Principal with much disappointment. I was born in the Romanian Capital and automatically was a Citizen by birth. I became bilingual in Bucharest so that no one could tell which was my native language. I had good grades from the Calvinist school to qualify me for further studies. But I was not good enough to enroll in the Municipal School. I believe such mistreatments made us decide to start a new life in Hungary so that I could have a better future than the one in the country where I was born.

I was often cornered in those days by Romanians with such questions as: "Tell me, Mişhu, are you Romanian or Hungarian?" To avoid the usual harassing remarks that accompanied my statement, "I am a Hungarian ethnic with Romanian citizenship", I responded: "I am neither. Because I have Transylvanian Roots! My father is Csángó (Chango) while my mother is Székely (Sekler); therefore one of my legs is Székely, the other Csángó." I usually got a forgiving laugh instead of a lecture for not declaring myself a Romanian.

Having spent some time in countries of the Middle East and in the Orient, I realize how close is Christianity to Judaism, Islam, Buddhism, and Hinduism. Each basically use among their major principles the Ten Commandments; also they preach charity and peace. One wonders, why can't we live in peace with each other after being indoctrinated since childhood in the same religious and ethical principles? Unfortunately, many of us as children also receive another type of indoctrination, one that emphasizes our differences and the supremacy of our race and faith. Why can't the United Nations pass a resolution demanding that each member nation rewrite the history books used in their school systems to emphasize brotherly love among people of different races, nationalities, and religions? Erasing chauvinism and nationalism from books would be our first step to avoid more wars. Our books should also point out a good reason to stick together: the real menace for all mankind on earth, namely, the harm to our living environment that is deteriorating from overpopulation, overuse of natural resources, deforestation, and air and water pollution. Unless we all work together to solve these problems, we all will be doomed! We should also be teaching in all our schools, starting in kindergarten, conservation of our natural resources and environmental ethics (Kosztarab, 1991).

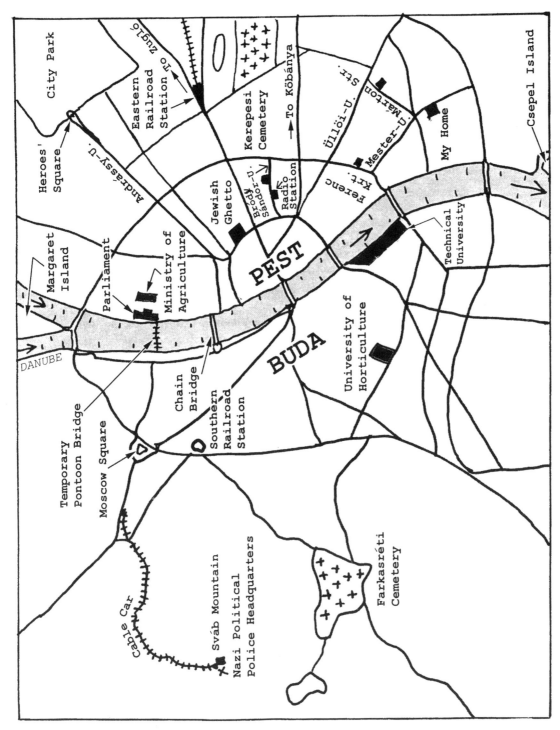

Figure 48. Section of Budapest with the locations mentioned in the text.

7— Refugee and Student in Hungary (War Years 1941-44)

The Arbitration signed in Vienna during the summer of 1940 divided the Province of Transylvania along ethnic population lines between Hungary and Romania. It was intended to partly rectify the unjust treaty of Paris (Trianon) in 1920 (Montgomery, 1947), when Hungary lost two-thirds of its territory, with over three million Hungarian nationals, to the neighboring countries: Austria, Czechoslovakia, Romania, and Yugoslavia. But Hitler in his foresight for influence in the area, wanted to avoid armed conflict between his would-be allies. The Pact also allowed for free movement of families in the affected areas between the 1st to the 15th of September, 1940. Therefore, Romanian nationals in Northern and Eastern Transylvania could move to the south and Hungarian nationals could move out from Southern Transylvania, if they wished.

My father's birthplace near Braşov in Southern Transylvania was to remain in Romania. Therefore he registered to move north into my mother's hometown in Eastern Transylvania. He was anxious to get out from the military work camp in Basarabia (now the Republic of Moldova), where he was used to build defense lines against possible invasion by Soviet troops. He was soon released from the forced labor camp, where he suffered from mistreatment with other minorities, including Jews. So he came back to our apartment in Bucharest and hurriedly packed his most essential gear, his backpack sprayer and other tools of a house painter. He left to my mother the job of selling the rest of our household items, to follow him as soon as we could. The small cash received from our last-minute sales was taken to the Hungarian Embassy in Bucharest for safety and for converting into Hungarian currency to be returned to us in Budapest.

We packed into three suitcases our essential belongings, and took the train to the new country border. Here on the Romanian side of the checkpoint, our suitcases were closely scrutinized for possible smuggling of "forbidden precious items." When the searcher found four bars of bath soap in the suitcases, he confiscated two, saying that four was too much to be taken out by two persons. We were at their mercy, so we swallowed the obvious unjust treatment and felt lucky to be allowed to cross the bridge to our new country on October 21, 1940. It was a dream come true for many of us, who felt mistreated in the country we were citizens of. Finally, we could live under a Hungarian Government, and be treated equally with the rest of the people.

We happily joined my father in my mother's birthplace town in Ceheţel. Here, my father stayed with relatives while painting the home of a closeby grain mill owner. For his work, he was paid in wheat flour and corn meal. He shared these with the family he stayed with. Temporarily we stayed in the same overcrowded three-room house. We took, with my mother, some potato harvesting chores for a portion (20%) of the harvested crop. It was a cold, wet, and windy November to work in the fields. But we felt good that we would not starve in the winter, if our basic staples (bread, corn mush, and potatoes) were secured then. For heating, only wood was used in that part of the country. So we asked and received permission from the town to fetch firewood from the

Commons area of the nearby beech forest. For this, we joined relatives who had horse-drawn wagons to bring firewood for each of us.

Christmas brought some new hopes for us. Uncle Feri and his wife, Aunt Julishka, from Budapest, visited Transylvania for the first time to see our host family. Besides the many Christmas gift packages they brought, they also offered to find work for my father in Budapest. When my mother requested it, they promised to sign a "sponsorship letter", required for us to be able to move to Budapest, overcrowded with refugees as it was. It was an assurance that we could stay in their apartment until we rented our own home.

It took until early spring to organize our move to Budapest, where we stayed in Uncle Feri's place at Bródi Sándor Street (Fig. 48). My father and I spent most of our days registering for work and hunting for jobs at placement offices and through newspaper ads. One auto repair shop mechanic/owner advertised for an apprentice for his shop. So I went with my mother to explore this possibility. The owner found me physically suitable, but he said he was really looking for someone with an 8th-grade education, and I had only completed 6 grades in Bucharest. He said to check back in a week or two. Probably he would hire me, if no 8th-grade graduate was found. Although I was somewhat disappointed, it turned out it was for my own good that he did not hire me on the spot. After discussing our adventure with Aunt Julishka, she strongly urged me to complete the missing two grades, to improve my status for a better-suited job.

Soon came the real break, that changed the course of my life. A single and retired Four-star General, Ödön Matheny, advertised for a gardener-caretaker for his hobby garden. He would provide the use of the caretaker's home, in exchange for some weekly work in his 2-acre garden. He would pay an extra hourly wage for my mother if she could cook for him when he was in town. After he learned that we were Transylvanian refugees from Romania, he "softened his heart" and offered extra yard space for raising vegetables, chickens, and for

a pig if we wanted, also 10% of the fruits produced in his garden and 10% of the sales from the fruits. The only drawback was that his place was in Rákoshegy, a middle-class garden town 15 kilometers east of Budapest, and was accessible by train only. We took his offer, especially when he agreed that we could take turns with my father with the gardening chores.

We were taken in his small car to his garden estate. What a joy! Finally we had our own home! Although it was a small, two-room cottage with a pantry (Fig. 49) and an attached garage for the General's car, it had an adjoining poultry yard and vegetable garden for us. The little house was entirely empty, except for a wooden cooking stove in the kitchen, so the first job I had was to push a wheelbarrow to the local railroad station and purchase two bales of straw for bedding. I did so. At least we did not have to sleep the first night on the bare floor. We used our winter coats for cover.

Soon, I enrolled in the elementary school as a 7th grader. Apparently, my preparation from the private church-affiliated bilingual school in Bucharest gave me a good academic background. I received excellent grades, even after having skipped most of the school year.

In the afternoons after school and during the weekends, I was the General's helper. He kept me under military discipline. I hated that, but I had no choice, and was compensated with training in horticulture and beekeeping. He raised strawberries, raspberries, blackberries, grapes, sweet and sour cherries, apricots, peaches, plums, quince, apples, and pears. All was professionally done, including the making and the use of compost, and of our home-made liquid "natural fertilizer." The latter was made from our own feces! Our outdoor toilet was placed on an elevated platform, like a "Royal Throne" that we could reach on three to four steps up. This allowed the placement of a well-sealed box on rollers under our seat. After each use, we had to throw a scoop of fresh peat moss over the fresh "stuff." There was a container with peat moss in the cabin. When the box was filled to the brim, we rolled it out to some concrete well rings with closed bottoms

Figure 49. Our home, the Gardener's cottage in Rákoshegy, under recent renovation.

that were sunk into the ground. The tanks were strategically located between the trees in the orchard and covered with woodboard lids. We added a certain number of fecal scoops into each tank and filled them with tap water from a hose. Bee-like flies soon laid eggs in the stinking syrup to produce rattailed maggots. When the maggots were fully grown, the syrup apparently was ready to be used as a liquid fertilizer. We diluted it with water and poured it into trenches made around the root system of each fruit tree. It was easy to make trenches and cover these up with a big hoe in the sandy soil we had. The summers were hot and dry (15-20 inches or 400-500 mm yearly precipitation), so irrigating our trees was essential for their survival.

As an always-hungry teenager, I filled my tummy when picking fruits: one handful of cherries into the basket and the next in my mouth. When my General realized this, he sarcastically suggested that I whistle while picking his cherries in the future. On Saturday mornings we weighed the crops for book-keeping, and I pushed the fruits in a wheelbarrow to the local farmer's market to be sold. After keeping 10% of the income for my family, I gave the rest to the General.

I realized that I could increase my income if I took an additional early morning job. Be-

fore going to school, I delivered milk from the nearby grocer to his customers. The weekly payments from my milk-route just took care of my father's weekly cigarette bill. I pedaled the 20-liter (ca 5 gallon) metal can on the grocer's bicycle, and measured out the milk into the covered containers left outside our customer's doors. Somehow, probably due to forgetful housewives or out-of-town folks, I usually ended up with about one liter of milk left over, that I happily gobbled down before returning the emptied can to the grocer. I considered this milk my fringe benefit for rising early each day. Soon I had a leased bicycle from the Selmeczy family. In exchange for chopping some firewood, they offered me for long-term use a bicycle that shortened my travel time to and from school.

One day my 7th grade class was put to a math competition for a prize. Because I was only average in math, I almost gave up the problem solving, when I discovered some shortcuts and found I could make the needed calculations. I won and got a chess set for the prize.

My excellent grades in the 7th grade and winning the math competition gave me the encouragement to transfer after the 7th grade to a Middle (Polgári) School with higher standards than the 8th grade in Elementary School. This school also prepared the students for further studies in Regular or Technical High Schools. So I talked to my parents, and they gave their consent to explore my chances for transfer.

The Principal of the Middle School agreed to my transfer if I passed the required exams at the end of the summer on subjects that in Romania I had not been able to take, such as Hungarian literature and history, constitution, and the German language. So I had to study these four subjects during the summer, what the students had already learned during the first and second grade at the Middle School, in order to qualify entrance into the third grade in this school. I studied during my free time all summer, passed the exams, and was able to start in a new school at Rákoskeresztur that fall. The bicycle from the Selmeczys came in handy, because my new school was in the next town.

A source of extra income fell accidentally into my lap. While I was at the coal and firewood yard in queue waiting to purchase some wood, several women approached me to take home in my wheelbarrow their just-purchased firewood. I soon realized they were either widows or their husbands had been taken for military service. Therefore I happily pushed their meager fuel supply home. I did not expect compensation for my help, but most forced on me some money or fed me with some of their culinary specialties. These ladies gradually became my charges. They often asked me to help them with other loads of firewood when it was available, also to chop these up so the chunks could fit into their cooking and heating stoves.

When snow covered the street, each home owner was required to remove it within a certain time from their section of sidewalk, and from half of the roadbed in front of their property. A number of elderly and incapacitated people needed my help to clean the snow; and I made myself available, often earning some money that we badly needed to start our new life from scratch in Hungary.

Because of my tree-climbing skills while picking fruits, I became known to older folks as one able to trim their large overgrown shade trees, often some dangerously overhanging their house roofs. So, I took all these jobs.

These chores brought more money because they were risky and required extra tools and often the skills of a monkey. Instead of charging a flat rate for such work, I took into consideration the financial status of my customer. My retired bank president customer paid much more for a similar job than the low-income widows did.

My father took a job as a night watchman for the town hall. He slept some during the day, and thus spent less and less on the garden chores of the General. Thus I had more work on my shoulder in exchange for our housing. One day after the honey bees filled the combs with the excellent tasting and light-colored black locust honey, I had to help the General with the extracting of honey. As a young trainee, I was still afraid of the stinging bees when they were buzzing around my head while transferring frames of honey-filled combs into the extractor. At one point 2-3 nervous bees were loudly buzzing around my face. I got scared and dropped the bee-covered honey frame to the floor of our apiary and ran out, closing the door behind me. The many bees shaken off of the dropped frame found the left-behind General. So the General got a number of stings due to my clumsy handling. In his anger with me, he loudly shouted in the drill sergeant's lingo. After this event, for some time, he declined to accept my assistance with bees, and I lost my chance to chew the left-over tasty honey-filled comb sections.

As the War effort brought a shortage of food, my father thought that we would have to produce more food for our own needs. Therefore, he leased two nearby empty house lots from the town hall. We spaded these and planted corn, potatoes, and other vegetables; some for our chicken and now also for a pig. Bread, sugar, flour, meat, oil, and lard were rationed. The war effort emptied the warehouses, but horsemeat products were not rationed and were more readily available from special butcher shops, as in Paris today. So, we ate a lot of horse meat bologna and joked that now we would be better prepared for galloping. Firewood and coal were also rationed

Figure 50.
Carved wooden chairs,
home-made (Sekler).

and often unavailable even with ration tickets. My father found out that we could get permission from the town hall to dig out the stumps of black locust trees along the sidewalks in our town. So we dug out and removed a few dozen stumps. It was hard work with hand tools, but we were happy to have more heating fuel piled up, for the winter.

By June 1943, I completed the Middle School and was facing the decision at age 16, where to go from there. Because of my indoctrination in gardening and beekeeping by the General, I wanted to study horticulture. My parents disagreed and told me that there were better-paid jobs in electrical or mechanical engineering, and I could apply to a specialized High School (H.S.) in Engineering sponsored by the State Railroads that my father started working for. I was disappointed with my parents' choice so, in my sadness, I gobbled down much cold ice cream, knowing from before that this usually started my tonsilitis. I was soon bedridden with a high fever. When I discovered my frightened mother's face at my bedside, I asked if she still wanted me to enroll in

the engineering H.S.? With moist eyes, she said that she did not care any more, just that she wanted me to get back on my feet. Soon I recovered, and happily enrolled in the Municipal Horticultural H.S. at Zuglo in East Budapest (Fig. 48).

The new school required that besides my grade reports, I also bring two letters of character reference from persons well known in our community. I got these from my General and the retired bank president whom I worked for. After my parents moved out of the General's cottage into a tiny rented house, I moved to the boys' horticultural boarding school. Because of my father's new steady job as a painter in the state railroad shop, I did not have to take temporary jobs. Anyhow, the school kept me very busy. We had classes daily from 8 to 12 and field practice from 1 to 4, including Saturdays until 1 p.m.. Every second Sunday, after church services, we had to water our school greenhouses, feed and milk our cows, etc. Most of the food for our school mess hall was produced on the school farm. This way the cost of boarding us was kept to a minimum.

About half of the students lived close enough to commute daily. The rest of us slept in three large dormitories, each with about sixteen beds. Our dorm supervisor was a bachelor teacher who slept next door in his private room. We had to take turns with house-keeping duties, so our parents were not burdened by high tuition and boarding fees. Because of my social background and good grades, my parents paid a minimal yearly fee.

Besides the basic H.S. subjects, we also took courses in horticultural sciences. After four years we would graduate with a special H.S. degree that qualified us to take a middle-man's supervisory position in a horticultural enterprise, or to enroll in colleges or Universities with agricultural, horticultural, or sylvicultural training. Because of the German influence and later occupation, the study of the German language was required, to be replaced by Russian, after the Soviet occupation of Hungary.

Gradually my parents were pacified, after seeing my good school grades and progress. I visited them on every second Sunday, unless I took a job with other students helping out horticulturists or, in my junior and senior years, doing some landscaping work, often lawn-establishing jobs for home owners.

The extra income helped me to pay the tuition for dance lessons, that almost all of my junior-senior classmates took. On Friday evenings, we dressed in our Sunday best. We picked flowers from the school grounds and greenhouses and made bouquets to give to our dancing partners in the Dance School. With the more advanced partners, we practiced ballroom dances that were in fashion — the tango, polka, foxtrot, waltz, etc. Because of our social status, after receiving our High School diplomas, we were expected to be able to properly dance and socialize with the ladies, and to use French table manners when eating our meals. The latter we practiced in our school mess hall by using the fork only in the left hand with knife in the right. I thought, after coming to the United States, that this was a practical and faster way of eating than the way most Americans handle silverware.

My training in horticulture was interrupted in the summer of 1944, after the German military occupation of Hungary. My school did not open in the Fall, and many of my 16–17-year-old classmates were taken into pre-military training. Even my retired General was re-activated into the military.

8 — Arrested by the Nazis (Budapest 1944)

In March 1944, Hitler invited the leader of Hungary, Regent Horthy, to a meeting in Germany. After the meeting was over, he detained Horthy under false pretenses. On March 19, while Horthy and his entourage of military and political experts were held, the German Army seized control of Hungary. Within hours the German political police, the Gestapo, arrested and imprisoned all Hungarian military and Government personnel who were suspected of resisting the German occupation. Hitler also demanded that all Jews be rounded up and shipped out of Hungary. Before his trip, Horthy had resisted this demand, and instead placed the Jews of Budapest in a restricted area, the Ghetto (Fig. 48), where they were kept under surveillance, but also guarded against deportation to foreign countries by the Germans.

My school was soon closed, and as a 17-year-old boy, I was in danger of being drafted for military service by the Nazis and sent without proper military training and weapons to fight against the invading Soviet army. My mother arranged to have a family picture taken before I was drafted (Fig. 51). Also, I started searching for a job that could provide military service exemption for me. Because many of the buildings in Budapest were damaged by the Allies' bombs, the reconstruction of these buildings became a high priority for the City Government. People working on such projects were temporarily exempted from military service, but mostly women and young men like me were hired.

I was able to find employment with the City's 9th District Reconstruction Office, as an untrained workman helping to repair damaged roofs. We had to remove broken roof tiles and other debris from an attic and pile them in the

Figure 51. Our family just before my arrest in the fall of 1944.

middle of the courtyard of a four-story apartment house at 35 Márton Street (Fig. 52). Then we had to carry up new tiles and other roofing materials. It was late fall of 1944, and we felt the cold on such outdoor jobs, especially on the windy roofs. There was an acute housing shortage in the city, and our foreman was ordered to make a number of apartment buildings habitable for displaced tenants before the winter weather set in.

Because of the labor shortage, we were able to hire some young Jews to come to help with these projects. They were pleased to be able to leave the Ghetto, at least during the day. While in public areas, they had to wear the large yellow Star of David on their clothing. They were supposed to return at night, but many asked to stay overnight in the partly reconstructed first floor of the building where they worked. They were granted this request, and we also purchased food for them on the Teleky Square black market. Jews could not obtain food with ration tickets outside the Ghetto. We were all hoping that they would survive during

Figure 52. Number 35 Márton Street, the site of my arrest by the Nazis.

out of it, explaining that I wasn't a skier, but they convinced me to take the skis and try to trade them for food on the black market. The Braun children were happy to learn about my successful visit with their parents and laughed about my story of the skis. Their parents were right. Because inflation had caused the value of our currency to plummet, farmers started bartering their food supplies for manufactured goods. I was able to trade the skis for a 20 kg bag of valuable potatoes in the nearby farming village of Rákoskeresztur.

One morning, while waiting at the railroad station in my home town of Rákoshegy for a train to Budapest, I noticed some young men being escorted out of the station by military police. The German Army needed their labor to dig ditches for a new defense line against the Soviets near the Ferihegy airport. The Nazis were also recruiting young Hungarians to reinforce the army. The next day I decided to move from my parents' home in Rákoshegy and start sleeping in the building where I worked, in an attempt to avoid being picked up by the Nazis or the Germans. I moved to a third-floor room with two other young men, both brick layers. One of them, Lajos Majer, was a former classmate of mine in the Middle School. About 36 Jews occupied the first floor rooms. Each night we locked and butressed the large and heavy house gate with a wooden beam for safety. We also started accumulating emergency provisions if needed before the arrival of the Soviet troops. One day we found out that a candy store on nearby Üllöi Street (Fig. 48) was selling out their Christmas candy. So, we lined up to stock up on candy. It turned out later that this candy probably saved some lives.

At midnight in mid-December, we were suddenly awakened by loud banging on the house gate, and shouting demands to open it. We were scared stiff, and no one went to open the gate. The Nazi guards then tried to open the heavy doors with crow-bars; failing that, they requested reinforcements from the local police. The Jews sneaked into the bomb shelter in the cellar of the building. They hoped to get out through the escape door of the shelter

the crucial weeks before liberation from the Nazis. Because of my upbringing and past experience as a mistreated Hungarian ethnic minority in Romania, I sympathized with the Jews and tried to help them, although hiding and protecting Jews was a serious crime, often punished by execution on the spot. I never thought about these consequences.

One day, members of the Braun family, a boy and four girls, asked me to smuggle some food to their parents in the Ghetto. Armed with packages of special cigarettes to bribe the guards at the entrance to the Ghetto, I got through and reached the elderly Brauns in their own apartment inside the Ghetto area. They were very happy to hear good news about their children. After delivering the parcel, they offered me a gift of a pair of old skis for which they had no more use. I first tried to talk them

and into the cellar of an adjoining building. Soon the Jews realized that escape was impossible because they heard police orders from the other side of the escape door.

My two roommates and I had our own plan to escape through the roof. Because we had been working on the roofs for some time, we were confident that we could jump from one roof to another. So, we got dressed for the journey and raised our heads through a roof hatch to figure out the best route. To our astonishment there were already some Nazi guards on the roofs of the nearby buildings.

Disappointed, we retreated to our room, just in time to hear the gate door being targeted by a series of gunshots. The locking mechanism was destroyed and, with the help of police reinforcements, our pursuers hastily entered the courtyard. Orders were shouted to all hidden occupants to come out of the rooms with hands high. We were now really frightened! Should we go out to the third floor iron railing with our hands up? Then we heard two series of machine gun firings. Two young workers were killed in the court yard: Mr. Fehér, a Jew, and a Frenchman who had deserted from the German Army. Both had tried to defend themselves with small pistols. Their screaming just froze our blood. After somewhat calming down from this event, I suggested to my roommates that we get back into our pajamas and into bed, and wait there for the arrival of the Nazi guards. This way they would not accuse us of being among those who shot at them. My comrades agreed, and with trembling knees we got back into bed to await our fate. We heard shots fired into the doors, before the invaders entered each room.

After a while, we heard shouts from one of the Jewish girls on the first floor. She offered to guide the Nazis to the occupied rooms and open the doors herself in order to prevent further shootings through the doors. Her offer was taken because she would be a shield between room occupants and the armed Nazis. Because of her brave act, no one else was shot, and the rest came out with hands up. Soon the guards reached the third floor, and the girl

shouted to us to open the door. We did so in a hurry. The Nazis were surprised to find us in bed and in our pajamas. They ordered us to grab our clothes. While dressing, I filled my pockets with the Christmas candy that I had recently purchased. That candy helped us survive while under arrest.

We were lined up in pairs by the armed guards, and marched to the 9th City District Nazi Headquarters on Ferenc Körut (Fig.48). On the way, while still on Márton Street, I remembered that, according to a new law, arrested foreign citizens were to be placed under the jurisdiction of the Gestapo. As a Romanian citizen, I was afraid I would soon be transferred to the Gestapo. In hopes of preventing this and because I spoke Hungarian well, I decided to claim Hungarian citizenship. So, while the guards were not looking in my direction, I got in the middle of the group, took out my residency permit that marked my citizenship, and tore it into small pieces. As we passed a ground-level grated window used for coal and firewood, I slipped the shredded bits of my document through it.

They locked us into a bathroom at the Nazi Headquarters. It was so crowded that I had to sit with three others in the bathtub, while waiting for the interrogation. The Nazis decided to separate us into two groups: Jews and Gentiles. Men were ordered to line up in a well-lit large conference room and to drop our pants. A woman, with a Nazi armband and a rubber baton in hand, inspected our penises for signs of circumcision. Because only Jews were circumcised in that part of Europe, those considered to be Jews were locked into a separate room. Many Jews had false baptismal certificates from Christian churches to save them from deportation, but such documents were not taken seriously by the Nazis.

The interrogations lasted until the early hours. The Nazis tried to extract from us the names of those who had procured the pistols used against them, as well as our leaders and organizers of the rescue operation for the Jews. Apparently, they already had enough compromising information on each of us, because a

Figure 53. The neglected Small Majestic Hotel building in 1977, the place of my incarceration by the Nazis.

young man, who had formerly worked on our construction crew, was talked into joining the Nazi Guards, and for some unknown reasons betrayed us.

Around 6 a.m. some of our group was taken to the headquarters of the Nazi political police on Swabian Mountain (Fig. 48) in Buda. We had to use the cable car for the steep mountain climb. I was locked up in a small hotel building, called Kis (Small) Majestic (Fig. 53). About 140 men were jammed into a two-bedroom complex. There was no furniture in the rooms and, because of the crowding, we took turns in sitting on the floor and taking a nap there. One by one each of us was interrogated in a separate building. Most came back badly beaten up.

In our group, I was the youngest, and last to be interrogated. When my turn came, I had just finished reading the only newspaper available to me at that time, the Nazi Party's daily. When ordered to go, I hurriedly stuffed the newspaper into my coat pocket, where it was half-way hanging out, as I walked out. In the interrogation room four people were waiting for me: a Nazi detective in front of me, a secretary on my right side typing my confessions for a document, and two large henchmen, one on each side. On a signal from the interrogator, they applied blows with rubber billy clubs filled with lead from each side to extract from

the prisoner the information they wanted. I believe that it was their hope and intention to obtain some new information from me that would further incriminate my older comrades, because I was the youngest in our group and possibly the easiest to "soften" for the right answers.

Yes, I must have looked frightened, because the typing woman looked at me with pity and pointed out to the interrogators my youth, and my high school student status. She even discovered the Nazi newspaper hanging out from my coat pocket. She asked how I happened to be reading the Nazi Party newspaper. I said that my father brings it home to read himself. I stretched the truth to save my skin, because in fact, my father only occasionally read it for certain news unavailable elsewhere.

After this episode, my interrogation proceeded without the usual "softening" blows. I could not deny, however, that I had intentionally helped the Jews, and as a "patriotic" Hungarian had not done my duty by betraying the operation to the Nazis. After signing my confession, I was taken back to the prison quarters. Here, I was cheered up by the delivery of a large loaf of bread and a jar of apricot preserves. It had been sent by my mother, who after four days of searching hospitals and jails in Budapest, found me here. She bribed one of the police guards with 200 Pengös, and he delivered the food to me. My comrades and I had a small feast on the unexpected food parcel. Our supply of Christmas candy had just run out, and the daily one cup of soup given to the prisoners was too meager for a 17-year-old boy. The next day at noon I stayed close to our main door to be among the volunteers to serve the soup. That gave me the "privilege" to wipe the emptied soup containers clean with my slice of bread.

Two days before Christmas we happily noticed that the Soviet Army's mortars were closing in on the city. Also, there were more nervous shouts being exchanged between our guards. Some of my companions got on their knees and prayed for our liberation. Others wished that one of the Soviet cannonballs would hit our prison wall, so that at least some of us could escape. We were afraid that our Nazi guards might shoot us before the Soviets took over, so that no witnesses would survive to identify them.

As a youngster, I probably needed more sleep than my older comrades. But, I had no room to lie down in the crowd because most of the floor space was taken by older people. Therefore, I figured out that if I climbed on the top of the large Dutch tile stove near the door, which was not heated, I would be able to have an uninterrupted nap! So I braced myself on its top in the corner, close to the ceiling, where it was stinkier but warmer than in the rest of the room. I took short naps there, while my jealous comrades made smart remarks to me. To my amazement, I discovered on the top of the stove a small file and in a paper bag some salt mixed with sugar, which I soon licked up and washed down with a lot of water. I gave the file to the people close to our iron-grated window (Fig. 54), encouraging them to use the file to weaken the iron grate in preparation for our possible escape.

To kill time, I got a book and read a Hungarian novel by Michael Földi, entitled *Toward God's Domain*. After finishing the book, I autographed the inside back cover, where 24 cellmates had already done the same (Fig. 55).

Figure 54. The iron-grated window on our prison cell, which some prisoners wanted to use to escape, after they weakened the iron grate with a file.

Reading the names, I realized what a famous group of people had been there; one was the Regent Horthy's private physician, another Karinthy's, the famous Hungarian writer's son, Gábor. Others became suddenly notorious as saboteurs; one even destroyed a bridge in front of the retreating German Army. So I was in good company. I treasured this book with its autographs for over 40 years; then I finally donated it to a Jewish acquintance Edit Roth, in Budapest, for inclusion into the state collection of historical documents from the Nazi era. I kept only a xerox copy of the pages with the autographs.

Just before Christmas we heard some commotion from outside our prison. Apparently the top Nazi leaders including the Commander, Peter Hain, packed up and left for Western

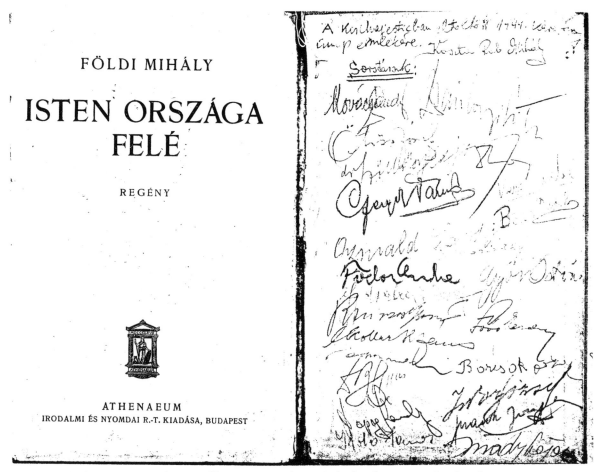

FÖLDI MIHÁLY

ISTEN ORSZÁGA FELÉ

REGÉNY

ATHENAEUM
IRODALMI ÉS NYOMDAI R.-T. KIADÁSA, BUDAPEST

Figure 55. Signatures of my cell mates on the inside back cover of a book.

Hungary (Hain was arrested by the new government in 1945, tried, and hanged for his atrocities). On Christmas Eve 1944, a group of minor Nazi officials entered our quarters. We were very excited, and everyone stood up, except for me. I was sitting on the top of the tile stove near the door. As the officials entered our room, one of them noticed my legs hanging from the top of the stove. Shocked, he stepped back and held up his pistol and shouted to me to roll off the stove. He probably thought that I was prepared to jump on him. That was a frightening experience for both of us, and I quickly slid off the stove. Then, an official gave a speech. He called us slimy worms who should have been hanged a long time ago, "but look how merciful is our nation's leader, Szálasi!" Then he read the Amnesty Declara-

tion from Szálasi, the leader of the German's puppet government in Hungary. Szálasi offered amnesty to Hungarian citizens imprisoned for minor crimes against the state, with the stipulation that they pledge to join the defenders of Budapest against the Soviet Army. A third official read the names of those of us who qualified for the amnesty. Many of us did, and we quickly pledged as required, collected our confiscated belongings, and ran for our lives down the mountain road into the city.

At that time there was no public transportation in the city. I had to cross one of the bridges over the Danube from Buda to Pest, but I was held up at the Chain bridge by German guards, who had already set explosives on each bridge. They were planning to blow these up to prevent further Soviet advances. It took some persuasion to allow our group of "would-be city defenders" to cross the bridge under guard. After crossing, I walked to my uncle Ferenc's home on Brody Sándor Street (Fig. 48), to tell them about my release from prison. They were delighted to see me, and told me about my Aunt Julishka's adventures with my mother. They had needed to knock on many office doors of Nazi officials in order to find my prison. Actually one of these officials told them to give up looking for me, because I would surely be executed for my grave crimes against the Fatherland.

From my uncle's home, where I had my first square meal in many days, I hurried to my parents' house, 18 km east in Rákoshegy. While walking through half of the city and then through the Eastern suburbs of Budapest, I noticed the military preparations for a last-ditch defense of the city. I was frightened and sad that I would have to join the military the next day for this futile fight. I had no military training, and the only available weapons were rifles to use against the advancing Soviet tanks. The Germans were using the untrained Hungarian youth to delay the imminent capitulation.

While walking on the foot path along the railroad tracks close to Rákoshegy, I ran into my parents, who had just started out for my jail. They were carrying a second food parcel for their hungry son. It was a joyful reunion. I did not tell them about the price of my freedom: the pledge I had been required to make.

At home, my father and I got busy gathering firewood, mostly black locust stumps from the nearby forest close to Ferihegy Airport. While out in the forest, we realized that the Soviet Army was closing in on us fast, and our town would soon be taken over. Because hungry soldiers are known for their pilfering habits, we wanted to hide some food. So, we hast-

ily dug some holes in the garden and buried food in enameled food containers, such as chunks of fried pork covered with lard and large jars of fruit preserves. I also found a Hungarian-Russian pocket dictionary, but realized that to use it I would first have to learn the Russian alphabet. I never learned so much so fast in my life, than under that pressure. Just before dark, the first Soviet patrols ran down our street. We were frightened of the possible consequences of this sudden takeover by the Soviet troops, but I was also relieved that I wouldn't have to participate in a lost cause, the defense of Budapest, and that my comrades and the Jews had survived until the Soviet troops arrived, and now would be protected.

Postscript. Members of the Braun family were taken to the 9th District Nazi Headquarters where they were put to work in packing the loot of the hurriedly departing Nazis. From there they were taken to the Headquarters of the Nazi Political Police, from where they miraculously ended up in the Jewish Ghetto in Budapest. There they survived until the Soviet Army took over Budapest in mid-January 1945. "Hungry and cold, but all of us survived" was written to me by Iby from Tel-Aviv. Iby (Mrs. Lewin) had already arrived in Israel by 1946 and was soon followed by Ella and Gyuri. The two younger girls, Magda and Ilonka, remained in Budapest, where Magda is still living (1994). The elder Brauns have since passed away, and unfortunately Ilonka died early in her life. Iby, now widowed, Ella, and Gyuri are alive and residing in Tel-Aviv (1994).

9 — "Liberation" and What Followed ...
(Escape from the Soviets — 1945)

The Soviet soldiers occupying our town, Rákoshegy, taken without a shot having been fired, were young Ukrainians. A few German soldiers left as a rear guard dug their trenches just outside the town's western border and manned three heavy caliber machine guns. They positioned these to cover the approach from our town.

I was soon "recruited" by the Soviet soldiers to keep the fires going both in their kitchen and their bath house. They brought a pile of furniture from vacated houses for me to chop up and use as firewood. They fed me twice daily from their kitchen, usually with canned meat dishes. The Soviet soldiers had also only two meals daily. But before each military action, *e.g.* assault, the soldiers were given cupfuls of vodka. I felt sorry for them because most of these young men lost their common sense ability to defend themselves under the effect of alcohol.

I witnessed the action when they were ordered to overrun and occupy the defense line held by the half dozen Germans left behind just outside of town. These Soviet foot-soldiers assaulted, *en masse* and without any protection, the withering fire of the three German machine guns. Instead of hiding behind trees or getting down to the ground when shot at, they ran ahead under the influence of the vodka and were butchered by the dozens. I learned that the number of casualties did not count in the eyes of many of their military leaders. This is probably why the Soviets lost in action the largest percentage of soldiers compared to the other warring countries. It was customary for Soviet Generals to make pledges directly to Stalin that they would occupy certain cities and areas of enemy territories within a set time limit; often in honor of Stalin's birthday, October Revolution, May Day, etc. Apparently they did not care how many soldiers they lost without "ground preparation." They often did not bomb the enemy's emplacements ahead of assaults by their soldiers. I can't ever forget the sad event, when, after the shooting was over, I was ordered to help collect the frozen, dead bodies of the six Germans and dozens of Soviets for a temporary burial.

The Ukrainian combat soldiers who arrived with the first wave were friendly to my family. They must have realized that my father was too old and I too young to have been drafted as soldiers and have fought against them in the Ukraine where most of them lost some family members to the fighting. Some were looking for enemy soldiers and "rich capitalists", but my family did not qualify. It also helped that I had a small Russian dictionary and was able to, although grammatically incorrectly, use a few words. My father had learned a few Russian and Ukrainian words as a young man, from prisoners of war kept in Transylvania during WWI.

My father's vague knowledge of their language almost proved fatal with the second wave of occupational troops. He was accused of beeing a refugee from their Communist system. We had a hard time convincing the drunk soldiers, even with documentation, that my father had been born in Transylvania. These soldiers under the influence of alcohol were pretending to search our home for hidden weapons, but were asking us to show our wristwatches. I told them that, because mine was broken, I had the pieces in a matchbox. One still wanted to see it. I showed the dismantled watch in the box and told them, "Caput, nye charasho!"(Broken, not good). He said, "What is not good for you is good for me," and pocketed it.

Many soldiers were looking for wrist watches to "borrow" from the civilians. A story that got around those days was about a Hungarian watch repairman who got into trouble. A Soviet soldier brought him a grandfather clock that he had "acquisitioned" from a home when no watch was found, and ordered the watch repairman: "This is big enough for you to make several wrist watches from it for me."

Another story from those days was about some Soviet soldiers from the outback of Siberia where no flush toilets had ever been seen. Such soldiers were housed with a Hungarian family in their home. The soldiers could not figure out the use of the toilet bowl, but seeing water in it, they placed their freshly caught live fish in it for keeping them alive until they were ready to be prepared. The home owners, not looking down, used their toilet and flushed down its contents. The soldiers, soon ready to fix their fish dinner, were surprised to find the bowl empty. So they named it "the stealing gadget of these crazy Hungarians."

As soon as the guns stopped in Budapest, around mid-January, I decided to visit my Uncle Feri and his wife Aunt Julishka. To find out if they survived the street fights and bombings of Budapest; also whether they needed some help and to offer our home for temporary shelter if their apartment was destroyed during the fights. My mother packed some food for them. When I told my intention to the Milne family, their daughter, Sara, joined me for the trip because she also wanted to visit some friends in Budapest. Her two brothers, George and Frici declined to come after their widowed mother discouraged them from undertaking "such a dangerous trip." They were an interesting family who were trapped in Hungary because of the war and were not able to move to England where Mr. Milne came from. He married a Hungarian woman but was an English citizen. As I recall, he was the only horse dentist those

days, internationally sought, especially for treating priceless racing horses. He advertised his special skills with interesting color postcards depicting a horse dentist at work in funny poses. I enjoyed my good friendship with the three children. They were about 13, 16, and 18 years old; Sara being the oldest, next George, and Frici the youngest. Unfortunately I lost track of them after they moved away, probably to England.

Sara and I packed our belongings into backpacks and walked the 18 kilometer long trek to Budapest. Enroute, while crossing some empty fields at Kőbánya (Fig. 48), we discovered parts of hastily buried soldiers sticking out from the ground after the snow melted. Some dead bodies of humans and horses were still on the streets. It was cold enough to stop the spread of the stink usually associated with large masses of decomposing bodies. We held our breath at those sites and were lucky to be able to reach our two destinations in Pest by noon. We found my relatives and Sara's friends all right. They were happy to learn about our families surviving at Rákoshegy and were grateful for the delivered food. On the way back, we were walking in a better mood and avoided the ugly sights we'd witnessed earlier that day.

We approached the Kőbánya Alsó railroad station, built on an embankment so that the city street traffic could cross the high tracks under a railroad bridge. Before reaching the pedestrian underpass under the bridge, we were stopped by armed Soviet soldiers. They asked for my documents and I showed these. After checking for my birthdate in these, they motioned for me to follow one of the soldiers for further checking of my papers. They motioned for Sara to leave; she was free to go home, but was hesitant to leave me.

The soldier to whom I was assigned already had 6 or 8 local civilians. He ordered all of us to follow him in a single file. Being the last to be added to the group, I stayed last while the guard was at the middle of our file. Sara followed us, close behind me. She wanted to find out where I was to be taken and rejoin me as soon as I was released. We had almost reached the corner under the railroad bridge (Fig. 56), when I spotted on the other side of the embankment, in the middle of the Liget Square (now Zalka Máté), a large group of local men being closely encircled by armed Soviet soldiers. It did not look like they were just taking us for checking documents, but rather to be taken as prisoners of war. I got really scared at the sight! Therefore, I made up my mind in a second to get out of the queue as soon as I could before reaching our well-guarded destination. So, as soon as our guard was making his turn around the corner and I was temporarily out of his sight, I suddenly turned around, grabbed Sara's arm, and started back toward Pest. By walking in a half circle, we avoided the soldiers who were just collecting their new shipment of prisoners. We almost ran the entire 12 kilometer trek home.

It was a really narrow escape, and I realized later how lucky was I for taking that sudden, last second, step. I learned that the men gathered at that site in mid-January were sent to temporary prison quarters without roofs, blankets, heat, food, or toilets. Those who survived ended up in the infamous camps near Gödöllö, where about half of the prisoners died from malnutrition and from contagious diseases. The survivors were taken to Soviet Prison Camps for 3 or more years. It was a practice of the Soviet Occupational Forces to collect civilians from the streets to be used as prisoners of war. Some were used to replenish the numbers when other prisoners escaped or died. In addition, they had a quota to fill to be used as free labor to rebuild Soviet cities destroyed by the ravages of war.

Soon after liberation from the Nazis, our new town administration was formed, mostly from Communist Party members and persons who had been persecuted under the Nazis. The Soviets would not trust anyone else. Most of the able-bodied men in our town were ordered to work for the Soviet forces at the nearby Ferihegy Airport or on repairing the destroyed railroad tracks. My father was working on the crew to cut off the broken ends of blown-apart rail tracks with hand saws. Thus they were able to put shortened rail sections together by replacing the sections blown up by the retreating Germans. I was picked up each morning in front of the Rákoshegy Town Hall by Soviet soldiers who transported our crew in the back of their trucks to the airport. There we had to remove the accumulated water from the craters in the runway, often by using empty metal food cans, and grade the ground surface with shovels so that Soviet military aircraft could use the airport for landing and takeoff. Around lunch time we were given a thick soup made of dried peas and were taken back to our town before dark.

Some of us, younger and more adventurous than the older folks, got into the habit of jumping off the back of the truck transporting our crew to the airport when it slowed for sharp curves. Often, only the half-way filled truck with only older folks arrived at its destination. Other times, when thick fog covered the airport, some of us pretended to go to the outdoor toilet, but instead ran home under cover of the fog.

To ease the food shortage, citizens were sent by the Town Council to participate in a variety of community chores that would help food production. Because of my background training in horticulture, I was assigned to assist a local gardener. We had to produce, in hot beds, young vegetable plants to be distributed at low cost to garden owners, thus promoting production of vegetables. I learned at that time how I could get 8 to 10 potato plants started from each tuber. We divided one tuber into several sections, each with 1 or 2 buds.

My family had a large garden, and with the extra greens I raised large-bodied Belgian rabbits for meat. No meat was available in the stores and none was in sight for a long time since the three armies (Germans, Hungarians, Soviets) killed our livestock. Therefore, one day my mother packed up our new meat grinder and sent me by train to a far-away village. I traded the meat grinder with a farmer for a 9 kg live piglet. The trading farmer let me make a small cage for my precious new possession.

The trains taking the many city folks for trading industrial goods for food stuff with far-

Figure 56. Railroad bridge at Köbánya, with the left corner concealing the guarded captive Hungarians snatched on the streets. It was my last-minute point of escape to avoid being taken to a Soviet concentration camp.

away farmers, were always over-filled, including the outside platforms and steps. Thus, many of us, especially younger folks, travelled on the roof of the train. This is how I transported my caged piglet home, where we hurriedly built a pig pen.

For another trading mission, I purchased salt and kerosene from traders coming from Transylvania. I added small containers of my father's home-made black shoe polish to these. As a house painter he made a paste from soot collected from inside our chimney and from other "ingredients" in his paint storage. The farmers needed black shoe polish for their farm boots, kerosene for their lamps, and salt to cure their meats. So, I took the overcrowded train to the Kisvárda area in Northeast Hungary. There I traded my goods for 5 liters of sunflower oil for cooking, a burlap bag (ca 40 kilograms) of potatoes, and about 10 kilograms of wheat flower. With some help, I climbed to the roof of the train and surrounded myself with the precious cargo. It took a long day to make the 200 kilometer ride home. When I arrived, my face was so black from the locomotive's soot that my family had a hard time recognizing me.

During the early summer of 1945, I made a deal with a local beekeeper to assist him for about six weeks with his traveling bee colonies

for a 20 liter (ca 5 gallon) can of honey, plus room and board. We started out in southern Hungary where the black locust forests were in bloom and moved, every 8 to 10 days, farther north, carrying the 60 bee hives on a horse-drawn cart to new locust forests just in bloom. With this method, we extended the black locust honey collecting season to about six weeks rather than 8 to 10 days when staying in one place. We moved the hives during the nights, after our bees returned to their hives and it was cold enough for the bees to travel quietly and keep the horses cool. One average-size hive was kept on a scale so we could estimate the daily output and time when we would extract the honey.

We slept outdoors, often in haystacks close to the beehives to guard them from poachers. We purchased milk from the local farmers, while honey and the fruits fallen from the trees along the road were free. I don't think it cost the beekeeper much for my six-weeks room and board. He got rich on that crop of honey. Because no sugar was available in the stores and money had become worthless due to inflation, honey was often traded for gold jewelry. My lucky beekeeper built a 2-story large brick house after that honey season. I got my 20 liters of honey, which lasted for a whole year for our family.

In the fall my Horticultural High School opened. Unfortunately, only half of my last year's classmates returned to school. Some had been drafted into the military as 16- and 17-year-olds, and probably became casualties of the war, or never returned from Germany where they were taken during the last weeks of WWII. Others might have ended up in Soviet Prison Camps.

Instead of German, now it was required to study Russian as our second language.

All students in our school were expected to pitch in to rebuild those school facilities that had been destroyed. With spades and without the benefit of tractors or horses, we also had to till the soil on a large area for gardening. The faculty and all farm hands worked with us.

We had to start growing enough food for our own school cafeteria. Our teachers also leased garden parcels to raise their own vegetables on the school practice grounds. The new history books arrived for us to re-learn the history of WWII from the Soviet point of view.

Our life slowly improved during the next year, and I happily graduated in June 1947. Of the eleven classmates who graduated, nine made it to the 50th class reunion.

I was ready, finally, at age 20, to support myself. (Yes, I was already 20 years old at the time I graduated from high school. In Romania we started school at age 7, and I also lost one year, when I had to transfer after 7th grade to the 3rd grade in the Middle School in Hungary.)

10 — As a Student-Educator-Researcher in Socialist Hungary (1947–56)

After graduation from the Municipal Horticultural High School of Budapest in 1947, I got a job offer to work as a foreman in a fruit tree nursery in Central Hungary. I declined that offer, because I wanted to stay in the capital where the "action" was and my parents lived. So, I took a lower paying job in Zuglo (Eastern Budapest) with István Papp, a floriculturist. We raised cyclamens, begonias, gladiols, and even early cucumbers in the greenhouses. Papp hired village girls for both their looks and diligence.

We shared views on how to revive our Nation: by enlisting the help of talented and unspoiled youth of the peasantry and by making Hungary into a horticultural garden to supply fresh produce, flower and vegetable seeds for the Western European markets. Both of us were active in the National Peasant Party (NPP). The party was formed by peasant/populist writers to include tenant farmers and those with small holding plots, and intellectuals who wanted to help the cause of the oppressed peasantry.

One day Papp asked me if I would volunteer to actively help the NPP during the 1947 fall election campaign. After I agreed, he kept me on his payroll while I was put in charge of reviving some or starting new NPP local organizations in the suburbs of Eastern Budapest and the surrounding towns. First, I was sent to an NPP Leadership Workshop in the Party Center across from the Opera House in Budapest. Here I met the famous, and some infamous, leaders of the NPP. Most were well-known writers, such as Peter Veres, Imre Kovács, Imre Darvas, and Ferenc Erdei.

They provided most of the lectures, and built confidence in us that the politically and economically neglected poor peasants would save our Nation. We were convinced that Hungary could do well independently without Soviet or other foreign interference. After the workshop, I was given a list of contacts in each town in my assigned territory, some cash for anticipated expenses, and a taxi-cab with a driver. This was a big step upward for me after the manual jobs I had with Papp. I visited the contacts in each community, rented an empty storeroom in the center of each town, got it painted, and hung the needed signs for the local Party Centers. I also sought volunteers to mind the office, whom I supplied with leaflets, and money as needed.

My more enjoyable "work" was in organizing entertainment for fund raising and to bring together Party sympathizers and support groups. Among these socializing events were grape harvest festivals. Here the supper was prepared by the local supporters, and live gypsy music was provided for the dancers. Usually the events were held in large gardens where steel wires were strung for a canopy to support fresh grape canes with colorful bunches of grapes hanging down over the heads of dancing couples. For a young bachelor, it was much fun to do these. Besides meeting girls, I also met a number of politicians whose public appearances and speeches I scheduled. Papp, my benefactor, was on the district ballot, and I was also offered a place on a local ballot that I declined to accept.

Our party received about 5% of the national votes, but had higher support in the suburbs and towns I worked in; that made me happy. Ten parties entered the 1947 Fall Elections; some of these had been artificially created by the Communists to divide the votes, so that no one party would attain a majority as in 1945, when only six parties entered the Elections, but only five got mandates.

Unfortunately, the Communist Party was able to increase their support rate by taking away voting rights from thousands of non-sympathizers with the help of their own Secretary of Interior who was in charge of police. They returned the voting rights soon after the elections. The Communists also obtained tens of thousands of absentee ballots that were repeatedly used in towns across Hungary by their party members travelling in trucks and buses to cast ballots in many localities. It was easy for them to use these tricks because the police were under their control, and they had the full backing of the Soviet occupation army.

It was distressing to see after the elections how politicians opposing the illegal Communist takeover of our Country were jailed on false accusations, or intimidated so they left the country. I decided to get out of politics and find a safer and more permanent professional job. I was lucky! The Colorado Potato Beetle had just crossed for the first time into Hungary and the Bureau of Plant Protection of the Ministry of Agriculture was hiring people with my background. I was hired as a "spray master" and sent to the "front line" at Hédervár (NW Hungary) to help eradicate this pest.

At Hédervár, I shared sleeping quarters with a young scientist, Dr. Tibor Jermy, who had just returned from a Soviet concentration camp. Tibor drank 2-3 liters of cow milk daily to regain his normal weight and strength. He tested insecticides against the beetles. He had many glass-topped Petri dishes with live beetles treated with different doses of chemicals. Tibor had an alarm clock set day and night to wake him up, or alert him every two hours, so he could check the activities and mortality rates of beetles in each dish. During the first nights I also woke up with him, but later I slept through those nights. I was young, and each day I had long walks in the fields while searching for beetle infestations.

My daily walks often took me close to the Austrian border, the aim of many Hungarians who wanted to escape to the West from Communist Hungary. I heard a number of dramatic stories from people who tried to escape. But one of the stories stuck in my memory. It was about a Gypsy musician who was caught by the border patrols while trying to cross to Austria. He had his violin tucked under his arm. The arresting border guards, to their great surprise, found inside his violin a picture of the ugly-looking Comrade Rákosi, the much hated Dictator of Hungary. So, they asked him why he was taking a picture of Comrade Rákosi with him. He said, "It was my security against getting homesick. Each time I look at it, I will surely lose my homesickness ... "

Our group had to eradicate all stages of the Colorado Potato Beetle at the site of infestation. We used soil fumigants for the stages of the beetle in the ground and DDT dust for those on the plants. The Soviet Government assigned one of their "experts" to check on us to make sure we did a good job and stopped the beetles in Hungary so they couldn't reach Soviet lands northeast of Hungary. This "expert" wanted us to spread dry straw over the infested acreage and, at his signal, all at once would be set aflame so the beetles would be torched inside a ring of fire. It took some persuasion by our administrators to talk the Soviet "expert" out of his medieval way of controlling insects. He did not take into account that the infested land was adjoining some thatched-roof farm buildings which could have been burned down, possibly with the rest of the town.

We counteracted with jokes all the lies spread by the Communist newspapers. After the Colorado Potato Beetle appeared in Hungary, Czechoslovakia, and Poland, the newspapers blamed the Americans for dropping the beetles from airplanes overnight. Potatoes disappeared from our markets at the same time. Our local Communists would not admit the true reason for the shortage: that most of the potato crop was being shipped to the Soviet Union. Why not blame the Americans for it?

One day my office colleague bent over to my ear and quietly asked, "Have you heard what happened last night?"

"No. What happened?"

He: "Oh! The Americans flew over once again … "

"Don't tell me — And what did they do this time?"

He: "Oh — they dropped potatoes for our hungry potato beetles!"

I much admired Tibor for his meticulous work, and he served as a role model for me that summer. By the end of the summer I had decided that in the fall I would go back to school to learn more in biology, especially about insects. After the field work ended and our crew had successfully eradicated the beetle, I was reassigned to assist in the Bureau in Budapest. Here I soon went to my Bureau Director Kalman Hinfner and the Section Chief Jozsef Szabó, asking them to reassign me as a night watchman at the Bureau Garage on Budafoki Street, so I could enroll during the day at the Horticultural Faculty of the Agricultural University in Buda. They sympathized with my goals and allowed me to enroll for classes, and to make up the lost time in the office with evening and weekend work. They also told me that the fumes generated by the gasoline used and stored in the garage would be harmful to my health. I was never able to properly thank these supervisors for their care and understanding because soon both were jailed on drummed-up charges by the new Communist Regime.

I happily enrolled at the University. My monthly regular salary from the Bureau, 360 Forints, just covered expenses for tuition, mess hall, and books. I had free housing at home. The first year I had to purchase just for my botany classes 3 books, 2 lab manuals, and 2 lab notebooks, costing half a month's salary. Surely, I could not have enrolled in the University on my parent's meager income even after my mother returned to work for a state hospital.

My work for the Hungarian Bureau of Plant Protection between July 1947–December 1949, was an educational experience with many surprises. On request by farmers I was sent to villages to organize emergency pest control projects and to provide the know-how and the free pesticides from the government, while the local farmers provided the free labor needed to exterminate the pests that had invaded their fields. At each work destination, I reported first to the town manager (=biró) and asked him to find me housing while I worked in their town. He would first ask if I were married. I would tell him I was still single. Then, he usually smiled, winked his eye, and said that he has a wealthy farmer with a single daughter, who would be pleased to take me in for room and board.

So I often ended up with such families, who were looking for an appropriate match, a young man from the city who wore a necktie, because they did not want their only daughter to marry a local farm boy with whom she would be stuck in the drab farming life. So, as a prospective son-in-law I was well treated by the family, I got the fancy front guest room, excellent meals, without paying any compensation for such service. On my departure, they usually said: "Oh, just keep in touch with us." After some days, when the family realized that I really did not show special attention toward their daughter, the quality of my meals would gradually decrease. The girl usually was a spoiled, average-looking gal with good intentions, but without many intellectual interests.

But they tried other methods on me. In Sajtoskál, for example, I was taken one Sunday afternoon by the girl's widowed aunt to be treated with food and drinks and to use the occasion to show me her property that would be given to the girl whenever she married. On another occasion the parents gave me a wicker basket to join their daughter on a mushroom collecting jaunt in the nearby forest. They were hoping that the isolation with their daughter in the forest would bring out my manly desires that would result in a "lasting friendship." It did not work. As soon as I could finish my official work, I packed and said good-by and left the town. This was just one of the several similar experiences in assignments in villages where there was no hotel or hostel for out-of-town workers.

One of my professional assignments was to organize field mouse controls in southwest Hungary. Here the mice had built such high populations that unless they were at once exterminated, raising field crops would be futile. I was taken in an old U.S. military surplus Dodge to a village, with hundred of kilograms of crushed corn baited with zinc phosphide. The town hall was filled that night when I gave my usual speech on how the field mice could be exterminated in one day with the government's free pesticide, with their own manual help. I also asked that each family send one able-bodied adult for the next day's work. They were to bring a tin can and a spoon to disperse the bait after lunch, but they also needed a hoe in the morning to first close the 8-12 entry holes that led to each mouse nest. This way we would save extra work and pesticide, because bait would be placed only in the freshly opened holes.

Some farmers challenged my method, stating that they would do a better job on their own fields if I gave them the pesticide ration. I responded that the treatment had to be general on all the fields, including the no-man's land along the roads and on the community-owned fields, or many mice would escape.

Next morning I often had between 200 to 300 persons available. I entrusted the town administrator to assign one elderly and respected man as supervisor for each group of 12 to 15 persons. They were to follow their own group and make sure that each person performed the assigned task. The others had to walk in a single row, about 5–6 meters apart, and close all the mouse holes on the strip of land in front of them in the morning. They placed the bait in the freshly opened holes in the afternoon. By late afternoon when we returned through the earlier baited fields, we found hundreds of slowly staggering mice and many dead ones.

Unfortunately I also found many dead raptorial birds at the side of creeks where they tried to neutralize with water the effect of the poison bait, which had reached them through the poisoned mice they had eaten. I wondered if we could find a way to avoid killing the beneficial birds. Probably we could, if the other half of the town could be out to collect the dead mice before the birds did.

The villagers were grateful for the assistance. Each evening and weekend I was invited to their wine cellars, to taste their wines. Most of the wine was too sour or dry for my taste, so I learned to quietly add some sugar powder before drinking.

I learned during the first week of my work that the villagers were disappointed when they found me to be a much younger person than they expected from the Department of Agriculture. I was only 21 years old, but I looked even younger. The farmers listened more seriously to those officials who had military service behind them, and I had not served yet. So I decided to grow a mustache. Soon, I looked 3–4 years older with my wide dark brown mustache. After that, I had less of a problem in convincing the old farmers of my professional competence and the value of the projects offered to them. Since then I have kept a mustache, which apparently lends me a distinguished look, even after 50 years.

I often wonder how I pulled through those years. It was a real hardship for me to be enrolled full-time at the University, while keeping a full-time job for 30 months. Also, we lived in Rákoshegy, almost 20 kilometers from my work place and 24 kilometers from my university. My father also had to travel 20 kilometers each way to his work place at the Rákosrendező Rail Shop. So, I proposed to my parents that we should ease our life by way of moving to an apartment in Budapest. This would cut down on our daily travel time from three hours to one and a half.

No apartments were available in Budapest unless someone wanted to trade one for ours, but our tiny apartment in Rákoshegy did not have the needed trading value for one in Budapest. To make it suitable for trade, I would need a two-bedroom house with a garden. Therefore, I applied at the Town Hall for a house with a garden. One such was abandoned, and the town rented it out to us. With my father, we fixed it up with fresh coats of paint. Then I started inquiring about trading possibilities. Luckily, I found an elderly couple who wanted to move back from Budapest into their own two-bedroom house with a garden in Rákoshegy, but their house was occupied by a tenant family. The latter family would not move out until a similar rental house was offered in exchange; and the law was on their side.

So I talked the tenant family into accepting our upgraded rental property in exchange for their rented house, so that the owners could move back into their house, and I would have the owner's apartment in exchange. It was a three-way move. The tenants bargained for the moving expenses, so I made a deal with the truck driver moving us, to move the tenants into our former house as well. It took some planning and some work, but we finally and happily landed in a bedbug-infested two-bedroom apartment at 65 Mester Street. Being a budding entomologist, bedbugs did not intimidate me. After discovering our new apartment "sub-leasers", with my father, we put all the furniture and belongings in the middle of each room. We filled the cracks with caulking mixed with DDT. We also re-painted the walls with lime white-wash mixed with DDT. We did not know about the bad properties of DDT in 1948. It worked like a wonder on the bedbugs. None showed up during our 8-year stay there.

My days were filled with studies and office work. We had only one temporary pontoon bridge over the Danube in Budapest, located near the Parliament, just across from my office. There were many days when I had to cross this bridge four times on foot to attend classes and laboratories, especially when roll-call was expected. Missing classes four times in one semester could have brought loss of credit for the course.

I was fortunate to team up for my studies with two very bright and diligent girls in my class. I made up the missed lectures by studying with them for exams. We also complemented each other's knowledge in the subjects studied. They were more advanced in biochem-istry and physics, while I was ahead of them in horticultural subjects and plant protection, where I already had some practical background training.

It was an ideal symbiotic relationship until one of my study mates was kicked out of the University after the freshman year. Soon after the Communist Party took over the control of Hungary in 1948, all University professors and students were politically re-examined, and about half of the students and faculty were sent away. Some of these students were ready to start their senior year. Eva, one of my study mates, was accused of wearing a cross on her necklace; that automatically disqualified her from further studies. The new Regime did not want students who had any kind of church affiliation to receive higher degrees. Other students were kicked out because their father was a former official of the old Regime, or their farming parents owned more land than they could cultivate themselves and had hired helpers for major farm work. Such parents were classified as kulaks, who "exploited" outside helpers.

Of the 130-member class only 60 of us were kept. I was allowed to continue my studies because, cautious after my experience with the Nazis, I never talked openly about my political views. Also, since my father was a worker in a railroad shop, I was classified into the "industrial proletarian" category.

The price for being spared during the re-examination was that I would have to give up my work at the Bureau to become a full-time student. I stretched my resignation time with many excuses: First, for example, I had to train my replacement. My other excuse was that we had run into a national emergency situation with the accidental introduction of the "American Fall Webworm" and my expertise was needed. I was even able to show Work Order Documents from the Ministry instructing me to assist with the Eradication Program. I made it known that I couldn't continue my studies without financial assistance. So they waived my tuition, and later I even received a 200 Ft monthly scholarship to pay for books and my school mess hall tickets. After these gestures, I was told that because I became a member of the "privileged class", there were no more excuses. So I resigned my job after 30 months service at the Bureau, and concentrated full time on my university studies.

The price to pay for "free" University studies was high. After graduation we had to take jobs assigned to us. My grades decidedly improved. I also wanted to continue specialized training in entomology. Therefore, I went to the entomology department head, Dr. Balás, and asked him to accept me as an unpaid helper after class hours and during weekends. He was impressed with my 30 months practical training in plant protection. Balás liked my Transylvanian ancestry because his folks had also come as refugees to Hungary from Transylvania.

He checked carefully my social background and asked at the end if I were a member of the Communist Party. I told him I was supporting the National Peasant Party. Apparently, he liked all these, because he confided to me that we would have to "trick" the Communist Boss, Comrade Szalai, a former streetcar conductor who was in charge of personal affairs at the University. So, Balás, who had just dismissed from his department a student who was a Communist Party member, had "gotten into the dog house" with Szalai. Therefore, if he were to recommend me to Szalai for acceptance into his department, I would not be approved by Szalai, especially since I was not a member of the Party. But, if I would go straight to Szalai to request his approval first and his recommendation for consideration to Professor Balás, we could succeed.

So, I went to Szalai with my request, told him about my background training in plant protection, and asked him to help me get into Balás' department as an unpaid trainee. He needed two weeks to make up his mind, apparently to check first my socio-political background, maybe also my scholastic status. The latter was secondary for his Party. After two weeks, when I returned to his office, he telephoned Balás in front of me and suggested my acceptance for specialized training in entomology. Balás must have had his big smile ready

when "complying" with the request of the Personnel Boss. This is how I started my six years career in the Department of Horticultural Entomology of the University of Agricultural Sciences in Budapest.

Balás had some unusual and strange habits. Each newcomer to his department was put to a daily 12-16 hour training. But the same person was suddenly dropped from the "favorite status" as soon as a newcomer arrived, with whom he repeated the same treatment. I was dropped after a year when the first assistant professor, an attractive young lady, was hired. She was the favorite until another woman came to join us.

His marriage, with three small children, was in shambles, and he expected the newcomer women to look after his personal affairs: keeping track of his finances, shopping, making snacks, coffee, etc. He made them feel sorry for his unfortunate marriage. He often slept in his office, where he gave himself morphine shots. Apparently he suffered both physically and psychologically from the effects of WWII. As a soldier he hardly survived the infamous retreat of the Hungarian Second Army from the Don River area of the Ukraine. He developed schizophrenic tendencies and sometimes slept during the morning hours after working all night. His assistants never knew if he would be able to hold his morning lectures. Therefore, we took turns in preparing to jump in, at the last minute, to give his scheduled lectures.

While I was in a favorite status, Balás pointed out to me the need for a scale insect* expert in Hungary. So, I chose to specialize on this poorly known group 46 years ago, something I have never regretted. My first publication on scales was printed in 1950, while I was a senior student. Balás was pleased with my work, so he proposed to keep me in his department after graduation.

---

* Scale insects are 2–6 mm long, plant juice-sucking insects. Most live under a shield-like or wax cove; thus, they are hard to detect. They are economically important because they can kill trees and other plants.

I accepted the assistant professorship offered from June 1951, but I was sent by the University Administration during the first summer to a training session to assist with the redistribution of farmland. It was a political maneuver by the Communist Government to convince the Hungarian farmers to give up the ownership of their land and join the new cooperative farms (co-ops) organized in their villages. To achieve this goal, first the taxes for farmers were raised to a level that many were unable to pay. This provided an excuse to intimidate these farmers with imprisonment unless they joined the new co-ops. A number of "richer" farmers, so-called kulaks, were removed from each village to work camps as part of the intimidation campaign. A few of them burned down their farm buildings or the harvested wheat stocks, rather than join the co-ops. This situation created a political upheaval the like of which had never been seen in Hungary before.

We were indoctrinated to calm the farmer's feelings against the co-ops, and to try to convince them of the beautiful future that the co-ops would provide them. As a last resort, we had to make them realize that the group of farmers joining the co-ops would receive a joint ownership of a large block of the closest and best land, in exchange for the many small strips of land they turned in. Those refusing to join would get their share from the remaining leftover and far-away parcels with poorer soil. We had blueprints of the available farmland for redistribution and a land surveyor to assist us.

The farmers did not have much choice. Even after they joined the co-ops or accepted the redistributed land in exchange for theirs, many sabotaged the new system, butchering their livestock and raising only as much food crop as was needed for their families. To stop this effort, the government introduced the new taxation to be paid in farm produce, and set very low compulsory prices for farm products. Many young farmers who could not manage their affairs left their towns to seek jobs in the cities. The government immediately put restrictions on moving to cities. The country that used

to export much food now faced acute food shortages due to the forced collectivization. In those days I saw many farm women purchasing their weekly bread in the cities, where they were often denied service in the state-owned bakeries and stores. The work incentives for farmers were killed and everyone suffered.

I was sent in 1953 with the senior class to field practice on state farms where, as teachers, we should have shown the good examples in farming of the socialized agriculture. Unfortunately, we were only able to point out the bad examples; how not to do it when they would be in charge.

One such example in my field of plant protection was in connection with spraying the apple trees on the state farms. Because the farm managers were not pleased with the quantity of work of the "spray brigades" or teams, who were paid hourly wages, they introduced pay based on the number of trees sprayed. After three years, the top branches of such apple trees were dying. When I checked more closely, I realized that the San José Scale had built high populations there and was killing the top branches that had not been sprayed by the hurried, unscrupulous workers. Next, the managers introduced another new pay system based on the amount of spray put on the trees, so the workers would not neglect spraying the tops. This became the most wasteful method because the workers soon enlarged the spray nozzle openings and were washing the trees instead of spraying. Finally, after more wasted years, they introduced profit-sharing for the workers, and that improved production. This is just one example of the many problems that socialized farming brought to Hungary.

The Socialist system in Hungary wasted a lot of the agricultural products produced on the Socialized farms. There were poor storage conditions on the farms, and often the lengthy transportation during freezing weather resulted in a large part of the produce getting frozen. The stored grain was often raided by rodents and infested by insects.

At the same time they introduced such ridiculous economizing measures as collecting hair from the barbershop floors to be used in felt making for the cloth factories.

But the economizing that produced the most laughs in the country was from the new rule requiring the collection and utilization of human excrement from outdoor toilets to be used in the production of fertilizers. It was the homeowner's duty to turn in to the state collectors the accumulations from their outdoor toilets. The State-owned collecting tank trucks came on a regular schedule each month. I was told that once at one pick-up point there was nothing to show for the month. The homeowner was accused of sabotaging the State's 5-year plan for fertilizer production. He was interrogated by the police about the absence of "stuff." The frightened owner gave his excuse: "Because all my family members are active in the Socialist movements, we hardly spend any time at home. For example, my wife spends her free time in the Democratic Women's League and she 'does her business' there, my son and daughter are active in the Young Communist Movement, so they drop their "stuff" there, while I am working everyday long hours in the Party Center, where I also, on a regular basis, relieve myself."

Our students still learned enough from us to become enterprising and survive under the harsh conditions and the many restrictions that the Socialist Communist system brought us. I learned about one of our students who wanted to bring from the Soviet Union some new varieties of conifers for propagation in his nursery. But the Soviet customs agents would not allow him to take out his live tree branches. So, he sat down outside the customs office and twisted his live tree branches into funeral wreaths. After that, he had no problem in passing through Soviet customs.

After the Communist takeover, the universities had a new admission policy, with a quota system for the incoming students. The freshman student body had to be made up in high percentage by students with industrial proletarian or landless-peasant background. Next came the sons or daughters of small farmers who were co-op members, and then a very

small percentage from intellectual families, usually officials or educators under the new Regime. It reminded me of the Numerus Clausus law introduced against Jews by the Nazis, restricting their number in certain professions. Only after many years did the Communists change their quota system, when the Communist New Rulers' children became disadvantaged for being classified as children of intellectuals. Some extra credit was given at the admissions to those youths who had first worked as laborers in factories or on socialist farms.

Also, those youths from the worker classes who had no High School diplomas, but were talented and recommended by the local Party organization for such a privilege, were put through intensive and short preparatory courses before acceptance for University studies.

As an unmarried young assistant professor, I was assigned as advisor to a group of 20 freshman, with about six of these students without regular High School training. I had to make sure that none dropped out, and that they could keep pace with the rest of the students. First, I took my group on educational, but entertaining, field trips on Saturdays. We had fun, picnicked, and got to know each other better. I tried to instill comraderie and a feeling of loyalty for each other. I told them that if the cumulative grade average for the group went down, we all would suffer and I would probably be demoted from working with them; but if we showed, in general, grade improvements, we would receive attention, and probably some privileges. I also asked those students with special knowledge in a subject to help, and study together with, one or two who had problems in that subject. So we voluntarily formed study groups. The spirit of "One for all and all for one" worked! Our group became first in the rate of grade improvements among the six such groups of the freshman class. We were publicly recognized for it, got free theatre tickets, and I received a monetary award that paid for my family's first more complete radio.

Unfortunately, my group fell apart after one of the most liked and helpful students disappeared. After some time, we learned that he was arrested and jailed without trial, probably on some false political accusations. One of the Communist methods used to "keep the lamb in line" was to periodically jail some people and thus intimidate the rest.

One way to indoctrinate us at Universities under Communism was the requirement for taking political courses. As a student in horticulture, I had to take five different political courses for my college degree. These included: Marxism-Leninism, The Questions of Leninism by Stalin, Socialist Economics, Socialist Agriculture, and The History of the Communist Parties in Hungary and in the Soviet Union. In addition, both as students and as faculty, we were required to show up 30 minutes earlier than the start of classes, to read and "evaluate" the latest news releases in the Party Newspaper.

Also, the faculty had to attend weekly political seminars conducted by one of the Party officials. Here we discussed and evaluated the latest political events in the country and abroad. The seminar conductor assigned us some home readings to be discussed at our next seminar. It was a way to make sure we were fully informed on the subjects that the Almighty Party found important for us, as well as to detect our disagreements with the Party's policies.

One of my young colleagues, Zoltán Baráth, had good acting skills and disliked the seminars. He memorized word-by-word lengthy texts from Stalin's speeches, so he could quote these word by word as an actor when asked. He did a wonderful performance one day, but was highly criticized that in his quotations he did not express enough enthusiasm for the subject. They wanted us to show openly that we supported enthusiastically the ideas of the Party.

Every day we made jokes of these indoctrination seminars. One such was that our so-labelled "Democracy" in Hungary was "like eating sour cherries; you spit one and then swallow one." We spit for disliking the system, but we had to swallow our thoughts because we were intimidated from openly criticizing the New System. Some people were jailed for telling political jokes not complimentary of the Re-

gime. It was during the Korean War, that a large map of Korea was displayed in the entrance hall of our University. The "glorious" advances south by the North Korean troops were marked daily on this map. Finally, the advances almost reached the southern coast. Then, a big sign informed us: "Tomorrow we shall push the American Imperialist Troops into the sea." But as soon as the American and other United Nations troops started advancing northward, the sign and map disappeared.

During the next winter our newspapers published articles with a picture of small insects on the top of snow in North Korea. According to the news release, these insects had been dropped from American airplanes to spread diseases among the North Korean troops. As entomologists, we recognized these insects from the pictures. They were "snow fleas" that had nothing to do with spreading contagious diseases. They feed on organic material, and often are blown by the wind some distance; as frost-resistant creatures they may jump on the top of the snow when disturbed.

Soon, my department head, Balás, was called by the Party to give a talk at a public meeting, and as a scientist, condemn the Americans for the atrocities committed by starting germ warfare. Balás could not say no and lose his job, so he called in saying that he was sick, bedridden, and unable to partake in the public meeting. We were intimidated enough to keep from telling that it was a lie about these insects, and that we could not help the Party by "confirming" the news stories.

The New Regime did not tolerate religious affiliations for students and professors. They wanted us to build the new atheistic society. So, when Tili and I were ready to get married, we selected a church far away from our home and office where no one would recognize us during the short and simple ceremony. Only our parents and the two witnesses were in attendance. At our university working place only our civil ceremony was made known. I could have lost my job as a teacher otherwise.

It was expected of us that we participate in the Socialist holiday celebrations such as April

4 (Liberation Day) and May 1 (Workers Day), to march through the city under red banners and with sign slogans, to cheer, wave, and show happy faces, especially when marching in front of the Communist leadership. The organizers from our office were checking closely to see if all of us showed up. Our office walls also had to be decorated with pictures of the Communist leadership and with appropriate slogans.

Despite the constant attempts to indoctrinate us in Communism, the Hungarians came up with new jokes about the Leadership, like the following one. Alcoholism was widespread in the Soviet factories; subsequently production suffered and on-the-job accidents were common. Khrushchev, to stop it, went to the factories and gave speeches against the curse of alcoholism. To make his point effective, he brought with him two live earthworms. In front of his audience, one worm was dropped in a glass of vodka, the other in a glass of water. Soon after, the worm in the vodka stopped moving, while the one in the water continued wiggling. "Look what happened to the one in the vodka. It's already dead!" said he. "What would you, comrades, conclude from the experiment?" One worker stood up and said, "Comrade Khrushchev, thanks for the demonstration. I now know why I have never had any problem with intestinal worms!"

Every time we turned around, we were asked to volunteer for some activity. For example, when the socialist farms had not enough labor for harvesting vegetables or fruits, we were asked to work free as volunteers during our weekends. They really twisted our arms, so we had no choice. In the same way, the Regime extracted from us "voluntarily" 10% of our yearly salary for government reconstruction "bonds". We were told that the extra money was needed to build new apartments for the hundreds of thousands of couples without proper housing. But most of the money was used for other, often military, purposes. I learned later that most of the marriages that broke up in Hungary were caused by young couples being forced to live in their parents' homes. We also had to live for three years in my in-laws' home, due to the apartment shortages.

In each work place and housing complex, for every 10 to 15 persons or families, one informant of the Communist Party was assigned to keep close tabs on our activities. Who were our friends? Do we belong to a church? Are we listening to the Voice of America or to the Free Europe radio messages? etc. These informants' periodic reports were included in the political dossiers kept at the Personnel Departments of our working places. We realized all this when, during the 1956 uprising, the personal files were taken out from the safes and given to us. Such a "system" still keeps the people in China, Cuba, North Korea, and Vietnam under control.

Because our Entomology Department did not have a Communist Party member yet — one to serve as a Party informant — I was "chosen" to become one. For a whole year, one of the informants assigned to work on me was using all kinds of maneuvers to soften my resolve. I would have probably lost my job if I hadn't soon accepted that "privilege," but the 1956 Hungarian Uprising gave me the escape route to avoid becoming a full-fledged member and informant of the Party.

(Our escape story is told in Chapters 1 and 2.)

11 — Starting a New Life in a "Strange Country" (USA 1957–)

The events preceding this text are in Chapters 1 and 2.

After our paperwork for emigration to the United States was completed in the refugee camp near Salzburg, we were taken by bus to the American military base at Munich, Germany, on January 22, 1957. We were much excited about this trip. It had taken two long and tiring months to reach this big step in our new lives. In the meantime we had such excitements as Tili's bus accident and hip fracture in Austria and smuggling Eva out of Hungary. And now we were worrying about starting a life from scratch (our belongings fit into two small suitcases), without money and without speaking English. Such questions were often on my mind: would I find a job as an entomologist? Would Aunt Juliska's relatives in Shelton, Connecticut, come through with the requested sponsorship letter? How could we survive the first months without a penny in our pocket?

We were already hungry when we arrived at the U.S. military base, but we were greeted by many encouraging and smiling faces and, to our pleasant surprise, the military band was playing welcome music at the base. After unloading our belongings at a temporary dormitory, we were taken to the Army Cafeteria for our first American meal! I had already lost a few kilograms on the meager meals provided in the Camp Roeder refugee camp near Salzburg. Now here, our first time in a U.S. cafeteria, we had a real choice in meals! We were given large trays with sections for different kinds of food. As I walked down in front of the serving counter, I discovered dozens of food items to choose from. There were smiling black U.S. soldiers behind the counter. When they asked me if I wanted the food in front of the server, I nodded each time and a generous portion from most items was given until my tray could not hold more. We ate and ate; we tried to make up for the last two months. It was an encouraging introduction to America.

Next day we were bused to a military medical evacuation airplane fitted with beds to transport invalids. Because Tili was just released from the hospital where she'd been treated for her hip fracture, and Eva had a mild cough, we were therefore taken to the U.S. by airplane instead of by boat. After all of us were seated, group pictures were taken of the passengers. We flew overnight, with a short stop at an airbase in Labrador, and arrived by morning in Newark, New Jersey. From there we were bused to Camp Kilmer, near New Brunswick.

En route, I admired the many TV antennae that I had never noticed in Europe. Also the many frame houses built mostly from wood, not from masonry as in Europe. The home yards had only grass and a few bushes, but there were no fences around the properties. Apparently there was no need for fences to keep out prowlers.

And the many family cars! Actually, each family home had at least one car, often in a separate garage. And I compared these in my mind with the conditions in Hungary where we were told by the Communists that "under the western rotting and declining capitalism, the workers go to sleep hungry..." Then it dawned on me that the highway signs were giving distances in miles, not kilometers as in Europe. What a strange world! And I thought, oh God, how will I adjust to all this?

Figure 57. The military barracks at Camp Kilmer, near New Brunswick, New Jersey, that served as a temporary home for many Hungarian refugees in 1957.

The empty military base was now fitted for the arrival of Hungarian refugees; up to 5,000 at a time. Here we were assigned a small private room in a barrack (Fig. 57). We were also given a printed greeting letter both in English and Hungarian signed by President Eisenhower. Soon, we received mess hall tickets and tickets for free purchase in the camp commissary of needed small items, including cigarettes.

After a short nap, the loudspeaker instructed us in Hungarian to register for contacting our sponsors and for English-speaking classes. We did both, and I started attending my first English class. Our teacher brought in two baskets filled with fruits, vegetables, and other groceries. She lifted these groceries one by one, and we had to repeat the English names of the items displayed by her. Then she pointed to each piece of furniture and item in our classroom, giving its name, and making us repeat the word after her, often individually.

I have never forgotten the acquisition of my first bottle of Coca Cola. During the class break, I discovered a soft-drink dispensing machine in the hall. I had not seen such before. As I was trying to figure out how these work, one teacher came over and motioned to me, asking if I wanted a coke. I said yes, but I had no American money yet. So, with a smile, he pulled out a nickel, inserted it, and out came my bottle of cold drink! I thanked him for his gesture. My first coke tasted like medicine; it took me some time to acquire a taste for this strange new drink.

In the camp's mess hall we often ate with Americans working in the refugee camp. We soon realized that Americans do not use the knife and fork as Europeans do. They spread butter on their bread and rolls, something we never did with our meals, although we probably made up for this with the sour cream generously used in our dishes. Also, Americans drink their diluted coffee from big mugs with cream. In the Old Country we had either a small strong espresso coffee or a "long coffee" diluted with much milk as milk-coffee at breakfast. Americans do not use toothpicks after meals. In Europe, toothpicks were on each table next to the salt shaker, and we used them after meals while covering our mouths discreetly. Use of chewing gum was so common here, even with adults, but I had never seen this in Hungary in those days.

One day we were informed by the camp authorities that our would-be sponsors, Aunt Julishka's relatives (Kiss) in the United States, declined sponsorship for us because they had already agreed to sponsor some other relatives. We were much saddened by the news, and hoped that some welfare agency would do this for us.

But our problem was soon solved. One day on the loudspeaker we heard an invitation for persons with an academic background to register in the office set up by the U.S. National Academy of Sciences. So I registered, and was given the opportunity to attend a more intensive language course at the nearby Rutgers University. Because we had a young baby, Tili was unable to attend. Instead, she was offered room and board with the Ashman family at Maybrook, in New York State, while I was taking the course. It worked out, and I visited my family on some weekends.

12 — Adopted Twice at Age 30 (Washington 1957)

The intensive language course at Rutgers was a real challenge to me. After 6 to 8 hours of classes each day, we had to continue our studies by listening to tapes and practicing in our double-bed dormitory rooms, each assigned to two students. My roommate was a middle-aged physician, Dr. Rózsa. We usually studied together. On weekends we were often taken to visit with American families, to learn more about the American way of life and to practice our new skills in English.

On one of these free weekends when no field trip was scheduled for us, I had my biggest surprise since arriving in the United States. A middle-aged man with a big smile (Fig. 58) visited with me in the dormitory and, after learning that my German was better than my English, conversed with me in German. He introduced himself as Frank L. Campbell, an entomologist, who worked at the National Research Council in Washington, D.C.

Frank, as I will call him here, had learned from his colleagues at the National Academy of Sciences that among the many refugees accepted to the United States was a young entomologist. He decided to go to New Brunswick, New Jersey, on the weekend to meet me and to offer his assistance. This is how we met the first time — one evening in March of 1957 in the new dormitories at Rutgers. I was amazed that a man whom I had never met before, would travel from Washington just to find out what my needs and dreams were and to offer his unselfish assistance. I learned later from others that, after Frank found out that I had worked on scale insects in Hungary, he gave this information to scale insect specialists in the U.S. Department of Agriculture's (USDA) insect systematics group. He was instrumental in placing me, with the aid of a National Research Council Fellowship, in the USDA laboratory until my English comprehension improved enough that I could take a position offered to me by a pest control firm in Baltimore.

Figure 58. Frank L. Campbell, an entomologist, editor, administrator, and humanitarian. With his wife Ina, he "adopted" my family.

For the five months that we were in Washington, Frank and his wife, Ina, found time to get to know my family. Also, Frank introduced me to many entomologists and sponsored my membership to both the Entomological Society of America and the Entomological Society of Washington.

One of the special events with Frank and Ina (Fig. 59) while in Washington was the invitation to L. O. Howard's 100th birthday celebration at the Cosmos Club in the summer of 1957. Howard was one of the best known and highly respected chiefs of the Entomology Section at the U.S. Department of Agriculture during the first part of the 20th century, and was Frank's much-admired chief for a while.

Frank learned that I would need a car of my own from September 1957 to start working as a consulting entomologist in Baltimore. He must have also realized that I had no money to purchase one. One Sunday afternoon Ina and Frank visited us and took my family on a sight-seeing trip which ended at their old home near the Potomac River. Frank showed us a beautiful blue, 6-year-old Oldsmobile (Fig. 64) in their yard and offered it as a gift so that I could take my first permanent position waiting for me in Baltimore.

My wife and I at first did not comprehend his wonderful gesture, and it took some time to sink in. Needless to say, we were overwhelmed. For the first time in our lives we would own a car. Frank had just had the vehicle checked in a repair shop; in addition, he included with it four winter tires and a one-year pre-paid insurance policy. I still treasure this car's Owner Service Policy in our family scrap book. We used this car without major problems for five years, and it was a sad occasion when I had to part with it in 1961.

I must have surprised Frank when I told him, after he gave us this car, that I would not be able to drive it for a while since I had never learned to drive a car. I was 30 years old. After the initial shock, he told me not to worry about it. But he himself must have worried because he called me soon to offer me driving lessons. He spent a number of his lunch hours teaching me to drive in a park near the Potomac River. Whenever I chauffeured him later, I joked that if he was not satisfied with my driving habits, he should blame my driving instructor and ask for a refund of my tuition.

After two years on the job in Baltimore, I decided to return to academic work, which I had left after coming to this country. I started looking for a place where I could complete my Ph.D. work in entomology. Frank was again instrumental in placing me in his old department at Ohio State University, where he had taught insect physiology and toxicology between 1936 and 1942. He recommended me to Professor D. M. DeLong, who offered me a $200 monthly stipend.

Frank kept up with my progress through graduate school, and when I was ready to take a position, he offered to be among my references. Jim Grayson, who would become my chief at Virginia Tech, had been one of Frank's

Figure 59. Ina Campbell, the most wonderful and supportive spouse that a scientist can dream of.

admirers since his early years in the profession. After reading Frank's letter of recommendation, Jim invited me for a job interview. This is how I ended up in the beautiful mountains of Virginia, where we are still living after 35 years. He often took my family to the Cosmos Club for special programs and dinners while in the area, and it gave Frank special pleasure to initiate and co-sponsor my membership in the Washington Cosmos Club.

A new chapter opened in our friendship with Frank and Ina after their retirement. Frank called this second period in our relationship the time when he became *my* protégé. Up to then I had been his. After his retirement in 1964, Frank decided to pursue research on the sensory organs of the German cockroach antennae, which he had left off 22 years earlier. While working on this subject in research laboratories in Europe and Australia, Frank needed more research samples from a new source. I offered to supply them and mounted on microscope slides cockroach antennae obtained from our colonies at Virginia Tech. Details on his research and the diary type summary of a two years' sabbatical work and a trip around the world were printed in their wonderful compilation: Campbell & Campbell (1973) "Better Late — An Entomologist's Postretirement Renovation" (371 pp.), printed in a limited edition of 16 copies at Virginia Tech, Department of Entomology.

After Frank and Ina returned from their "sabbatical" abroad, I realized that in order to publish his research results, Frank needed to prepare some illustrations but lacked the facilities. Therefore, we offered the available instruments and space for work in my laboratory. This is how, for a shorter period in 1969, and for longer times during the summers from 1970 to 1974, Frank and Ina spent time at Virginia Tech and in Blacksburg. They not only completed the preparation of needed illustrations, but pursued new research work. Results of his research were published in the Annals of the Entomological Society of America 63(1): 81–88 (1970), 65(4): 888–92 (1972), 72(5): 580–82 (1979). While Frank was at Virginia Tech, Jim Grayson, head of my department, bestowed on him the official title "Visiting Professor." Our entomology faculty and graduate students enjoyed his company, including his generous help with advice and assistance.

Through the years we became close friends, and I was able to learn more about Frank. His father, like mine, worked in a railroad shop. He got into college with a Pennsylvania Railroad scholarship that started his splendid academic career. He developed a number of exemplary habits and unusual hobbies. To enlarge his vocabulary, he played scrabble with Ina whenever he could, and also played by mail with a cousin and two of his former students.

Actually, he kept in touch on an annual basis with 37 of his former students. The Campbells were prolific writers. While on the sabbatical trip they kept in touch with many friends and mailed about 1,700 letters and cards between July 1, 1964, and September 9, 1965. I always admired his skill with the English language — which was probably the reason he was selected to edit a number of professional journals. One of these was *Scientific Monthly*,

in which he had a Monthly Commentary during 1945–48. Each evening, before going to bed, he dictated the daily events to Ina for inclusion in their extensive (36 volume) diary that was donated to a historical society after Frank's death. For fun while on trips, the Campbells collected a sizeable menagerie of small statues and artifacts of camels (their "namesake").

Frank enjoyed tasting, in moderation, wines after dinner. He made it into a scientific endeavor, searching out new ones and evaluating them, often with friends. His evaluation of each wine was typed by Ina on a 5"x8" card with the wine label mounted on the other side of the card. About 1,200 wine bottle corks strung on 40 twines made a curtain for the entryway between their kitchen and dining room. It was a most enjoyable event when visiting Frank, to join him on visits to the Central Liquor Store to select new varieties of wine for tasting. After his death, the annotated wine label collection on 5,683 cards in storage drawers was donated by Ina to the Virginia Tech Library Special Collections to be used by classes taking courses in oenology.

It would make this story too long if I listed all the occasions and details of Frank's and Ina's generosity to my family. I will simply summarize by noting that Frank and Ina spent much of their time and effort to help others. Besides helping us, they raised two adopted children. Before he met me, Frank had assisted a refugee Chinese professor of Zoology with resettlement and a job. Frank passed away at age 80 in 1979. Before his death, he made arrangements for his body to be given to a medical school for research. Here is another example of a great man serving science even after his death. Ina moved to a retirement community in New Jersey, where we continued to visit her until her death in 1991.

The association with our second adoptive parents started soon after I accepted a Fellowship to work at the USDA for five months, while improving my English. The monthly $200 Fellowship from the National Research Council (NRC) was not enough to set up a new household from scratch, and to pay for rent, transportation, and food for my family. When I raised this problem with Frank, I was told that some additional help would be provided soon. So Frank called on Mr. Spector at NRC, who called the Catholic Relief Agency. The latter directed him to the Blessed Sacrament Parish, near Chevy Chase Circle. Apparently the Parish was prepared to sponsor a Hungarian Refugee family. The parish priest, Father Roach, found the Leonard family, who volunteered to coordinate the assistance with financing from the parish. We were moved for a two-week stay into the Leonard's house in Chevy Chase. John and Frances Leonard (Fig. 60) were well known for their big heart in helping people in need. Besides adopting and raising three children, they took in from the street an alcoholic handyman, Mr. Johnson, who lived with them for years until his death. Later, when John was widowed, for several years he provided a home to a Polish newcomer family.

We were shown an apartment that could be rented for us by the parish. It was an empty two-bedroom apartment on the corner of 14th and Longfellow Streets in Northwest Washington, D.C. We were delighted with the prospect of moving into our own apartment after 16 temporary shelters in six months. The parish offered to pay our rent for the five months we would be in Washington. Knowing that all of our belongings fitted into two suitcases, Father Roach called for assistance. Fortunately, in two weeks, the parishioners donated all the needed household items to furnish our apartment, including a washing machine to help with Eva's diapers.

When they realized that we could improve our English faster if television were available, one family offered their second TV set, which needed minor repairs. Another family repaired it, and a third one delivered it to our new home. It was unbelievable for us to see all the help that poured in. We still have the large but incomplete English china set and the ironing board from these original donations. The Leonards coordinated all these efforts. Frances took my family to free medical exams and

Figure 60. John and Frances Leonard, our second adoptive parents.

dental work provided by physicians who volunteered to help refugees. John and his ride-sharing colleagues transported me to my downtown D.C. workplace, while John's sister Mary-Lou and her husband, Francis Dollymore, were always there when we needed further assistance. John, as a chemist, worked for the U.S. Navy.

John and Frances, far beyond their church commitment as volunteers, acted like our true adoptive parents, and their assistance came when we most needed such help. We still keep in touch with John and visit him when in the Washington area. John is proud of my family's accomplishments and never fails to say so. After being widowed, he served actively as deacon in the parish near his home until the age of 83, when an accident slowed him down.

It was made easy for us to adopt the United States as our new homeland. Meeting generous people such as Frank and Ina Campbell and John and Frances Leonard, showed us excellent examples of the American spirit and compassion in helping people in need.

13 — "Apprenticed" Again
(Washington and Baltimore 1957–60)

A Fellowship from the U.S. National Research Council gave me an opportunity to continue improving my English while working in the Insect Identification Laboratory of the U.S. Department of Agriculture between April and August 1957. With a carpool arrangement, paying my share for the ride, I reached our downtown USDA Laboratory from my home at 1400 Longfellow Street. After work I walked to the American-Hungarian Federation building on R Street NW to take the early English course offered to us by professors of the American University from 6 to 8 p.m.

After my 6 o'clock class was finished, Tili handed over our one-year-old Eva in a folding stroller at the gate and attended the 8 o'clock class. I took the bus ride on 16th Street to our street corner. The bus driver often was the same who brought Tili down to class; now seeing the same stroller and child, he greeted me with a big smile. Probably he was wondering if we were separated and were playing "Ping-Pong"

with our child. We just could not pay for a baby sitter, and both of us wanted to take one of the two language classes.

Because of the relative closeness of Rock Creek Park, we often took turns in taking Eva with the stroller (Fig. 61) to that Park. Normally we were the only ones walking on foot on the streets and in the park. It was unusual in those days to see people walking. America was still enchanted with the automobile.

My temporary work in the Insect Identification Laboratory was to mount on microscope slides aphids and whiteflies that were to be identified and studied by Louise M. Russell, the specialist on these groups. In the same preparation room where I was seated, a young woman, Miss Ruth Saunders, was making slides for Harold Morrison, the scale insect specialist. Morrison was unique for owning the only air conditioner in the building. He, as an amateur electrician, had installed this new gadget himself. Because of his air conditioner, we used

Figure 61. Eva, the "ping-pong" baby, with Tili and her folding stroller, in Washington, D.C. in 1957.

Figure 62. The picture printed with my story in The Washington Post *in 1957.* © *1957,* The Washington Post. *Reprinted with permission.*

every opportunity to sneak into his room and cool off. The summer heat, and especially the humidity, in Washington was too much for me, after the dry and cooler Central European climate. This is one reason we settled, later, in the Appalachians.

Miss Saunders was getting married and invited my family to the wedding and the reception that followed in the church social hall. Miss Russell offered to drive my family to the wedding. I accepted the offer and was excited to be going to our first wedding and reception in the United States. I shared the good news with my American neighbors. When I told them that we had been invited to my "roommate's" wedding, I was greeted by unexpected laughter. I thought in those days, after only a few months in the U.S., that persons working in the same office are called "roommates" in English, as

they are in Hungarian. This was not my last malapropism while learning English.

Morrison's neck must have suffered from peering through the microscope for long hours every day for many years. Therefore, he, as a good engineer, made an iron frame with a cushion to rest his forehead while he was looking through the microscope. To block out the sun and electric light that could interfere with his vision in the microscope, he attached a black cloth to his forehead-resting frame so he could cover his head and the microscope while studying the insects. We often found him with closed eyes, or sleeping, while resting his head over the frame with his head covered with the cloth.

Emily, Morrison's wife, was his assistant with the cataloging records and literature, and in translating foreign language articles. She even learned Russian to be able to assist him.

Morrison kept a drawerful of candies for himself and visitors, especially children. My daughter, Eva, always had her fill of candy whenever we visited him.

A newspaper man selected me with other Hungarian refugees in Washington for an interview. After the story with my picture (Fig. 62) appeared in *The Washington Post*, I was offered assistance by a Congressman. He would introduce a bill in Congress so I, as a foreign citizen, but a rare scale-insect expert, could be hired by the Federal Government. I declined his offer because a job was waiting for me in Baltimore.

We moved in September to Baltimore and I started working as a consulting entomologist for Insect Control and Research, Inc., in Catensville. After introduction to my new job and a short course in industrial pest control at Virginia Tech, I was assigned to visit a number of "clients" each month. I had to inspect the premises for evidence of insect and rodent infestation and take food samples for laboratory analysis to detect possible insect and mite fragments and rodent hairs. I had to provide the management with a report on my findings and make recommendations. This way our clients avoided problems with the local Health Department and the Food and Drug Administration.

When needed, I also sprayed or fogged with insecticides or set traps or poison baits against rodents. Occasionally, we also fumigated infested grain or other food shipments before these were used in the plants. First, I had to identify the pest and the rate of infestation. Among my regular clients I had a hospital, two breweries, several bakeries, and many restaurants.

A different division of the Company was involved with termite control, one with insecticide preparation and sales, another one with food analysis in our laboratory. Occasionally we fumigated railroad cars filled with grain and boats in the Baltimore harbor.

One day, during a downtown bakery inspection, our inspector was just saying goodbye to the baker who was serving over the counter his many early morning customers. A nervous woman was inching her way to the front, to face the baker. She shouted to the baker, "Look what you sold me in the cake yesterday, a cockroach," and she was shoving the baked insect over the counter. The baker, with a pale face, asked for the roach. She put it in his palm.

The baker took a close look at it, and hastily threw the brown thing in his mouth, chewing and swallowing it, to the amazement of his customers. With a smile he said, "This was only a raisin." No one in the store doubted his finding, except our inspector who had recognized the intact head and broken legs of a German cockroach. This is a good example of how quick-thinking people can save their business reputation by swallowing the evidence that could be used against them.

Most bakeries were infested with cockroaches, fire brats, and silverfish. Flour and Sawtoothed beetles were also common in such establishments. We discovered in one brewery that the labels had been chewed off of stored beer bottles. The cockroaches liked the natural glue used for the labels. It was made from animal products, probably bones, in those days.

While I was inspecting one of the bakeries in the Jewish neighborhood near the Pimlico Racetrack, the owner of the bakery asked about my nationality. I told him I was Hungarian. Then he asked me, why so many of my countrymen had participated in the persecution of Jews during WWII. I told him he should not generalize because then he would be no better than the Nazis. I also said that I knew a number of Hungarians who helped Jews during the German Occupation of Hungary. He said, "Name me one!" I replied, "Here I am, because I was arrested by the Nazis for helping Jews to escape." I had to tell him in short my story in Chapter 8. After that, he invited me to his home and offered me a job to fix his lawn. I earned some extra money with such weekend jobs.

One of my new Jewish acquaintances in Baltimore was Ruth Newman, a widowed attorney and insurance agent, who invited me to join in the effort to pack and mail used clothing to Hungary. She obtained the clothing from the local Jewish community. I was pleased to participate in this effort, knowing that many families had lost their belongings during the Uprising.

In my free time, I collected scale insect samples from trees in the Baltimore area, but I had no microscope to study them. When Mrs. Newman learned about my problem, she asked me about the cost of purchasing a used microscope. I told her the closest I had seen was marked for $160 in a downtown shop. She made a few phone calls and raised the funds. I got my beautiful brass microscope and used it for six years, until I got back to academic work. All such help gave me encouragement to finalize my first English language scientific article, which was published in 1959.

While in Baltimore, we made some new friends among Americans and learned more about their customs. One day Jim, a bachelor friend, invited Tili and me to our first steamed bluecrab dinner in a downtown place called the Pump Room. We had to walk through a bookstore to reach the dining area. Here we were seated and Jim ordered the house specialty, "all-you-can-eat crabs" for all of us.

Tili, dressed in her Sunday best, then got a real surprise when our tablecloth was removed and replaced by newspaper sheets. A large basket of spicy steamed crabs was emptied in the middle of our table. After we received high aprons, small wooden hammers, and claw-crushing tools, Jim introduced us to the mastery of opening the crabs. Because the crabs were so spicy, we had to neutralize the spices. I believe that the owner made most of his money from beer orders, not on the crabs. After two hours, Tili, who never really mastered the handling of the crabs, was still hungry, even after I helped her to open some hard shells.

We learned some more strange customs while visiting with American friends and attending their parties. Heavy drinks were served before dinner, but no alcoholic beverages were served with dinner, as wine is in Europe. I believe it is safer to drink after the meals. Americans usually sleep together in double beds, while Europeans normally sleep in separate beds; that

Figure 63a. Happy Eva in the arms of her Hungarian rescuer, Attila Bessko, in Baltimore, Maryland, in 1959.

may be the reason for fewer children in Europe. Also, Americans as a rule take showers in the mornings, while in Europe, we did it in the evening.

We ate pumpkin and sunflower seeds during the feature movie presentation in Europe, while here popcorn is the real thing for moviegoers. The keys often turn to the left in the locks in America, while in Europe keys turn only to the right to lock doors. I was much impressed to find many "do-gooder" organizations in America, in comparison to European countries. But dictatorships in many European countries killed the spirit of volunteerism for some time because it was forced on us to "volunteer." Only more recently have "do-gooder" organizations been given a chance to start again in East Central Europe.

Tili and I enrolled in evening English classes at the nearby college. Gradually, we were able to improve our English speaking and comprehension. My report writing from my inspection work also helped, not to mention the conversations I regularly had with our clients and my colleagues. Tili had similar practice opportunities while working as a cashier and book-

Figure 63b. Attila Bessko, Baby Eva's smuggler, reunited with us in Bishop Hannan's office in Washington, D.C. Bishop Hannan was Attila's sponsor to come to the United States. Photograph by Joseph F. Siwak for the Roman Catholic Press. Reprinted with permission.

keeper for the Catensville Robert Hall clothing store.

We conversed with Eva in Hungarian only, and we took her to a Hungarian refugee woman for babysitting. We tried and succeeded in making her bilingual. She learned English from American playmates and their families in the neighborhood. Thus, she did not pick up our Hungarian accent in her English. She also practiced Hungarian with Attila (Fig. 63a), who had smuggled her out of Hungary. He stayed with us in Baltimore for six months while he studied English (Fig. 63b).

Our company had a research laboratory where we raised pest insects in jars and cages to be used to test new pesticides. Some manufacturers wanted their new products tested by an independent research lab before submitting them for Federal approval. After my first year with the company, I was put in charge of this laboratory as assistant director of research. The director/owner of the company, Gene Gerberg, had a Ph.D. in entomology. I had no Ameri-

can graduate degree yet, only some teaching and professional experience along with eight publications.

Because of my training and experience with landscape pests from Hungary, I suggested to our Director to open a new division in landscape pest control, where I could fit in with my expertise. He declined to do so because of the liabilities involved in case we accidentally killed someone's favorite tree or shrub. His decline of my proposal made me start looking around for an opportunity to return to academic work.

But, in order to teach and do research at a University, as I had done in Hungary, I needed an American Ph.D. degree in entomology. My "adopted father" in Washington, Frank Campbell, learned about my wish and wrote to colleagues at some universities, including Ohio State University (OSU), where he had taught insect physiology before moving to Washington. I was soon accepted to do Ph.D. work in entomology at OSU, starting the Spring Quarter, in March of 1960.

14 — Back to School at Age 33
(Columbus, Ohio 1960–62)

Figure 64. Eva ready to move from Baltimore to Columbus, Ohio, in March 1960. Note the 1951 Oldsmobile, a gift from Frank and Ina Campbell in 1957.

We packed our furniture and belongings into a rented trailer and the Oldsmobile given to us by Frank Campbell (Fig. 64). While we were driving through Pennsylvania in mid-March, an unexpected treacherous snowstorm forced us off the highway into the closest motel. The next morning I realized our tropical fish had frozen. I had forgotten and left them in a covered aquarium in the car. I did not tell Eva until we unpacked in Columbus.

Our first nights were spent in the home of my graduate advisor, Dwight DeLong, while we looked for an apartment. We rented one just two blocks north of campus. This way we both could walk to our work places. Tili soon had a

job with *Chemical Abstracts,* which was housed close by. Eva was enrolled in the city nursery, and later in the University's nursery. We had trained her from an early age to be carefully independent. Now, at age 4, she learned to walk alone to the City Nursery, three blocks from our home.

Our house had six small apartments on two levels. Four apartments were occupied by graduate students from India and two by Hungarian Refugee families, including us. We had a back yard for our children to play in and our cars to be parked. As a former insect control man, I soon found many cockroaches harboring in our neglected basements, from where they staged their nightly raids into our kitchens and pantries. I proposed to the landlord that I would spray the entire house against the roaches if he would provide the pesticide. He agreed. I asked the tenants to agree on a date when all of us would be home so I could spray throughout the building at once to be effective. Some of our neighbors from India were uncooperative; because of their religion, they couldn't assist with the killing of living creatures. Therefore, my pest control operation was only partially successful. We learned to live with these pests, but I set up traps to catch live roaches.

Most of the Indian students were bachelors, or had left behind their wives while studying in the United States. Some of my Indian neighbors had the habit of doing their chores during the night, including cooking with Oriental spices with open windows in the hot summer. So I smelled a lot of curry and freshly fried chapati (a bread substitute). The preparation of the latter was a daily routine for Indian wives, and some hated it. The wives wanted to go home to India as soon as possible. One reason was apparent to me. Because of their darker skin, some landlords confused them with Blacks, and would not rent apartments to them in 1961. Wearing a sari helped these women to be distinguished. I learned later while visiting in India, that scientists and engineers who returned to India from the U.S., where they had completed graduate work, were discriminated against on the job market by Indira Ghandi's government agencies. The official reason, as I was told, was that they were too highly trained in the use of expensive gadgetry, which is not available in many Indian laboratories; therefore scientists and engineers who had received their degrees from the Soviet Union were favored.

My teaching assistantship provided $200 per month, for which I had to assist with the courses taught by my advisor, Professor DeLong. I once instigated a loud round of laughter in his class when I dropped a large teaching chart on DeLong's head while trying with shaky hands to move it to a new place on the board. He soon asked me, rather than assisting with his classes, to prepare many microscope slides with small insects for his laboratories. Later, he transferred me to a research assistantship of the Ohio Biological Survey. For two years I had to collect scale insect samples from most counties in Ohio. I also obtained the parasites and predators of the scale insects found, made biological observations on the studied species, mounted the insects on microscope slides, and studied, described, and illustrated them. I did these chores continuously for 28 months while taking courses as required.

Because of my research publication record and teaching experience in Hungary, I was given 30 extra credits and allowed to skip the MS work and work toward the Ph.D. degree. It was a 12–14-hour daily engagement for 30 months. My other Hungarian student friends compared the Graduate School at OSU with coal mine work in Hungary. Our native language was not accepted for credit as a foreign language. So, to satisfy the language requirement, I had to take a comprehensive language exam, translating zoological texts from German to English and vice-versa. An added difficulty for me was that both languages were foreign to me. I studied all summer for it, between daily swims in the cool University pool. Since then, the language requirement has been replaced with computer science courses or just deleted, to the delight of our graduate students.

I was given the Biological Survey's station wagon during the weekends to collect my samples from across Ohio. Sometimes the family joined me on these trips. The car had a manual transmission, so I asked my labmate, Paul Freytag, to help me learn how to use the gears. I believe I shook Paul's nerves a few times while learning the use of a straight shift car. Paul was my helper with many other chores too. But first, he introduced me to drinking coffee twice a day. While both of us were working in the same corner of the large graduate laboratory, he often made fun of my Hungarian accent, but also corrected me so I could gradually further improve my English. Because of my slow comprehension of lectures in classes taken by both of us, my lecture notes were incomplete, but I was able to make up the rest from Paul's notes. He was a good artist in illustrating insects, and taught me some skills that enabled me to do my own drawings for both the classes and for my dissertation.

DeLong was often out of town, so I was able to get some advice from Paul, and from Professor Donald Borror, who served on my student advisory committee. DeLong, to supplement his income for his extensive research projects and field trips, had a contract with A&P Stores in the region to keep the insects away from their merchandise and stores. During weekends he would inspect the stores and warehouses and fumigate when needed. I was told by his greedy colleagues that his income from the A&P was higher than his University salary. After he learned more about my experience in pest control, he put me in charge of pest control in the fraternities and sororities on the campus. I used to "brag" to my classmates that I had passkeys to all the sororities on the campus, so the girls could call me day or night, if insects or rodents were bothering them.

I received a small fee for my pest control services. People learned about my skills, so I was called a few times to do termite control for small houses of friends. It took me a whole Saturday to treat both sides of the concrete-block basement walls of a three-bedroom family house. I used Chlordane. My fee was $100 instead of the $300 or more charged by companies in 1961. My expenses were under $50. The $6 hourly income was a good one those days. Tili's monthly salary from *Chemical Abstracts* was $360. So we were able to save our bank deposit, kept for emergencies.

Our gift Oldsmobile was 10 years old by the fall of 1961, so we decided to purchase the smallest and most economical American car available in 1961. By purchasing in September a new last-year's model, when the new cars came to market, I got a 15% discount, so our new American Rambler cost only $1,700. Eva called it the Silver Bullet when, after 10 years, she was taking her first driver's lessons in it.

During the summer of 1961, Paul Freytag invited us to join him on a trip to the Rocky Mountains Entomological Conference. His parents and brother were living in Laramie, Wyoming, so we could also stay almost free after the meetings in one of his brother Bob's cottages at Snowy Range. We happily accepted his offer and rolled in a Volkswagon van to Laramie, where we spent two days at the home of Paul's parents before leaving for the conference at Cameron Pass in Colorado.

The meeting was held in the wooden barracks left from a POW camp for Germans. We all pitched in on the food preparation and housekeeping chores, so expenses were kept to a minimum. The sessions were informal. Most of the participants brought their families along, so it was an ideal combination of an inexpensive vacation for the families while the men (for I can't recall any women entomologists in attendance at this meeting) had the opportunity for professional discussions. Our children were entertained in the Crafts Shop, where they learned new artistic skills. During the evenings we were entertained with movies.

After the meeting, we returned to Paul's parents. His father was a retired professor of chemistry in Laramie. We met other entomologists working for the University. One of the wives asked Tili to show her how to make a real Hungarian chicken paprikás with dumplings. Tili agreed to do it, and we were taken to their home for the demonstration. Tili was shocked when she found only two chickens available, especially after learning that our gracious host, without telling her, had invited other families for the dinner to be fixed by Tili. After recovering from her dismay, Tili asked for more chicken, which was hurriedly thawed and fixed for the unexpected crowd of 12 people. There was an unfortunate delay in the food preparation. Because of the high elevation, over 2,000 meters, it took 50% more time to cook our meal. We spent 10 days at the Snowy Range Lodge, living in a wooden cabin at approximately 2,500 meters elevation. Paul took me trout fishing, and twice we had a good meal from our catch. Eva discovered a friendly chipmunk living under our cabin that, to her delight, even entered our rooms. Paul took us to an abandoned gold mine and to a number of unique mountain attractions, like beaver dams. On the way home we stopped in Fort Collins and Denver.

By the end of spring 1962, I had completed the required courses and was ready to finalize my dissertation. I set a daily routine, to be able to complete morphological descriptions and illustrations with distribution and biological records on 52 species of armored scale insects, with four new to science, in 52 days. By then I had the host, distribution, and life-cycle records accumulated, and the specimens were slide-mounted and identified to species. I just had to organize my data. The rest of the work for each species had to be completed in one long day. Therefore, in the morning hours I checked my samples and selected the best specimens to be used for illustrating the species. The selected slides were placed on a microscope slide projector. I projected in a darkened closet to a drawing sheet the image of my insect, and traced it with a soft pencil. Next, while studying under the microscope, I added the details from more specimens. When satisfied, I finalized my drawing in India ink. During the afternoon hours, I used my samples and my illustration to describe the morphology of the species. After dinner, I returned for another 3–4 hours to include with my description the records on life cycle, host plants, distribution, and natural enemies found in Ohio. My literature cards with synonym names for each species were already chronologically arranged for typing.

By 10 p.m. I usually went home with the handwritten description, etc. on the species just studied. Tili bravely deciphered my poor handwriting and typed a rough-draft of each description the next day. After corrections, the final typing was completed by a professional thesis typist. After 52 days I had the bulk of my manuscript and had two weeks to complete the abstract, introduction, methods, identification keys, conclusion, and the list of cited references. I reserved two weeks for emergencies and to take my manuscript to Dr. Harold Morrison in Washington for his comments. He leafed through it, while I was returning the borrowed specimens to his drawers. At the end, he handed back my manuscript and drawings. When I asked about his special comments, he said with a big smile, "You're no worse than the others." By then, I had gotten to know Morrison for his kidding and often sarcastic comments. I thanked him, and named a new species (*Acutaspis morrisonorum*) in his and Emily Morrison's honor.

It was during my last haircut in Columbus, Ohio where I was just completing my graduate studies, that my six-year-old daughter, Eva, who usually accompanied me to such events, informed our barber friend John that we were to hurry home because that day was her birthday. John smiled, pulled out a silver dollar, and gave it to her as a birthday gift, telling her that she would get another silver dollar next year for her birthday if she came again. She smiled, thanked him, and asked: "If I can't come next year, would you mind mailing it to me?" She was already showing the skills that would lead her to become a lawyer.

While struggling with my written final examinations, Tili took off with Eva to Vienna, to meet her parents for the first time after five years. Because refugees from the 1956 Uprising were blacklisted by the Communist Hungarian Government, we were not allowed to have personal contact with close relatives, and only after five years could our parents visit in neighboring Austria, where most of us met with close relatives. I realized that time how lucky we had been to be able to smuggle Eva out of Hungary in 1957. Otherwise, we could not have seen her for five or more years.

I applied to six academic openings, and three came through with invitations for personal interviews. A fourth job in the Midwest was in a Wesleyan college. They showed interest in me by sending their standard questionnaire. When I reached the question on whether or not I drink alcoholic beverages, I just tossed away the questionnaire. These folks should know better, that Europeans, especially in wine grape-growing areas, normally have a glass of wine with their dinner. This habit does not make them alcoholics; and some even consider wine in moderation as a medicine. I went for job interviews at Illinois universities at Carbondale and Normal. Both sent me an offer. Next I went to Blacksburg, the place I had visited for a short course in 1958. This time I took my family along. I got a salary offer that was 10 to 15% less than the two offers from Illinois. Before making a decision, I looked up the weather station reports from the three towns and found Blacksburg the most attractive — less heat and humidity here than in Illinois. The head of the Entomology Department at Virginia Tech, Dr. James McD. Grayson, after reading Frank Campbell's reference letter, gave me credit for my eight printed research papers and a bulletin in print, and for the six years of college teaching experience in Hungary, and "sweetened the pie" by offering to appoint me as an Associate Professor. I took his offer and have never regretted it.

After the graduation ceremonies at the end of the summer, I rented two moving trailers, and with a friend's help, moved to Blacksburg. Jim Grayson reserved a two-bedroom apartment in the University's Faculty Center. I moved into the empty rooms, but soon I had an offer to use for two years the furniture of another Hungarian Refugee family in the same building. They needed to store their furniture for two years while in Vienna for graduate studies. I took the offer and carried the furniture to our apartment.

By the time my family returned from Vienna, the apartment and the needed furniture were secured, and I could start on my new job on the first of September, 1962.

15 — As Teacher-Researcher-Administrator (1962–92)
(Never give up; do it, but now!)

A full-time teacher —

During my first five years at Virginia Tech, I had to teach nine different courses. I was the only full-time teacher in the department. This meant 4–5 courses each year during three quarters, but some of the advanced courses I taught every other year only. Because most of my courses were in insect taxonomy and morphology, I faced the problem of how to present the relatively dry material in a digestible form to the mostly non-taxonomically-minded undergraduate and graduate students, who were often taking my courses because they were required. I also soon realized that not many students like to memorize a glossary of morphological terms or learn about the number of tibial spines on the hind legs of a cricket, not to mention learning the characteristics of more than 1,000 families of insects.

To achieve my teaching goals, I tried my best to transfer to my students the enthusiasm I had for the subject. Apparently it rubbed off on them. I also wanted to sell them the material, but how? By applying the material to their everyday professional problems! I found out the students' areas of specialization and selected my examples from their fields of interest, and referred to these during my lectures.

How did I do this? During the first meeting of each course my students had to complete a questionnaire in which, besides standard information, they had to state their interest, field of specialization, and the proposed title of their thesis or dissertation, if a graduate student. For example, when I learned in one course that three of my students were interested in insects of forage crops, two in parasites of pest insects, whenever I had a chance,

I provided examples on the pertinent insects in my lectures. Also, when I once, as a substitute instructor, had to teach applied agricultural entomology and realized that all the graduate students enrolled were from tropical countries, for their benefit I changed the course material into tropical agricultural entomology.

When I treated the morphology or classification of the insect families, I discussed the more interesting aspects of their biology, their economic importance, and the damage produced by some. In a few of my courses the students worked on individual projects selected by them from my list of topics, or sometimes even suggested by the students themselves, who were interested in learning more than I could provide through the lectures and laboratories. For example, when one of the students told me that his family owned a rose nursery, I asked him to prepare a paper on the pests of roses for extra credit. He did so.

I encouraged graduate students to present papers at national meetings and to publish their work. It created more interest and enthusiasm for the class projects because they set higher goals than merely preparing a class assignment. The professional experience from oral presentations and from publishing was, of course, valuable and provided an additional learning experience not usually included in most classes. I was fortunate to see some of my students presenting papers at professional meetings and publishing several papers as a result of research which originally started as class projects. These students were highly motivated and worked hard on their projects.

For example, in my course in Advanced Systematic Entomology, the individualized problems to be completed during the laboratory periods involved 60 hours of work, which would satisfy the standard requirements set in the course for 30% of the final grade. Instead of 60 hours, the average time students spent on the problem was 131 hours. It was not because they could not complete the assignment in 60 hours, but because they wanted to do a more complete job than the minimum requirement in the course, because it was on a problem they had selected themselves, and because a spirit of competition had risen in the class.

I usually treated undergraduate students as I treated graduate students, something students appreciated. My office door, which adjoined the graduate lab, was always open for consultation. Some of the best research papers were edited for presentation at one of the professional meetings. I helped to publish some of these, and thus provided the students with an opportunity to co-author their first research paper.

To make my courses lively and interesting, I developed a number of teaching aids and other methods for my lectures and laboratories. With students who were on the payroll, we prepared about 80 home-made, colored wall charts. These saved me time during lectures, and the students could re-use the charts when studying because they were stored in a box in the classroom. Later, the charts were put on color slides for use in far-away class rooms. I also developed a departmental color slide collection of approximately 4,500 slides on insects and other arthropods. These were available for use and/or duplication by the faculty and teaching assistants.

Duplicates of my 25-year collection of specimens of insect and mite damage on plants, on herbarium sheets, were used to prepare "Riker mounts". About 450 such were prepared in glass-topped boxes, where besides the dried damaged plant parts, the preserved life stages of pest insects were also displayed with pertinent text. These Rikers were especially useful in my laboratory exercises. Several colleagues used these display boxes and duplicated many of them.

Students appreciated more my laboratories in "horticultural entomology", especially when I held these in an orchard or arboretum under an insect-infested tree. Here, I discussed the insects' life cycle and the damage they produced. Some of the field trips ended in the Virginia Tech Arboretum and/or Orchard where I demonstrated to students how to roast their Transylvanian Kebab with onion over the fire.

To retain the students' attention and interest in the subjects covered, for years I collected jokes and humorous stories on insects and told some when pertinent to the subject matter covered in my lecture. I believe such humurous stories on insects told with my Hungarian accent gave some spice to my presentations.

Working with Graduate Students

I have developed close working relationships with my graduate students by having their work area next to mine. Only one student, who liked to work during the nights, did not fully benefit by this arrangement. The latter, probably to save on rental expenses, started working after 5:00 p.m. Before starting to work, he gave his girlfriend the key to her apartment. He worked all night in my laboratory until his girlfriend showed up in the morning to drop the apartment key off with him for the day. This is just one of many examples of how some graduate students saved on their rent.

I organized joint scale insect-collecting trips, often with out-of-state colleagues participating (Fig. 65), and went together with my students to professional meetings where most of us presented papers. I made a special effort to see that my graduate students published some research papers before they started shopping for a position, but some students were hesitant to write papers. So, I introduced a new course for graduate students on how to write and illustrate publications, including their theses; also on how and where to find the needed literature. It must have helped, because almost all of my students found appropriate positions fairly quickly. Their theses and dissertations were already published or were in print soon after graduation.

Figure 65. A group of scale-insect collectors at Seashore State Park in Virginia with our graduate students and colleagues from Maryland. From left, Sueo (Steve) Nakahara, Michael Kosztarab, Douglass R. Miller, James O. Howell, John A. Davidson, Dale K. Pollet, Michael L. Williams, F. William (Bill) Gimpel, and Paris L. Lambdin.

Because of the high cost of printing their extensive works, I initiated a research bulletin series for taxonomic papers from scale insect research. We printed 18 such bulletins, some of book size. I also encouraged my students to correspond directly with researchers in their field around the world. Such personal contacts for young beginners were stimulating.

I realized that almost all of our predecessors had worked only on the taxonomy of the adult female scale insects, neglecting males and the immature stages. So, we divided the chores when revising most groups. One student worked on the adult females, another on the immature stages. But none worked on the adult males, because we did not have appropriate background for the males, which are entirely different from all others. Therefore, I invited in 1966 an expert on male scale insects, Dr. Sherif Afifi from London, as a Postdoctoral Fellow. He brought not only special knowledge for all of us, but also exchanged ideas with our group on the training methods at the Universtiy of London.

I often ended up in my graduate classes with foreign students who were taking their first classes in the English language in America. Because I have studied six languages, most of

them phonetic, and have lived in foreign countries where I learned to communicate with people speaking languages foreign to me, they had fewer problems in understanding me than they did the professors who were from America.

One of my first foreign graduate students was having language problems. When I tried to explain that, for her research assistantship and also for her thesis problem, she would need to work on the morphology of immature stages of the same group of scale insects where I had already started working on the adult females, she just shook her head, being unable to comprehend the information. Disappointed, but not giving up, I decided to simplify my explanation. So I said: "You will have to work on the babies, while I will be working on their mothers." Her face brightened up, and with a smile, she said: "Now I understand!"

I was kept very busy in teaching. For example, in 1969, besides teaching 3 courses, I also served on 19 graduate students' committees and as a major advisor for four. My course teaching and graduate training methods brought three university recognitions during my first 12 years at Virginia Tech.

Some comparisons
with the European School System

Because of my background and interest in further improving our educational system in the USA, I will make here some comparisons with the European system, with suggestions. As college teachers, we are not able to fully utilize the four years available for professional specialization and training of our students. The reason is that there are no national minimum standards for High School graduation. I was pleased to learn, just before my manuscript went to press, that U.S. President Bill Clinton has just arrived at the same conclusion, and will try to do something about it!

Each state and community, often depending on the available funds, sets its own standards. Unfortunately, because funds for education normally come out of real estate taxes, poor communities can't afford to attract the best or even sufficient numbers of educators. Therefore, students arrive at our universities with varied and often insufficient background training. As a result, the first one or two years at many U.S. universities are often spent in making up the scholastic deficiencies of our students. The High Schools in most European countries and probably Japan have already covered enough math, chemistry, physics, and their native languages to render remedial courses unnecessary at the university level. This way they can concentrate intensively for four years on professional training, instead of having only two, or at best three years for it, as at many colleges in the United States.

Final exams at European universities are usually oral, normally administered by two faculty members, while in the USA these are often written exams, often of the multiple-choice type. The lack of oral presentation skills shows up especially during job interviews. Although it is more time-consuming to give oral exams, they should be introduced wherever practicable.

Because of the high level of education in Europe at High Schools, and at many universities, normally no course work is required from graduate students. Professors can expect more research from their students, often resulting in sizeable dissertations and other publications. I feel that European graduate students could benefit from taking some courses, so as to be brought up to date in the field of their specialization, especially if they have been out of school for some years before starting graduate work. Therefore, I believe that if our U.S. high schools and our undergraduate colleges could adopt the European academic system, followed by traditional graduate work under the U.S. system, we could provide better trained engineers, scientists, and other specialists than we are now doing.

In addition to the part-time vocational training currently provided by many U.S. high schools, it would be useful to introduce in the United States more-specialized Vocational High Schools, where students for four years (ages 15-18) would receive intensive training in a profession, besides the basic High School curriculum. For example, I can visualize the need for a High School in Textile Engineering in the southeastern United States, or a horticultural High School in Central California, etc. Graduates could fill the middleman position in their discipline or continue with further college training. Students would have more incentive to finish a Vocational High School and would more easily find jobs with the four years of intensive training in their profession. The fringe benefits for the entire country would be a lower unemployment rate for High School graduates, and, because of longer class/shop hours in High School, fewer youngsters would find time for misbehavior on the streets. I attended one such school in Europe where the students were trained 48 hours per week, and even during the summers we received vocational training. To reduce the cost of our upkeep in the Horticultural Boarding High School, we raised most of our own food on the practice fields of the school.

Our public school buildings often suffer from vandalism during the summer vacation time, but also from equipment breakdowns when no one is in the buildings. I recall the case of our local PTA landscape project, when dozens of parents pitched in to landscape the bare yard of our local elementary school. Most of the trees and shrubs planted there died during the first summer for lack of watering by the school system.

The five schools I attended in Europe each had a caretaker family living in an apartment on the school premises. The wife helped with the cleaning of the classrooms, while the husband was a handyman to repair and replace broken-down electrical equipment or plumbing, and to keep the heating furnaces in working order. In addition to the free housing, they also received salaries. In two schools during class breaks, the caretaker sold us sandwiches, milk, and soft drinks. The family took special pride in maintaining the school rooms and the school yard in good order. I can't recall any case of vandalism in these schools. The above may be a good system to adopt for some American schools. I have never seen in Central Europe flat roofs over school buildings. In our county, the taxpayers paid for roof repairs several times over the price of the original flat roofs that leaked too soon after construction.

I have not found the teacher and course evaluation sheets to be completed by students at European universities or in developing countries. When I introduced this kind of evaluation after teaching a course in Sri Lanka, I was shunned by the professors. I think it is a good idea, and I used such even before they were introduced by our universities. But paying too much attention to course evaluations has resulted in grade inflation at some universities, as I found when I chaired an ad-hoc Committee on Grade Inflation.

There is a new emphasis on undergraduate training, a healthy trend, I believe, after having witnessed just the opposite emphasis for 25 years. In the mid-1960s professors were told that our promotions and salary increases depended on how much money we brought in from granting agencies, and on how much we published. Surely the quality of course teaching suffered. One drawback of that emphasis was that many of us with research assignments went for outside grants and then catered to the requirements of these granting agencies,

neglecting the research that would benefit our taxpayers in Virginia.

Most academic departments do not employ a caretaker for their collections of teaching aids and instruments. This is a big mistake because it requires instructors to individually accumulate and store the materials used in their courses, often duplicating items that could be used in several courses, *e.g.* teaching charts, color slides, software, *etc*. Many teachers depend on their teaching assistants to keep such materials in order, but these assistants run away as soon as the course ends, leaving behind piles of unsorted teaching aids which cannot be easily found the next time the course is taught. Thus, during the next semester, the new course assistants often have to start from scratch, developing a new set of teaching aids for the same course.

Research and Publications

My original 10-month academic appointment letter in 1962 did not include research responsibilities. Only two years later, when I had obtained a National Science Foundation grant, was 25% time added for research, and I was reassigned to a 12-month appointment. It happened during the year when our young university president started placing more emphasis on research grants and publications by the faculty. I was fortunate to receive almost continuous grant support from the National Science Foundation (NSF) after 1963 and from 1970 to date from the U.S. Department of Agriculture. I needed the money to provide the salary for a technician and stipends for my graduate students. Because my research was considered more basic than applied, I received minimal funding, except for part of my salary, from the Virginia Agricultural Experiment Station (VAES). At least for a while the VAES published our research bulletins.

Soon after coming to Virginia Tech, I realized that there had been only one comprehensive study published on Virginia insects. This was on butterflies. So I decided to make a special effort to inventory our Virginia insect fauna and to produce publications on the topic. I learned that Dr. Richard L. Hoffman, Professor of Biology at Radford College (now University) had the same dream. So we got together and initiated at Virginia Tech the series *The Insects of Virginia* in 1969; we published 13 bulletins in ten years. Simultaneously, I started another series, *Studies on the Morphology and Systematics of Scale Insects*, that continued through 16 bulletins until my retirement. The latter proved to be a good outlet, especially for publishing my students' theses and dissertations. The manuscripts for both series were reviewed by specialists and edited by Hoffman and myself. The first series is being continued through the Virginia Museum of Natural History at Martinsville.

After I came to Virginia Tech, I was offered a better-paying job as a scale insect specialist of the U.S. Department of Agriculture (USDA). I declined the offer because I liked the combination of teaching and research work, the academic atmosphere, and the cosmopolitan small-town life. I offered to assist the USDA by training future specialists and to help out during two summers with the upgrading of the scale insect collection, which I did.

By 1970, I had five graduate students working with me on scale insect research; in 1972 we reached the peak of our publication output with 463 printed pages that year. Out of the cooperative projects with the USDA, we published four research bulletins during 1974-88. My students' research benefited from having the world's scale insect literature processed in our laboratory. Because they received from me the needed abstracted literature for their research, they saved time that enabled them to produce more in their graduate research.

To introduce my graduate students to research on scale insects, I twice offered a Special Studies course on the subject. From 1974 on this course was replaced by the Coccidology Training Sessions at the University of Maryland, where I started sending my students. I taught some topics in these sessions.

Recognition

In recognition for my research work I was elected to membership in the Washington Cosmos Club during 1970, for my studies on Virginia insects, I was made a "Fellow of the Virginia Academy of Science" in 1975, and for my work on scale insects in Central Europe, I was granted Honorary Membership of the Hungarian Entomological Society in 1979, named an Honorary Doctor by the University of Horticultural Science of Budapest in 1993, and granted External Membership of the Hungarian Academy of Sciences in 1995.

I served as an Exchange Scientist to Hungary for the National Research Council in 1975. While working during the three summer months there, I prepared in coauthorship with Dr. F. Kozár a manuscript, *Scale Insects of Hungary* (Kosztarab and Kozár, 1978). Later, this was expanded into an English language book, *Scale Insects of Central Europe* (Kosztarab and Kozár, 1988).

While in Hungary in 1975, I realized that the United States could benefit from the introduction, as a new natural enemy of scale insects, of a beetle that is common in Hungary. The beetles feed exclusively on scale insects that are often pests in horticulture and silviculture. Releasing these beetles would reduce the need for using pesticides. So, in 1977, with permission, I introduced to Virginia a new beetle, *Anthribus nebulosus* (Fig. 66). It was named the "Hungry Hungarian Beetle" by a reporter. I reared these in our Quarantine Laboratory and released their progeny to two sites in Virginia. These insects were reported in 1991 from as far away as the New England states as effective predators of scale insects.

By 1996, I had authored or coauthored 165 papers and research bulletins, including three books, for a total of 4,368 pages. By 1996 I had also named a new family of scale insects and, often in coauthorship with my students, 12 new genera and 57 new species. In recognition of my research, entomologist colleagues

Figure 66. The Anthribus *beetle, which kills pest scale insects, was introduced to the United States from Hungary by the author in 1977.*

have honored me by naming after me one genus and 13 species new to science. This is a common practice by systematists to name new species after the persons who collected the samples or who assisted their research.

Effects of Acid Rain

For some time I had wanted to learn about the possible effect of acid rain on our biota. So after observing the decline of our trees in the Appalachian Mountains, I decided to study what is happening to our soil microinvertebrates under different plant communities and under different acidification pressures. I applied for a 3-year Miles C. Horton Research Fund grant and received financial support for a student without scholarship. After quantitative assessment, our samples were sent to specialists for qualitative analysis. Decidedly fewer insects and mites were found where higher acid (3.5 pH) was present in the soil sample. Actually, acidi-

fication increased in our area after the oil embargo (1982-1983) when oil furnaces were converted back to coal burning. I believe that scientists should study this phenomenon further. What is going to happen to our food crops if with the acid rain we kill the microorganisms that help convert organic materials into essential nutrients for our plants? Also, more effective legislation should help reduce present air pollution levels.

Curator of the Insect Collection

One of my original job assignments in 1962 was to look after and curate the insect collection of my institution. I started with about 70,000 dry and alcohol-preserved insects in 1962 that, with help from many colleagues and graduate students, had expanded to more than one million by the time I retired (Kosztarab, 1992). I was proud to be able to curate the state's oldest (started in 1888) and largest insect collection. About half of the new acquisitions were scale insects and mites that required slide mounting. I also developed a small "Herbarium of Insect and Mite Damage" that helped to identify some pest species even after they were gone. It was called our "FBI File on the Smallest Criminals"; instead of fingerprints, we saved on dried plant material their galls, leaf minings, characteristic chewing patterns, etc. that were species-specific to these pests. We also used these in teaching demonstrations. Because of the university's failure to hire a replacement systematist, I have been serving as curator for the collections since retirement.

The school administration recognized my curatorial efforts by naming me Chairman of the Museum Study Committee in 1986, Director of the Center for Systematics Collections in 1987, and Founding Director of the Virginia Museum of Natural History at Virginia Tech in 1991. For my initiation of a symposia series on scale insect studies, I received a Life-Time Achievement Award at the 11th Sternorrhycha Symposium of the Entomological Society of America at Baltimore in 1992.

To promote insect studies at my university, I prepared live insect exhibits for public view-

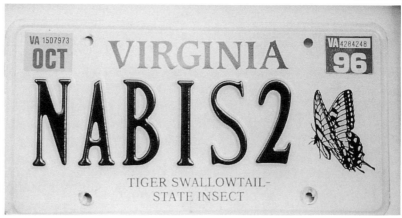

Figure 67. My Virginia automobile license plate with the NABIS insignia, to promote the National Biological Survey, and with our state insect.

ing. One such was a beehive behind glass, placed in the Virginia Tech Library, and a carpenter ant colony in a terrarium, placed in the entry hall of the Entomology and Biology departments in 1972. In 1976 I also organized and chaired a departmental committee to prepare an exhibit: "Insect Inspirations and Photography" in two art gallery halls of the Student Center. In a few days, about 4,000 students visited our exhibits. As a result of the public exhibits, enrollment in some courses increased to such a level that we had to teach in large classrooms across campus. With the drastically increased teaching load, the department gradually hired three new faculty members. So my 16 non-teaching or research assignments in the department were reduced to eight by giving some of these to the new colleagues, and my research time allotment was increased to 60%, with two of my courses being reassigned to new faculty members.

The National Biological Survey (NABIS)

After comparing the efforts of the Europeans to inventory their animal and plant life, with our U.S. efforts, I realized that we have fallen behind many nations, especially since 1939, when the Bureau of Biological Survey was dissolved. Therefore, in 1975 I proposed to the Entomological Society of America (ESA) that they help initiate a project on the Insect Fauna of North America (IFNA), and tried to further this goal as a member (1979) and as chairman (1982) of the Standing Committee on Systematics Resources.

In 1982 with my Canadian colleagues, I organized a joint symposium in Toronto to learn from each other and initiate coordination of efforts for North American insect studies. I soon realized that besides the insect fauna, other groups in our biota were also grossly neglected — especially lower plants and invertebrates. So, I asked representatives of other disciplines to join with me in an effort to initiate work on the entire flora and fauna. They enthusiastically joined me. We formed a "Planning Committee for the National Biological Survey" to include 11 members, 10 advisors or government agency consultants, and myself as chairman until 1987.

We worked together to establish communications with government agencies working on related subjects and to obtain their endorsement. Nobody objected to our goals and efforts. I received positive responses from representatives of a large number of organizations and individuals after they read my editorial in *Science* (Feb. 3, 1984). Actually, 38 professional associations and other organizations, representing more than 200,000 scientists and educators, passed resolutions or sent me letters supporting the concept for the initiation of a National Biological Survey.

Between 1984 and 1994, on behalf of initiating the NABIS Project, I made many presentations to prospective groups, legislative offices, societies, government agencies, and radio and TV programs. I also published some articles (Kosztarab, 1988) and organized meetings; even the two license plates on my cars bear the NABIS logo (Fig. 67) (Kosztarab, 1988). Our own Virginia senators and congressmen were supportive, and one offered to work toward increasing the Smithsonian's budget with money earmarked for the initiation of the NABIS effort. The Smithsonian, however, declined to take on a new responsibility. Unfortunately, a "turf fight" slowed down progress in Washington, although a large number of U.S. legislators supported the effort (Kosztarab and Schaefer, 1990).

It took ten years, after my initial editorial letter in *Science*, to have the National Biological Survey (NBS) started by Interior Secretary Bruce Babbitt in 1994. He had to change its name to the National Biological Service to calm down some of the critics. In the fall of 1996 the NBS was combined with the U.S. Geological Survey, and became the Biological Resources Division of the U.S. Geological Survey. It is a strange "marriage", placing NBS, which deals with our living natural resources, under an organization that worked for over 100 years on this nation's non-living resources. I hope future wiser legislators will realize the mistake made by the Congress.

I received a number of recognitions for my 10-year effort toward the initiation of NBS, but the one closest to my heart came from the Association of Systematics Collections (ASC). They selected me in 1994 to receive their Annual Service Award. This is a large framed and hand-painted, personalized color certificate.

Our Virginia legislators in the U.S. Congress asked me to show examples of products that could result from the NABIS effort. So, with some coauthors, I produced three book-size publications and a book as contributions Nos. 1 to 4 (1985, 1988, 1990, 1996) to the National Biological Survey. The last one was completed after my retirement (Kosztarab 1996).

Extracurricular Activities

My other two extracurricular activities included the promotion of the establishment of a Virginia state museum of natural history and the designation of a state insect by our Virginia legislators. It took me 20 years to see the first come true, but only 15 years for the state insect. I have described in the *Virginia Journal of Science* (Kosztarab, 1993a), in detail, the 20 years leading to the establishment of the museum; I only summarize the story here. I had served in 1968 and 1969 on an ad hoc committee of the Virginia Academy of Science to study the feasibility of a state science museum and a natural history museum and to make reccommendations. Our committee supported both museums. The science museum was established in Richmond in 1977, but our Virginia Museum of Natural History at Virginia Tech was started only in 1989.

To achieve the latter goal, we combined the needs of several departments having problems housing and curating their natural history collections. First, a Center for Systematics Collections (CSC) was established in 1973. After some financially lean years, I was asked to reactivate the CSC in 1985. Curators formed a Museum Study Committee in 1986 that I was asked to chair. We made a special effort to publicize through newspapers the plight of the Virginia Tech natural history collection. Most of these collections were stored in a warehouse, and others were stored in hallways of campus buildings.

At about the same time, I was asked to serve on the Scientific Advisory Board of the privately supported Virginia Museum of Natural History (VMNH) in Martinsville. I realized our chances to have a branch museum at Virginia Tech would increase if we joined VMNH in their efforts to become a state-supported museum, especially since VMNH had a godfather in Delegate A.L. Philpot, the Speaker of the House, in Richmond. We could contribute to a joint effort by boasting that we had Virginia's oldest and largest natural history collections, with nine curators for those, although none of our curators were ever paid for their extracurricular work on the collections. Our efforts succeeded when, in 1988, the Martinsville museum was taken over by the state, with branches at Virginia Tech and at the University of Virginia.

The question on the adoption of a state insect came up in the Virginia General Assembly in 1976 when a delegate, to educate school children about the government, was promoting the praying mantis for this distinction. As an entomologist, I realized that what they had in mind was the imported Chinese mantis. The Chinese mantis would be inappropriate for a state insect because it is of foreign origin and feeds on both pests and beneficial insects. It is also cannibalistic. The Chinese mantis will eat other mantises, and often their mates after the honeymoon.

Therefore, I proposed for the state insect the Tiger Swallowtail butterfly. The House adopted the mantis, and the Senate adopted the Tiger Swallowtail butterfly. These two opposing actions created a legislative deadlock in 1976. It took 15 more years of keeping the idea alive to see progress. In 1991, I was fortunate to be able to join efforts for the same goal with the Virginia Federation of Garden Clubs. After lobbying efforts and testifying in the bill's behalf by both the representative of the Federation and myself, the bill was passed with strong support in both houses on February 2 and 9, 1991. The Tiger Swallowtail butterfly became Virginia's state insect.

I have often been asked why I selected the Tiger Swallowtail. My answer is that it is the first insect that was named and described from North America, and the specimens sent to the famous Swedish biologist, Linnaeus, were from Virginia. It is a colorful, and graceful insect. It is widespread throughout the state and is active from April to late October. The adults help to pollinate flowers. It also symbolizes the fragile living environment which suffers from degradation (Kosztarab, 1993b). Since 1995 Virginia drivers have been able to obtain their car license plates with the colorful state insect on them (Fig. 67).

16 — Four Trips Across the United States (1964–88)

Some of my research projects required the taking of live scale insect samples from plants. Studying species in several genera and families of scale insects with distribution across North America took me to many states. I usually had my family on these trips. This way I had free assistance with the driving task, and for collecting, labeling, preserving, and shipping my samples. Because I had only partial funding for such trips, I usually combined these travels with some family vacation in the areas visited and paid the difference for the extra expenses from personal funds.

During the first three trips, I also consulted with colleagues enroute, inventoried the scale insect collections of their institutions, and borrowed their pertinent material for the studies. I obtained ahead of time the necessary collecting permits for the State and Federal Parks. During my last trip in 1988, instead of flying to an International Conference in Vancouver, Canada, I drove my car so I could collect insect samples enroute and observe the effect of air pollution and acid rain in five National Parks. We usually took off on these trips as soon as my teaching ended in June to avoid most of the summer heat on our southern route to the West Coast.

First Trip — 1964

Our first trip (June 7–July 11, 1964) was to the "promised land" for me: California. Because of my work on scales, for some time this state had appeared to be the most attractive to settle in, for scale insects are considered a very important pest in California agriculture. I thought: this could be the state where my expertise would be most appreciated!

We packed up with much care the needed belongings for three of us to last five weeks, plus my professional gear. I attached a luggage carrier frame to the roof of my 1961 Rambler American. Most of my professional stuff was put up there and covered with an old plastic sheet for protection from the elements. After about 25 miles south on U.S. Interstate 81, the plastic cover started disintegrating and gradually the draft carried away most of it. So I had to place the gear from the roof on the back seat occupied by seven-year-old Eva and move Eva, to her delight, to the front seat between us.

We slept in Sweetwater, Tennessee, and continued our trip the next morning around 7 a.m. I tried to avoid the mid-day heat, not having an air conditioner, and usually extended our lunch time in an air-conditioned restaurant. Thus, we reached Texas by noon, and on the good roads, often driving at 70 miles per hour, arrived at Ranger, Texas, by evening to sleep. While Tili paid for the accomodations, I checked our room more closely for insects. To my amazement, I found a scorpion hidden behind a picture over our bed. I got out my pocket knife and with shaky hands made harmless the scorpion by cutting off its tail. I dropped the still pumping stinger tail and the body of the scorpion behind our bed, just in time, as my family entered the room. I told the family that I checked the room, but no mosquitoes were found. I did not dare tell them about my discovery. The next morning I tried to place the dead scorpion in an alcohol vial for a souvenir, but the tailless scorpion had walked away, and only the still-moving tail was available for preservation. Then, I dared to show the catch to my family.

It got so hot that day that we spent at least two hours in a cool restaurant in Colorado City (still in Texas), where we ate our first hot Mexican meal. We arrived in El Paso, Texas, by evening and enjoyed the cool swimming pool of our motel.

The next morning, we visited Mexico for the first time in the city of Juarez, across the Rio Grande from El Paso. A different world greeted us here as we did some shopping. My skills from the Bucharest bazaars came in handy here, as I bargained on the prices. At evening, Tili and I were able to see a Mexican dance performance because we found a babysitter for Eva in our hotel.

Next day we drove to my first professional engagement, at the Southwest Research Station of the American Museum of Natural History, at Portal, Arizona. Enroute we saw many roadrunners (birds) and ran into sandstorms in the desert habitat. We found the research station at Portal to be ideally located. It is at the meeting place of a semi-desert and the high Chiricahua Mountains with beautiful green vegetation and crystal clear streams.

We rented a small cabin and could eat meals with the rest of the researchers and their families in the cafeteria. I met a variety of biologists there. A research group was studying the behavior of soldier ants. For their work they were out during the night and slept during the day. Another group of young folks were collecting rattlesnakes which they kept in burlap sacks under their beds. One day this crew provided us with much excitement. We all had to hunt for some of the snakes that had gotten away and were hiding under our cabins.

One evening I joined M. H. Muma in collecting tailless whip scorpions. It was a new experience for me, although I was afraid of stepping on a snake in the dark. With some others, I also went to inspect the lights in the area. A lot of interesting insects and their predators accumulated around the lights. So I filled my vials and jars with new creatures for our Virginia Tech zoological collections.

It was the first time I ran into representatives of a family of scale insects that I had never seen before. They looked like mealybugs when I removed them from Prickly Pear cactus. But

Figure 68. Cochineal scale insects, the source of red dye, on prickly pear cactus in Arizona.

as soon as I dropped them into my alcohol vials, the alcohol turned a brilliant red color. I realized these were the Cochineal scales (Fig. 68) that I had always wanted to collect. The dye produced by these insects has been used for centuries to dye clothing. Actually, Montezuma, the Emperor of the Aztec Indians, required that his enslaved tribes produce cochineal scales and pay their taxes in part with them. When the Spaniards had to leave the New World, they transferred the cultivation of cochineal scales to the Canary Islands, probably to obtain a monopoly of this product for the European market, where it is still in production today.

Another scale insect family new to me, the Lac Insects, was well represented on Creosote bushes in the area. It produces a true lac. Although our native species does not produce sufficient lac for commercial cultivation, its relative, the true lac insect, *Laccifer lacca*, is commercially cultivated in India, Sri Lanka, and Burma. The resin produced by these insects has been used since ancient times as lac or shellac for varnishes, and as sealing wax and insulating material in electrical work. The resin from the native species has medicinal value in Mexico.

After my exciting discoveries in the hot sun, I settled in the cool laboratory where I identified and labeled the already-collected scale insect samples of the Research Station and enlarged the collection with my new samples from

Figure 69. Cerococcus quercus, *the first source of chewing gum in the southwestern United States. Actually it is a wax- and sugar-coated scale insect, found on oak trees in southern California.*

the area. After the lab work, it was a relief to swim in the station's cold, creek-fed swimming pool. Eva found friends close to her own age with whom she took over the work of periodically re-filling the humming bird feeders. We all went out in the evenings to watch the deer attracted to the feeding station set up at the edge of the compound.

Because the rattlesnakes kill too many cattle, twice yearly the local ranchers organize rattlesnake hunting parties to thin the population size. A number of local people told us that they eat rattlesnake meat, considered by many as delicious, called the "chicken of the desert." It was reassuring to know that our station crew wanted only live rattlesnakes for study.

After a long and hot day of driving (105°F at noon), we reached Yuma and rushed into the swimming pool of the local motel. In the evening after it cooled off, I had a successful collecting session under the motel's neon lights. The next day we started out before 7 a.m. Soon we crossed the Colorado River, which, after most of the water had been taken out upriver for towns and irrigation, had become a pitifully small creek.

My car was closely inspected for insects and possible plant or soil shipments before crossing into California. We soon realized what "smog" means in the Los Angeles, California, area. This was the first time we had run into smog, and it was difficult to see the closeby mountains, even at noon. We crossed an interesting dry, semi-tropical environment, seen by us for the first time; with blooming Olean-

ders dividing the highway, and patches of date palms forming an oasis on the horizon over the desert. The many Spanish style homes with red tile roofs were also a new sight for us.

After settling in a motel, I was ready to start my second professional engagement. This time I visited the famous Biological Control Research Station at Riverside, California. The scale insects on the scrub oaks in this area provided the first chewing gum source for Native Americans, so I had to collect samples (Fig. 69).

I met here a number of famous scientists, including Paul DeBach, and my Hungarian compatriot, Carl S. Papp. The latter was just engaged in finalizing illustrations for a High School biology textbook. It was a well-coordinated family affair. All of his children had made their own artistic contribution toward the completion of the drawings. He proudly showed me his extensive beetle collection from that area.

By noon on June 18, we reached Anaheim, a suburb of Los Angeles. Because Eva's 8th birthday was coming up, we went during the weekend to her dream place: Disneyland. In eight hours (2 to 10 p.m.) we had seen enough excitement to last for a lifetime. The next day we visited the Knotts Berry Farm, another unique day filled with adventures for Eva. By evening we were ready to roll to the northern end of Los Angeles to visit with friends, the Thiery family. We had not seen each other for six years.

We reached the Pacific coast at Ventura and went to Santa Barbara to visit one of the

Figure 70. Dick Wilkey, entomologist, a great humanitarian, and our friend.

oldest American Missions. We stopped at Buelltin in the late afternoon and tried out the famous Anderson pea soup. We liked it so much that we purchased a box of 12 cans for future use. Our next stop was at Solvang to visit this Danish village with its windmills. As it was late on a Saturday afternoon, most of the stores were closed and we saved money by not indulging in shopping in the many gift shops there. After a long walk, we drove to Los Alamos for the night. The next morning we went to Santa Maria for a short visit, then drove toward the Guadalupe area, enjoying the sight of many fields covered with commercially grown flowers.

The weather along the coast was cold and required the wearing of long slacks. But, I had made up my mind that I couldn't leave the West Coast without having a dip in the Pacific Ocean. So, at Pismo Beach we got into our swimsuits and, with Eva, I went in as far as up to my knees. It was so cold that we soon ran out of the water and back to the car, much to Tili's delight. Next, at San Simeon we tried to purchase tickets for a late afternoon visit to the Hearst Castle. All tickets were sold out for the day, so we had to return early the next morning. After one and a half hours waiting in queue, we got in. It is a unique castle, so it was worth participating in the 2-hour-long tour.

Wherever we went in California, except the high mountains and the irrigated areas, we found brown, dry grass cover. It was a disappointing sight after ever-green Virginia. Even after driving the 17-mile-long Scenic Drive at Carmel and Monterey, I decided I would not try to get a job in the Promised Land. We stopped for a free wine tasting at San Jose before arriving in Daily City, a suburb of San Francisco. Here, I packed and mailed home the recently collected insect samples. To our delight, we found San Francisco to be closer to our European hearts than most other U.S. cities that we had seen before. The hilly streets with many flowers, the streetcars with their bells ringing, the good wines, sourdough bread, and the snack counters at the Fisherman's Wharf reminded us of Europe.

Leaving the family in San Franciso, I went to Davis to work on the famous scale insect collections housed at the University of California. I selected and borrowed many legless mealybug specimens that needed slide-mounting before I could study them. Douglass R. Miller's family invited me one evening for dinner. He was completing his Ph.D. work on scale insects. Next, we went to Sacramento where Dick Wilkey (Fig. 70) ran the scale insect identification laboratory for the California Department of Agriculture. Dick and his family treated us like their own family and continued to do so later, each time we visited them. While at work, I looked over Dick's shoulder often enough to learn his techniques, but I could never master his unique microscope slide-making skills.

We arrived in Las Vegas late at night, but we could see the lighted sky over the city from a 20-mile distance. For the first time in our lives, Tili and I took our chances on the slot machines while our motel helper was baby sitting sleeping Eva. Two hours was long enough to lose the change set aside for this purpose. The next day we drove to the Grand Canyon. Enroute, we visited Zion National Park. We were enchanted by the multitude of colors on the rock formations, and the sight of the Grand Canyon at sunset. It was the Fourth of July, and the motel personnel provided an evening program to entertain the guests. The next day we went to Bryce Canyon, which we found to be the most beautiful among the Western canyons we had seen. With a day-long ride, we arrived in Gunnison, Colorado. This small mountain town provided relief after the long drive through the hot weather.

Next day we crossed the Rocky Mountains at the 13,000-foot-high Monarch Pass, where we enjoyed a snowball fight. It was good to cool off before crossing hot and flat Kansas, where I stopped to visit the Kansas State University Entomology Department in Manhattan. After inventorying their scale insect collections, I borrowed specimens for our research. Our next official stop was in Columbus, Ohio, visiting my Alma Mater. We were disappointed to find out that the university's expansion had swallowed up the street where we lived while at Ohio State University. We arrived home on July 11.

My collecting on this trip resulted in about 6,000 insect specimens which I mailed back to my office in five packages. My description here of our first trip benefited from Tili's detailed record keeping.

Second Trip — 1969

In 1969 I started a new research project that required samples to be collected from the field and specimens borrowed from institutions en route. To avoid discomfort from the heat, such as we had suffered on our 1964 trip, I purchased another used Rambler from a neighbor. This one had an air conditioner, and seemed to be in mint condition, with a stronger engine than my other car to power the air conditioner. But as soon as we reached the warm southern states and turned on the air conditioner, the engine started overheating. So I used the air conditioning system only sparingly, but still had to stop en route for a few minor repairs.

On this trip I tried to reach some new areas to collect my samples. We spent one week at the Research Station at Portal, Arizona. Here I discovered for the first time the presence of

Figure 71a. Collecting scale insect samples from oak trees using a long pole pruner, in Portal, Arizona.

an unusual gall-forming scale insect on scrub oak leaves, and collected large samples with a long pole pruner (Fig. 71a). When I opened the galls, I found inside the galls a wonderful association of half a dozen organisms. Some were predators, others parasites living off the scale insects, but others had just "sub-leased" the living space provided by the galls, a good shelter. Some ants were visiting the galls through a small opening and were feeding on the honeydew produced in quantity by the scale insect females. It was a beautiful symbiotic relationship. The ants fed on the honeydew and the scale insects depended on the removal of the smothering honeydew by the ants. Sometimes I found the gall opening closed so the ants could not enter. In these cases, the scale insects were drowned in their own accumulated honeydew (excrement). I saved large samples of the organisms found in the hundreds of galls opened.

It turned out that two species found in those galls were new to science. One thrips species (a tiny fringe-winged insect) has since been named after me, while the other new species of tiny aphid flies reared from the galls is still under study by a scientist in Canada.

At Portal, being so close, we crossed the Mexican border and did some sightseeing and shopping in Mexico. By now I was prepared to be stopped and questioned by the U.S. Border Inspectors at Douglas, Arizona, because of my Hungarian accent. The Border Inspector asked me: "Are you a natural-born U.S. citizen?" I jokingly replied, "No, I was delivered by Caesarean! -but naturalized in 1962."

It was a miracle that my used car purchased in "mint condition" for this trip lasted until Sacramento. There I was told that the block was cracked and that it was not economically feasible to fix it. So, I needed a new car to be able to return to Virginia, but I faced the problem that I had no credit card yet, cash, or bank deposit to pay for a new car. When the Wilkeys learned about my problems, they offered to lend me the needed cash. They said that I could repay them the loan after we arrived home. I took Dick's generous offer and negotiated the price for a Chevy Nova. Then I learned that I couldn't use my old Virginia license plate and that I could not get a California license plate unless I paid the required 5% tax on new cars. In addition, I would have to pay such a tax again in Virginia. I was not prepared to pay twice for a new license plate.

I shared my dismay with the car salesman. He said that he was willing to use his dealer's license plate to drive my car to the first border town in Nevada, where he could turn it over to me after finalizing the sales contract in Nevada. I agreed, and followed my new car by driving his automobile. In the first town in Nevada, we found the local justice of the peace sitting on the doorstep of his house waiting to notarize for a small fee such sales contracts as ours.

So, I ended up with a new car without a license plate. I was told by the dealer that if I were stopped in any state by the police for not having a car license plate, I could purchase for $3 or $5 a transient license plate in each state that I was stopped in. I made up my mind to get by without a license plate until we reached Virginia, but we still had to cross nine states. We made a challenge for ourselves to avoid being caught en route home without license plates. To achieve this goal, I placed a copy of my sales contract inside the back window, with the text: "Newly Purchased Car". I also parked my new car by backing close against walls, so the police driving by would think I was from a state where only one license plate is required, and that presumably was attached to the back bumper that they could not see

My problems were compounded each time I had to purchase gasoline on my credit card or register in a motel. There was a question each time about my car's license number. So I put down my town tag number that was on a small metal plate those days. I also displayed it behind my windshield. Nobody noticed the difference when I marked on the slips: Blacksburg Town tag No. 427." So we had much fun avoiding being caught without a car license plate while crossing from coast to coast.

Our two-week-long return trip included Reno, Nevada; Salt Lake City, Utah; Jackson Hole, Wyoming; The Grand Tetons and Yellowstone National Parks; the Black Hills of South Dakota; Sioux City, Iowa; Urbana, Illinois; Indianapolis, Indiana; Columbus, Ohio; and Huntington, West Virginia.

Back home, I finally got my Virginia license plates, after paying only 2% of the purchase price. After arranging a loan from our local bank, I returned the borrowed money to Dick Wilkey. I will never forget his family's gracious help when I was in a really desperate situation. I honored Dick (Fig. 70), by naming a new species of mealybug *Chorizococcus wilkeyi*.

Third Trip — 1976

Eva was enrolled at the University of Virginia and did not join us on this trip. Tili and I chose a somewhat different route than we had travelled before. This time we had a new Plymouth, a somewhat stronger car. Our route to the Southwest included Knoxville, Tennessee; Atlanta, Georgia; Auburn and Mobile, Alabama; New Orleans and Baton Rouge, Louisiana. Our next stop was at the University of Texas at College Station, where I inventoried the scale insect collection and borrowed some specimens for study. I suffered much here from the heat and humidity, when I tried to collect samples from local vegetation.

We continued our trip through San Antonio, Texas, to the Big Bend National Park. I obtained the necessary collecting permits and made cabin reservations ahead. This park was and is a favorite research area for many scientists. It has many unique habitats for the preservation of wildlife big and small. I watched with much excitement the fight between a large tarantula spider and a spider wasp. The wasp won and, after paralyzing her victim, she carried the large spider away. It looked like an overloaded airplane, hardly making the end of the runway, grazing the tops of the "trees", in the wasp's case, the tops of the tall grass. Such spiders are taken to the wasp's underground nest; after the wasp lays an egg on it, she closes it in a mud cell. The hatching wasp larvae will feed entirely on the spider, pupate in the mud cell, and emerge as fully developed adult wasps.

I had pre-arranged to meet with my New Mexican entomologist colleague, W.A. Iselin, on the lawn of the City Park in downtown Carlsbad. He brought me plastic bags filled with live gall-like scale insects on twigs from oak trees. It must have been an interesting sight for people to see two entomologists trading information and the catch on the park lawn. His samples included a species new to science that we named in his honor.

We hunted for a locality, Beulah in New Mexico, that had provided to Dr. G. F. Ferris a new species, but because no suitable specimens had been left for us to re-describe and illustrate, we needed to re-collect fresh samples, which we did.

After that stop, our route included Santa Fé, Los Alamos, and Albuquerque, in New Mexico before we reached the Research Sta-

tion at Portal, Arizona. I arrived early enough this time to be able to re-collect young specimens of gall-like scale insects, suitable for slide-mounting. Some specimens from each sample were preserved in alcohol, while the rest, on twigs in water, were mailed to my laboratory each Monday, in care of my graduate students working on the project, with instructions on how to keep the colonies alive for further biological observations.

Our next route passed through Tucson and Phoenix, Arizona, and Death Valley, to reach Owens Valley and the Mono Lake Area. Here Dick Wilkey joined me in collecting insect samples for both of us. Again it was so hot in the field that, by noon, even the ants disappeared. Earlier, I had trailed the ants on the plants to lead me to the mealybug colonies that are tended by the ants as their honeydew source. From here we travelled to the state insect collections at Davis and Sacramento, California, to search for needed specimens in air-conditioned laboratories.

Our return trip included the Botanical Garden in Seattle, Washington. This was the northernmost point where I could still find gall-like scale insects on oaks.

Fourth Trip — 1988

Before this trip, we purchased a new Plymouth Reliant with an air conditioner to take four of us to Vancouver, Canada, where I was scheduled to meet colleagues and give two talks. It was the International Congress of Entomology that is held every four years in the summer. I wanted to collect some insect samples en route, and my cousins from Budapest, István Csere and his wife Lili, happily joined us. Tili had made reservations for accomodations in the spring, to assure the best rates in Vancouver and other cities, and also had reserved cabins for us in several national parks across the United States.

Four suitcases were transported in a waterproof canvas bag on top of the car, thus we were able to carry the needed personal belongings for a 5-week trip, including some insect-collecting gear. Fortunately, the new car performed well on this 8,000 mile (12,800 kilometer) trip. We departed Blacksburg on June 17th, and returned on July 24th. Our first stop was at Mammoth Cave National Park in Kentucky, which we visited the next day. The two-bedroom cabin worked out well. A few scale insect samples were added to our collection.

After two long days, we went up to Estes Park in the Rocky Mountain National Park. Here, we enjoyed some memorable views of crystal clear lakes and snow-capped mountains. Other fantastically beautiful views greeted us at Grand Tetons, from our cabin facing the lake and the mountains. I noticed the effect of air pollution on the conifers along the often-travelled roads of the park, and took some soil and branch samples for further analysis at Virginia Tech. I believe that such roads should be restricted to electric-powered vehicles or at least natural gas-powered buses equipped with efficient catalytic converters and carrying full loads of tourists. I observed similar signs of the effect of air pollution in the Yellowstone, where Tili's early cabin reservations really paid off.

More beautiful scenery en route was at Coeur d'Alene, Idaho. In Seattle, we visited with two old-time friends. The next day at Port Angeles, Washington, we were lucky to avoid waiting long hours in queue and to gain passage for our car as the last one boarding the ferry boat to Victoria, Canada. There we stayed for three nights. One rainy day we visited the famous and beautiful Burchard Gardens north of Victoria. This garden is probably the most attractive one I have ever seen.

When Tili made the housing reservations for us in Victoria over the phone, she did not realize that the Cherry Hill Hotel she had picked out for us must have served as a typical western bordello around the turn of the century.

All the walls were covered with red velvety cloth and the bar had all the furnishings of a 19th-century western saloon. We had much fun walking through the narrow, dimly lit passages to find our room. Another ferry boat ride took us close to Vancouver. The week spent in Vancouver gave us some time for relaxation and for local excursions. I also met many colleagues from around the world. My two slide presentations were delivered and printed in the Proceedings of the Congress.

The route home was new for us and included parts of southwest Canada. Here we spent the first night in Osoyos, where we discovered a large Hungarian-speaking community. These people were raising grapes and other fruits, selling their own wine, and supporting a museum on their history in Canada.

The next day we reached Glacier National Park, which turned out to be another most beautiful attraction of the Rocky Mountains. There we got close enough to some mountain goats to take pictures. It was windy and very cold on the mountain-top road.

On our return trip we visited major cities: Chicago, Cleveland, New York, and Washington, D.C. and ended up with our daughter's family in Falls Church, Virginia. Our visitors, the Cseres, returned to Budapest from Washington, D.C. While they were in the United States and Canada, we served as their hosts. István Csere is my cousin through a great-grandmother of mine. We attended the same school in Bucharest and have kept up with each other since we both moved to Budapest after World War II. István volunteered, for some years, to look after my aging mother on my behalf in Budapest. Our friendship was further strengthened through the five weeks we spent together on this trip.

17 — Adventures as a "Farmer-Landlord" (Blacksburg 1968–1988)

Because of my experience as a teenager with my grandfather who farmed in Transylvania on about 10 acres, I always dreamed of having my own farm. This desire was reinforced by my eight years' training in horticulture and by my having often worked on land owned by someone else. While living for a few years at the edge of the Appalachians, my horticulture training and the poverty there developed my desire to try to improve the living of the impoverished mountain people. I thought I could prove to these folks that they could make a living on 5–10 acres of mountain land, if they grew labor-intensive plants for the East-coast markets. Such plants would be strawberries, raspberries, blackberries, small fruits, nuts, grapes, and unique nursery stock or Christmas trees.

The opportunity came when I learned that "more or less" 8 acres of land with two small farmhouses was on sale on Brush Mountain, near Blacksburg. With the help of a 4-year bank loan and some savings for a down payment, we purchased this land in 1968. The land came with some guinea fowl that were roosting on trees and were substituting for watchdogs for the owner, because they made a noisy racket whenever strangers approached the farm. Although these birds were offered for sale for 50¢ each by the previous owner, no one could catch them until some neighbors used their shotguns. I felt sorry for them, because I considered the guinea fowls better than watchdogs. They are cheaper to feed and they are good for biological control of pest insects on the farm, since a good part of their daily diet is made up of insects.

I was delighted with the land, which had a great view to the southeast toward Blacksburg and the Tom's Creek basin, and to the northwest was surrounded by forest. One small intermittent stream was running through the forested area with about one-third of the land open, and flat enough for my intended hobby farming. There were some old apple trees, sour cherries, 2 pears, 2 old grape vines, and even a group of chinquapin. For years I was able to pick some sour cherries, until the black knot fungus killed them. I considered the two old houses and wooden shacks a nuisance, but they came with the "dream" land.

To realize my original dreams, I selected 9 grape varieties from the Virginia Tech farm, and asked for spring cuttings that I rooted and planted in four 100-foot-long trellises on a south-facing slope for good drainage and full sun. My trellis-supporting posts were cut from black locust trees felled from the land. After 3 years I started harvesting and evaluating my grape varieties. I experimented to find out which were the most promising ones for our local conditions. At the height of my vineyard's life, one fall I had 600–700 pounds of grapes to give away, eat, sell through a local grocery store, and to make wine and some vinegar (sometimes unintentionally).

My experience with grapes in Virginia made me realize why President Jefferson's original vineyards did not last long. Because of our relatively humid climate and long rainy seasons, the grapes are attacked by a variety of fungi that the pioneering growers could not control; the needed fungicides were not yet available.

I also planted a row of dwarf Golden Delicious apple trees that provided enough for eating and cider-making in the fall. Some blight-resistant Chinese chestnuts were planted in groups of three for pollinating. These gave us the source for making the European's favorite chestnut purée and filling for chestnut cakes. But soon I learned that I had to freeze or boil the chestnuts as soon as they were harvested to avoid the full development of chestnut weevil maggots in them. Before I learned this, we often ended up with fully developed fat weevil maggots crawling out from the bottom of storage bags.

To provide my honey bees with an extra pollen source, I planted Russian olive trees on the hill. My two hives of honey bees gave me, as an entomologist, a special joy, and also supplied my family with extra sweets. At that time, because of the physical work on the farm, I did not have to worry about becoming overweight from sweets. I also experimented with thornless blackberries, but I found the available varieties too sour for enjoyment.

For some time, I was puzzled with the question of why Virginians in the mountains are not raising hazelnuts (filberts). This plant is very common in the home gardens of Central Europe and along the edges of forests. This nut is easy to grow and could be an ideal food supplement not only for people, but also for wildlife, especially now that the American Chestnuts are gone. So, I obtained permits from two government agencies to import hazelnuts from Hungary for propagation in Virginia. I planted the nuts in my vegetable garden where I could keep an eye on them. I waited anxiously for their germination.

One day, I was shocked to see that gray squirrels, which had never tasted hazelnuts before, with their radar-like sensing ability had gone over my planted rows and dug out each nut exactly where they'd been planted, just 3–4 inches below the surface. They happily munched on the just-discovered new food source. I was enraged, so I chased them away with much clapping and throwing of stones from my terrace overlooking the vegetable garden. I was lucky; they ate only about a third of my nuts. So I still had about 100 nuts left in the ground, that I had to cover with wire mesh to stop the diggers.

Almost all the left-over nuts germinated, so I ended up with about 80 plants. Of these, 50 were transplanted into 2 plots at the edge of my farm forest. I did my best to nurse these to nut-bearing stage, when I started evaluating each shrub for quality and quantity of nuts. I intended to select and propagate only the progeny (clones) of my best shrubs. After 5 years I was pleased with the results. And no insect pests had attacked these newly introduced plants.

Unfortunately, soon I discovered that a fungal disease, not known in Europe, the Eastern Filbert Blight, started killing the branches and in a few years all my shrubs died, except two that are still struggling and appear partially resistant. Removing and burning the diseased branches in the spring and spraying for three years with a fungicide did not stop the disease. I learned too late the reason why there are no filberts in cultivation in the Eastern United States: a few struggling native filberts in the forest are the source of an infestation. Because of this fungus, commercial filbert orchards were moved to the Northwestern U.S., where a few years ago even these became infested. Researchers often say: "Even negative results of an experiment are considered educational", but I had to give up my dream of following in the footsteps of Johnny Appleseed with my European hazelnut introduction project to the Appalachians.

My more successful and even money-making hobby was Christmas tree farming. In the 1960s, most of our Christmas trees in Virginia were imported from the West coast or other far-away places. I realized that we had the land, so why grow only weeds when we could experiment with pines and spruce for the local Christmas tree market? Also, we could use the extra income for my daughter's university education, and I might be able to make it into a family project, involving even my teenage daughter. Eva liked the idea, but never got involved, as is common with a teenager. I or-

Figure 71b. Our Christmas tree plantation, with Australian visitor Helen Brookes, December 1971.

dered 1200 2-year-old seedlings to fill an acre at 6 x 6 feet (1.8 x 1.8 m) spacing. Tili and I planted 650 with some help from a neighbor during a long day at the end of March. We had to rely on rain for irrigation because we could not water the plants. Due to lack of watering, the 24-experimental spruce seedlings were decimated by the end of the summer. However, except for 3–5% of the Scotch pines, the rest survived. Because the young trees were quickly covered by tall weeds, I had to mow the grass and weeds 3–4 times each summer, and shape the trees with large shears after they were three years old. We had to prune them to a 70° triangular shape, with 12 inch (30 cm) long leaders (Fig. 71b). I thought that I could save on mowing if I kept some beef cattle on the land, and I started seriously calculating the pros and cons of starting such a new enterprise. Soon I learned that you cannot combine cattle with Christmas tree raising. My neighbor's cattle were able to reach over the bordering fence and graze on my pine trees, shearing them severely along that side. Apparently, cattle like to browse on the new pine shoots. I had to sell these trees for corner locations at a discount price.

Many of my trees were raised to about 10 feet in height and I cut these down just above the lower branches. By leaving a 18–24 inch trunk with 5–6 branches, and tying the strongest branch to a stake for the first summer, I was able to "resurrect" a new tree. Because of the strong root system, the tree was marketable in 3–4 years. Thus, I had a number of trees that produced 2–3 Christmas trees from the same trunk. I was also able to calm the feelings of some tree lovers, who did not want to kill a tree each Christmas. As a conservationist, I also tried, but only during one season, to sell live trees with burlapped root balls to be planted in the yard after Christmas. I did not realize that Scotch pines have very deep tap roots and are impossible to dig out and burlap with hand tools after they are over 4–5 feet tall.

During the years of raising Christmas trees, our summer vacations included their shearing at the end of June or the first part of July, and marketing during December. In conclusion, it was much fun to raise and shape over 1000 trees. It also required the purchase of a 15 HP riding mower and a pickup truck to transport the mower and the trees for marketing. Most of my trees were sold through a local grocery store on a 20% commission.

I found a wet spot at the lower end of the vegetable garden that was not suitable for other plants, except bamboo. So, I transferred some plants from a friend's yard. I like to eat the young bamboo shoots in the spring, and I was able to provide friends and their children with bamboo fishing poles. I learned after a few years that the bamboo could take over the entire land if not controlled.

For a while I kept a vegetable garden on the farm, until the new student-tenants wanted to grow their own food. Another good reason for students to move to my farm was that they were kicked out from apartments when their little pups got too big for the four walls and neighbors.

I always wanted to build a small log cabin for a quiet retreat in the middle of my forested land. Luckily, I found enough native pine trees on a slope to give me the needed logs. But, unfortunately I waited too long with this project. In a few years my pine trees started declining, instead of growing to the size needed. Some dry years, and acid rain, could have been the cause.

The other project that did not materialize was the building of a dam to stop the flow of the stream and to create a pond for water storage and for wildlife. Some of my graduate students volunteered to help. I provided the food and beer. We felled some trees for the dam, and used stones and soil with underlying strong plastic sheets. After the spring rains, the water accumulated behind the dam to about four feet, so I was pleased with the results until a storm that fall washed away most of the dam. I was told that beavers could have built a better dam than ours!

I also developed a "nature trail" in the forest that included patches of native flowering plants, such as flaming azaleas, lady's-slipper orchids, some dwarf Iris, and Sedum, and along the creek a few native rhododendrons. For the wildlife, I planted wild plums and wild grapes. The creek bed with its salamander population served for my daughter's science project.

With much delight, I discovered a patch of chanterelle mushrooms near the creek. I consider these to be the most delicious mushrooms. Apparently, one of my predecessors on the farm used the cool stream for a small moonshine operation, because remnants of the still were detectable and the copper coils were left in a burlap bag in the attic of my smaller farm house. I found this while spraying wasps nesting in the attic. This old house was taken apart somewhere and re-built on this land about 35 years before I purchased the property. While doing some improvements, I found the construction date (1934) on the shredded newspapers used for insulation inside the house walls.

Both houses had a deep, home-made, milk-bottle-shaped cistern in the ground for storing rainwater from the roof. An outdoor hand-operated water pump brought up the water for the tenants. The periodic cleaning and disinfecting of the cisterns was my least favorite work project. But, I had to do it myself, to avoid risking accidents for my helpers. So, I lowered my 18-foot aluminum ladder, climbed down with the needed tools, and cleaned out the bottom residue while one of the tenants pulled up a rope tied to a bucket filled with the accumulated leaves and other organic materials. Sometimes the residue included frogs and even snakes. We used Chlorox to disinfect the cistern. The tenants often forgot to cover the pump in the winter, so the pump froze and created headaches. So, I asked the student tenants about the possibility of upgrading the water system by bringing in city water on an 1800-foot pipe and raising the rent $5 more a month. They talked me out of it, saying that they never drink water. The many beer cans around the house testified to the truth of their statement! So, only after the student tenants were replaced with small families did I invest in connecting up to the city water.

My farm apparently became an attraction to students in the late 1960s and 1970s when many wanted to "make a living off the land." Another bonus was that they could keep pets not allowed in the apartments. They also liked the privacy (I lived three miles away) and the low rent. They also learned that if they were unable to pay rent (although they never lacked money for beer), they could get by, doing some improvements on their rental property in exchange for rent.

So, I had the use of a number of semi-skilled painters and carpenters. One student built a porch that later became a greenhouse for raising plants and tropical fish by another one. Some helped mow the weeds from my Christmas tree plantation or sprayed my grapes. Others painted their rooms, often in ridiculous colors, and together we painted the metal roofs. It was also a joint community project to dig a new hole and position the heavy but moveable outhouses over it. We told jokes and had much fun together on such projects, especially when four entomology graduate students took over the property and acted like a fraternity.

One student was a VMI graduate who invited girls to the farm for "target practice". He owned a few small firearms whose use was offered free to the interested girls for teaching in how to handle them. Through the farming years, I met a number of my tenants' girlfriends who used to pitch in with the boys' household chores by cooking and washing for them and by keeping the house in better order than the boys would have done alone. Some of the girls, after a time, gave up on the free-loading boys. But soon these boys appeared "lost" without their helpers and begged them to return. Some of the spoiled boys, rather than learning to do housekeeping, married their girlfriends. I was invited to a number of weddings that resulted from such associations.

Gradually my farm became a dog and cat kennel. Friends, especially girlfriends, of my tenants often asked the boys if they would keep their pets on my farm just for a weekend while they were visiting home. Some never returned for their pets. Other tenants felt sorry for their dogs being alone all day, so for company they brought another dog. I learned that large dogs, kept all day indoors alone, can ruin screen doors and the furniture, and also mess up walls and floors during their lonely frustration. So I had to introduce a new rule in the leases, that the status quo of one dog and one cat which they brought with them originally was acceptable, but no "newcomer" pets were allowed.

One non-student tenant asked me to allow him to build a plexi-glass-roofed shack. I gave my blessings, until I found a few potted marijuana plants in the new shack. After another tenant moved out, I found marijuana leaves frozen in ice cubes in his defrosted refrigerator. Another tenant surprised me when I discovered a large healthy marijuana plant that he

was nursing in an opening of my Christmas tree plantation. I think my tenants had their fun in constantly challenging and probing me to find out how far they could go ...

My lease for the tenants included an obligation for them to help twice yearly with the maintenance work on the farm access road. With picks and shovels, the "road gang", as we called ourselves, filled in the ditches after the spring and fall with crushed stone. We had much fun doing community chores together; this brought us closer, easing the traditional tenant-landlord association. In the fall, we ended our work with tasting the new wine made from the grapes raised on the farm and my home-made beer.

I had a good relationship with my "native" neighbors, who often smiled at my "funny" accent and kept a sharp eye on the " professor's hobby farming". Because one of them, John, never had a car, I often found him on the road walking home from town, where I picked him up. Once, I even went for John with his wife to the county jail, when he was released, after serving time for pulling his shotgun on a trespassing neighbor. John had two small children, and they lived rent-free in a shack-like home just above my farm. He had the habit of taking off from his job in town at the start of hunting season in October, and not returning until the spring. John also had a drinking problem. His landlord and neighbors felt sorry for his family, and often helped out with food parcels during the winter. When he saw my wife and me planting pine seedlings, he volunteered and helped.

The chores on the farm and farmhouses increased when I went to an auction next door and purchased the adjoining 17 acres with 2 gutted-out two-room block houses. I wanted to increase my forested area, and made a deal with the owner to accept my 10% down-payment and a 5-year mortgage with him. I was afraid that if I didn't, someone would get the land to put up a trailer court and ruin the quiet neighborhood. So, for self-protection, after consulting with Tili over the telephone, I made the deal.

Soon after the new land purchase, the Virginia Highway Department condemned and purchased five houses to widen Price's Fork Road just across from our street. The condemned houses had the same window and door types that my four old farmhouses had. So I purchased these and replaced the old doors, windows, storm doors, and storm windows.

Everything went well until the owners of an adjoining large tract of forested land decided to develop their investment. Our farm access road, to which I had a right-of-way in my deed, crossed a small corner of the Commons Area of the land under development. The developers gradually closed all the old roads crossing their property that had been used as access roads by natives of the area for over 80 years. Our own farm access road was also closed three times, even after the owners were given a copy of my right-of-way. They probably thought that they could get a higher price for the unsold lots along our access road. When I complained after the first closing, they made me an offer to exchange my 6.3 acres with 2 small houses for a choice lot of 5 acres on their property. After I declined the offer, the road was closed twice. So, I had no choice but to go to court. After two years, and many depositions made by local inhabitants, the Court confirmed my right-of-way through the Commons Area, but I still ended up paying my attorney's fees. Through this unfortunate experience, I discovered here what we called in Transylvania the "wolf pack syndrome". I knew well two of the owners of the land under development. Individually, they were all nice to me, but after banding in a pack with developers, they became greedy. Wolves, as individuals, do not attack people in the Transylvanian Mountains, but they do in the winter when hungry and in large packs. The difference is that these wolves are hungry and need food during the harsh winter; the people I dealt with were financially well-to-do individuals.

So, I was pleased when my daughter, Eva, decided to study law. Now, I have better protection against "greedy wolves". Soon after I brought the town water lines to my small houses, I sold the properties. To console myself for the lost hobby (farming), I now have a greenhouse attached to our house that gives me a chance to grow plants all year long.

18 — Down South With the Birds
(Costa Rica — Winter 1969–70)

I had heard legends about the fauna and flora of tropical America, but I had never had a chance to see it myself. After I learned that about 80% of the scale insects in the tropics have never been described, I made up my mind to collect and study these as an introduction to future work in the tropics. One ideal target country that was not too far and not too expensive was Costa Rica. This small country, which boasts both the oldest democratic government in the region and an exemplary nature conservation policy, served best to make my dreams come true. Moreover, it had the headquarters and field research stations of the Organization for Tropical Studies (OTS). So I decided to go south with the birds for overwintering; but the real reason for choosing the winter months for my studies was the dry season during the winter months, essential for my field work.

I applied to the OTS for a small ($2,400) grant and received it. In preparation for the trip, I shifted my course teaching loads from the winter quarter to fall and spring. Also, we knew a family, the Walkers, with three daughters, friends of my daughter, who agreed to provide room and board for Eva while we were in Costa Rica. We thought that for Eva, as a single child, it would be a good experience to live with a larger family for three months. To manage our life in a Spanish-speaking country, we took some language lessons in our school language laboratory. I found a lot of similarity with the Romanian language that I had studied earlier in my life.

At first, I planned to drive my car down to Costa Rica, but after months of frustration in seeking transit visas from several embassies, thank God I gave up that plan. Later while in Costa Rica, I realized that the famous Inter-American Highway was so poorly maintained that my small car could have been lost in the giant ditches in the road.

After purchasing hats against the tropical sun and rain, and high boots for snake protection, we packed the needed insect-collecting gear (Fig. 72) and took off by plane to Miami. Because of delayed connecting flights to Costa Rica, we had to spend the night at the airport, but utilized the time by doing some last-minute shopping.

Figure 72. Author with insect net, side bag, and notepad for research, boots under blue jeans for protection against snakes, and tropical helmet to avoid sunstroke (1970).

137

At the airport in San José, Costa Rica, on December 8, we were picked up by the OTS jeep driver, Señor Alvaro Cordoba, who was later assigned to take us to some of the field stations. We rented a small apartment close to the University and OTS office, and moved in to finally make up for lost sleep. After recovering from the trip, Tili was ready to make us some coffee and turned on the electric stove that apparently had not been used for some time. As soon as the stove got hot enough, hundreds of cockroaches ran out, seeking cooler shelters in our apartment. Tili jumped up on the bed to avoid the fleeing roaches running up her legs. I performed some Hungarian dances to stomp on as many roaches as I could. So, we got our first introduction to the "tropical biota."

Because of my earlier work with cockroaches I kept calm, but Tili was ready to move out of the just-rented apartment. We talked to the apartment owner, who promised to get an exterminator. I told the other tenants about the owner's promise, warning them that spraying in our apartment alone would just chase most of the roaches into the other un-sprayed apartments. All signed up for pest control. In a few days, most of the apartments were sprayed; but that, apparently, was not effective enough. I had to set up my home-made roach traps by using large empty jars with banana peel in the bottom for bait and vaseline smeared in a band inside the mouth so that the trapped roaches got slippery feet and were unable to get out. Each morning I shook out into the toilet the dozens of cockroaches trapped in each jar. So, I was thinning the population, but never succeeded in exterminating them all.

I told Tili that we had better learn to live with them, because humans had intruded into their natural habitats in the tropics, and they also served as sanitary workers here. During the night, they remove the organic materials from the garbage bins in the alleys, thus saving us from the flies and the smell of decomposing garbage. I don't think that my explanation entirely calmed Tili's apprehensions. She probably would have deserted me then and there had she known that we were later going to face living with cockroaches 20 times bigger at two field research stations.

My studies in Costa Rica were scheduled to cover the scale insect fauna of a variety of habitats around five field stations and a banana plantation of the Standard Fruit Co. at Rio Frio. The yearly precipitation varied between the areas from 1,300 to 4,300 mm. My work goal also included the publication of biological information on their parasites and predators, as well as on the host plants of scales in Costa Rica. Another goal was to prepare an analytical comparison on the composition of the scale insect fauna of the dry forests of Western Costa Rica with that of the eastern rain forest areas. Many of the large, 30- to 50-meter high trees in the tropical rain forest provide support for hundreds of orchids, bromeliads, and other plants (Fig. 73). Unfortunately, I had to remove some of these plants and a thick layer of moss from the branches to be able to find the scale insects living under their protective cover. I used a ladder to reach some of the higher parts of the trees, but sometimes I had to climb the trees themselves. Climbing the trees is not a child's game in Costa Rica. Many trees are armed with sharp thorns on the trunk and even the monkeys avoid climbing them. But it was easy to reach my insects when a tree was uprooted after a storm. I especially looked for those.

I realized that I could increase my daily output if I hired a young farm worker. The daily wage on the coffee and banana plantations for my 16-year-old helper was $2.00 per day; so I paid $2.25. He was able to climb trees when we needed host tree twigs for species identification.

Some of my female scale insects were under 5-15 cm of soil at the base of the trees, others were on the top twigs, but most were under the thick moss layer covering the trunk and branches. The moss was collected into plastic bags to be placed in large funnels, each with a small light bulb heating the moss to chase the insects from the moss into the bottom of the "Berlese funnel" to fall into alcohol in a vial or small jar. Samples on the twigs and bark

Figure 73. Epiphytic plants (bromeliads, orchids, mosses) covering trees in Costa Rica and providing shelter for scale insects.

were placed in cellophane or plastic envelopes or jars, to collect the emerging scale insect males, parasites, and predators. We used binoculars to detect scale insect infestations in the high canopy of the tall rain forest trees.

In the evenings I set lighted white sheets up on a hillside to attract and trap night-flying insects. Tili helped me to mount, label, and pack these away before the ants and cockroaches could chew them up. Many large-bodied insects had to be dried before packing, so I used metal garbage cans as drying ovens with hanging light bulbs for heat during the night. We often placed our wet clothes and boots in the same "ovens" to dry them for the next day.

Since the roofs over our field station dormitories were made of sheet metal, the heavy tropical rains made such a noise that we often woke up in the middle of the night. It was too much for Tili to endure through many nights such as those, so she beat a hasty retreat twice from such places before I completed my work. For example, at our next stay in Rio Frio, even in the middle of the "dry season" we had 2-3 rains each day. The furniture was covered with mold, and our bedding felt moist and had a musty smell. The built-in clothes closets had large holes in the bottom of the doors for ven-

tilation and several light bulbs were constantly burning there to dry our always-wet clothes and boots. I often ran out between rains in a rain coat and hat and sometimes under an umbrella to hastily collect insect samples, before the next downpour. Yes, it was miserable housing, and I realized that Tili probably should not have been blamed for fleeing with the first available flight to our dry apartment in San José.

Because of the low clouds, air flights were cancelled for three days in Rio Frio. The flooded rivers took down the only bridge providing the needed passageway to the outside world. So, the ripened bananas could not be shipped out to the ports from the Rio Frio plantation. It became a desperate situation for the management, and I heard the cries of workmen who soon would lose their jobs. I was pleasantly surprised to see the problem solved by Robert H. Davis, Jr., the American engineer/manager. He strung steel cables over the flooded river. Then he sent across the bunches of banana, 30 to 40 kg each, via pulleys on the cables. The bananas ware loaded into trucks at the other side of the river and shipped to the ports.

At our next station in Turrialba, we were housed in the most pleasant red-tiled bungalows at The Inter-American Institute of Agricultural Sciences, which also had modern research laboratories. Here I was able to study mealybug infestation rates on different varieties of coffee, besides checking the scale insects on many fruit trees and crops. Mealybugs build large populations on the coffee varieties with tight bunches of fruit, so the insects were protected inside the bunches from sun and rain, and probably from parasites and predators. It was a beautiful sight when the coffee fruits ripened and changed color from green to red. During the coffee harvest even the schools closed so that the school children could help. I found about 11 species of scale insects on coffee and approximately 13 species on bananas in Costa Rica.

In order to assess the composition of the scale insect population in the forest canopy, I had to climb to the top of the trees. Here, I very much enjoyed the beautiful views over the tree tops; but not for long. One day I spied a long skinny green snake (very poisonous as I learned later) sunning close to me and probably waiting for birds and insects to prey on. I realized immediately that I would have to hurriedly descend because my boots, bought for protection from snakes, would not help here. From then on I neglected scale studies in the canopy.

I have been bitten by many insects, chiggers, and ticks while on collecting trips. In the areas where I found the mealybugs and some soft scale-insect colonies, there were usually ants that fed on honeydew produced by my insects, and they were vicious biters. Some of them left their marks on my skin. Their soldiers have large biting mandibles to protect the thousands of worker ants in the colonies. I have watched army ant workers marching as if on parade on the rain forest floor, flanked by their soldiers. It was another curious sight when I saw the trail of leaf cutter ants, carrying sections of tree leaves, cut to a manageable size for transporting in their mandibles, often giving the impression of large sails over their heads. They use the masticated leaves to grow fungi in underground cavities to feed their

young and themselves. Thus they practiced agriculture much earlier than mankind.

I was surprised to see many felled tree trunks of giant trees between the rows of banana plants. I was told that these trees had been felled to make room for the banana rows. But the tree trunks were often left in place and adjusted to fit between the banana rows. In a few years, moisture, fungi, termites, cockroaches, and other small creatures would hasten the process of decomposing the wood and enriching the soil.

One day, while being taken in a small flat boat over the flooded Rio Puerto Viejo to the La Selva Field Station, I got my surprise for the day. A small, skinny creature just ran across on top of the water in front of our boat. I was told this is the "Jesus Christ lizard" that is able to walk over the top of the water.

To our delight, we were finally taken to the dry lands of the West Coast area. The high humidity and frequent rains in the central lowlands had gotten under our skin. The semiarid cattle grazing areas of Guanacaste Province, with patches of tropical dry forest, were a welcome sight. I even got the courage to take a dip in a crystal clear creek here. Most of the scale insects in this dry area have an armor that protects them from dessication. The trees were also lower (up to 10–15 m) than in the wet forests and easier to climb. I watched for ticks that are often on the cattle.

While walking on a trail I unintentionally chased a 3-foot iguana out from a small ditch. The poor creature was immediately grabbed by a dog following us on the trail. We felt sorry for the fate of this unique animal, and both Tili and I started shouting at the dog, but it would not let go, so I started beating the dog's head with the handle of my insect net until it finally released the iguana, which happily scurried away. We congratulated ourselves for the good deed. However, when we related this adventure to our hostess, she was not impressed; she said that we made a mistake in letting the iguana loose because they are considered pests for eating the vegetables from their garden. The local folks like iguana meat as a good substitute for chicken meat.

It was getting close to Christmas. We had not heard from Eva, after sending her a number of letters and cards, and we were starting to get worried. Finally an 8-page letter brought news from home. She explained that she had needed some time to adapt to her new living environment. There were more activities for the four girls in her new family than in our small household.

The weather was summer-like. We just did not feel that it was Christmas, except for the huge tree-size Poinsettias that were blooming in the front yards. As substitute for a Christmas tree, we decorated some Poinsettia branches in a vase in the apartment. Instead of preparing a Christmas dinner with our meager kitchen dishes and utensils, we went to a San José restaurant as a Christmas treat. The standard menu in most resturaunts in Costa Rica included small black beans, rice, fried plantain, and fried chicken. This menu was always available, even in the most remote restaurants in the villages. So, for a holiday treat we ordered Wiener schnitzel of calf meat with potatoes and salad, and pastry and wine. It was a delicious dinner.

The Mercado Central (Central Market) of San José, with its wide range of fresh fruits and vegetables, was our favorite shopping place. We especially favored a most delicious miniature pink banana that only the local markets sold. We soon learned that most of the available beef in the market was too tough. The farmers butchered the cows after they got too old for efficient milk production. We were told to tenderize the meat overnight between pineapple slices — and it worked! While on field trips, we often got our fruits directly from the farmers who were selling at the roadside. Some would take us into their pineapple fields to select the fruits, which were cleaned for us with machetes on the spot.

For traveling within the city and to the suburbs, also once to the west coast, we used the local buses. These 20- to 30-year old buses were often overcrowded; local folks carried with them their live chickens and other small animals to and from the market. Often it became a real adventure for us to travel with the natives. Passengers and bus drivers were always attentive to us as obvious foreigners. We had a chance to practice our meager vocabulary, but if we got in trouble, some college students who spoke English eagerly helped us out. The buses would stop at any place where passengers wanted to get on or off.

I found the Costa Rican people very friendly. The tradition of democratic government and the relatively low living expenses attracted thousands of North American retirees. The latter were welcomed for resettling in Costa Rica, and received special privileges, e.g. duty-free importation of their household gadgets.

It was such an impressive sight for us to see the Presidential election campaign. Residents carried on their cars and hung out from their homes the banners of their favorite political candidates. After living under two dictatorships, we really appreciated this freedom to express political views without intimidation.

The middle-class houses in the city had marble floors, sometimes even in the garage, thus keeping the premises cool. Such floors were easy to clean. People in the villages usually had a sugarcane patch in the backyard that, besides providing sweets, probably also was used for rum-making. The machete was seen always at hand and in Costa Rica has become a multi-use agricultural and household tool. Seeing groups of men on the road with machetes at their sides often gives an outsider the wrong impression of men going to war. The taking of machetes into pubs was forbidden. The machete apparently replaces the scythe, the sickle, the clippers, saw, and hoe that are used in other parts of the world in agriculture. Here the tall weeds, vines, shrubs, even small trees that would choke cultivated fruit trees, coffee, and banana, are cut down with the machete. Even the lawns in parks and around middle-class homes are cut with the machete.

Figure 74. The airplane (Cessna-180) for our local travels in Costa Rica.

The Las Cruces Field Station, close to the Panamanian border at 1,200 m elevation in San Vito, could be reached by airplane only. So we reserved our seats in advance, and showed up early at the small San José airport for local flights. It was a single-engine Cessna-180, 4-passenger plane (Fig. 74). To our surprise, not only was our luggage put on a scale, but so was all our hand luggage and, in the end, each person! After Tili and I took our tight double seats, we were shocked to be ordered to make room for a third passenger. With much wriggling and placing our arms over the shoulders of our neighbors, we made it. Our overloaded plane hardly made it over the mountain-tops, but the view was great and compensated for the shaky ride.

The tropical rain forest available for research occupied 336 acres. It was next to a 50-acre botanical garden developed by Mr. and Mrs. Robert Wilson, horticulturists who donated the land to OTS for teaching and research. It was a biologist's dream to work in such a tropical paradise, and we took advantage of the facilities for two weeks. It was the most peaceful place to do research. While searching for scale insects at the base of giant rain forest trees, and watching closely for hidden snakes, I found a shiny golden front wing of a beetle. I jumped for joy to find traces of the Golden Scarab, so rare because of over-collecting by people who sell these to collectors of rare and beautiful insects for over $100 each. I searched in vain for intact specimens for our university collec-tion. Still, our catch increased tremendously, even without the Golden Scarab, during our stay there.

During my field work, I had many curious children following me. They tried to assist with my insect collecting. I decided to make their volunteering "official." I purchased a large variety of candies and piled up local coins. Then I prepared insect-killing jars safe for children, using only ethylacetate and paper strips. The next day I showed my little assistants what kinds of insects I wanted them to collect in the jars, promising that before the evening they could trade with me for coins and candy. All my insect jars were filled when the children showed up with the daily catch. There was the funniest horse trading that Tili ever witnessed. But I did not mind her comments as long as I increased ten-fold the daily catch. I think most of the children also got assistance from their family members working in the fields. When we were ready to leave the Field Station at Las Cruces, one of my little collecting assistants showed up with a beautiful bouquet of orchids, sent by his mother with thanks as a goodbye gift to Tili. We were both pleasantly impressed by the friendliness of the Costa Rican people.

Tili helped with many of my professional chores. She became an expert in sorting, labeling, and packing the collected insects. She kept up with the bookkeeping and correspondence required for the project. In addition, she prepared delicious meals from the available sources, some free, like bananas, plantain, and citrus fruits.

Because the generators providing electricity worked only during the nights, our refrigerator was cooled only for about 8-12 hours each day. We kept most of our food supply in the safest place, the refrigerator, to avoid insect infestation. Soon, I found out that some large cockroaches had moved into our refrigerator and were surviving in the only-partly-cooled facility. So we had our time to clean the refrigerator and scrutinize our food kept there.

Each evening at Las Cruces, some small lizard-like geckos walked up our white bedroom walls to catch small insects attracted to the ceiling light. I told Tili not to be afraid of them because they provide a good service for us, and were the reason for not having too many mosquitos. However, my calming efforts went unheeded when giant cockroaches, *Blaberus giganteus*, also walked up and roosted on the wall just over our beds. Though they stayed there all night, they disappeared by daylight. I told Tili that it must be their mating season for congregating on walls where there is no food. It would not be fair to chase them away during their honeymoon. I pulled our beds away from the walls to avoid the 75 mm long "honeymooners" accidentally walking over our beds.

Actually, I also made an effort to collect and preserve a number of native species of cockroaches for study by my colleagues at two universities. It turned out later that some of my cockroach specimens were new to science. My inventory from this trip included 239 scale insect collections from over 114 plant species. In addition, I preserved several thousand insects for studies by other colleagues. Many I sent to specialists, but most to the Smithsonian Institution. Later, after mounting the scale insects on microscope slides, I identified these to families and genera as far as I could, and gave to colleagues for further studying. Since then, a number of mealybugs new to science have been described from this material.

At the end of our trip, we took a longer weekend on San Andreas Island "just for vaca-tion" as I promised Tili. We rented a tricycle to seat two adults, and went around the island, enjoying the beautiful beaches, swimming, and snorkeling. I still picked up a few scale insect samples that looked promising for my collection. The old plane taking us to the island creaked so much that I was afraid it would fall apart over the sea. On the way back to San José, the plane was overloaded with large items of merchandise purchased by visitors on this duty-free island port.

The Costa Rican prison-island system really impressed me. Here the convicts live in home-made shelters and receive seeds and tools to grow their own food. If family members or girlfriends want to join them, they are allowed to do so. The island prison requires minimal guarding, because it is surrounded by shark-infested waters. I believe this punishment method is more humane than ours and probably results in fewer "returns"; also it is surely less expensive for the taxpayers than the prison systems in most other countries. The United States has many uninhabited islands in the Pacific and along the Alaskan coast, where hard-core convicts could hunt and fish their daily food, and even save for the harsh winter months without freezers in the North.

On my return flight from Costa Rica, I had about a dozen pieces of carry-on luggage, because I would not dare check my precious brittle insects. When the friendly stewardesses saw my bulky carry-ons, for which there was no room around my seat, they took 10 insect boxes and tied these down into an empty first-class seat. Apparently, only my insects could travel free in first-class on the Costa Rican airline.

Eight years later, in 1978, Tili and I returned to Costa Rica, as tourists just for 8 days, so I could re-collect some unusual insects at Las Cruces and clarify the biology of a misunderstood species. The trip was successful and resulted in another research article. I hope we may return in the future to Costa Rica as tourists and enjoy the friendly hospitality of its people.

19 — Around the World in 72 Days
(July 14–September 24, 1972)

Two of my graduate students and I had just completed a National Science Foundation (NSF)-supported study on a false pit-scale insect genus with worldwide distribution. The results of our studies provided new proof for the theory of continental drift. We were excited about the discovery. It was suggested that we present the results in a talk at the 14th International Congress of Entomology in Canberra, Australia during August 22–30, instead of waiting until our findings were published. The presentation would give me the opportunity to attend, for the first time, an International Congress of Entomology. I also wanted to collect in the field and select and borrow from museums new scale insects for study. So, I asked our sponsor (NSF) for approval of the trip and received their blessing with partial funding. I was prepared to supplement the cost of this travel from personal funds.

Because I had to travel to Canberra, halfway around the world, I decided not to return on the same route, but continue eastward from Australia on my return trip. I wanted to stop en route and consult with as many colleagues as possible who were not going to attend the Congress. Also, I thought I should organize the first international gathering of scale insect specialists (coccidologists) from among those attending the Congress. I believed that knowing each other in person would promote cooperation; also, we could avoid duplicating each other's work, if we knew who was doing what.

It took almost a full year of preparation to re-schedule my official work load, obtain permissions, arrange finances, shop for the best travel offers, get visas and shots, schedule meetings with institutions and scientists, and make air and hotel reservations. Finally, I had made arrangements to visit 21 entomological institutions, and to meet 27 coccidologists and a number of other entomologists, in 10 countries and 3 states of Australia.

The least expensive airfare ($1,726.10) for my trip was offered by PanAm Airline as a package called: "Around the World in 80 Days." The restrictions for this fare were: to return within 80 days; travel in one direction only, east or west, without backtracking; and to make en route at least four stops with a minimum of 48 hours each. I qualified because I wanted to visit colleagues with whom I corresponded professionally, or had known in person. Some had also expressed their wish for me to visit their institutions. I described my plans to colleagues and offered to consult on research of mutual interest, and to give talks at their institutions on some selected topics. I asked permission to survey their scale insect collections for material to be borrowed for our future research projects, and to prepare an inventory of their scale insect collections. Copies of the latter were deposited in the U.S. Museum of Natural History.

The contacted colleagues sent letters of invitation and, after receiving my travel schedule, made housing and local travel reservations. Some offered free or inexpensive housing and/ or board in their homes or in their institution's guest house for visiting scientists. My average overnight housing cost on this trip was about $6 per night; the lowest, 55¢ in New Delhi; the highest, $14 in Bali.

After consulting with my co-workers and graduate students, I discussed a 72-day work schedule for each. Tili and Eva, partly to compensate for not being able to join me on this trip, went on a 7-day vacation cruise to Bermuda. I also promised Tili that she would join me on a similar trip when the next opportunity arose. Luckily I was able to make good my promise seven years later.

My first stop going east was London, where I had three hours until my connecting flight to Madrid. Doug Williams, my English colleague, and his wife came out to the airport for a chat to bring us up-to-date on each other's projects. Williams came later to the USA for a year, and I spent a number of weeks in his laboratory at the British Museum. At the Madrid airport I had my first disappointing experience with a taxi driver, who added an "0" to my expected fare to the hotel of 100 Pesetas. Therefore, I took the bus for 20 Pesetas. Later, I almost got used to the attempts to extract higher taxi fares from unfamiliar tourists in different countries.

My local contact, Dr. Templado, an aphid specialist, was kind enough to put me up in a government hostel, where many of the Spanish language teaching foreign instructors spent their summers while improving their Spanish language skills. I collected my first scale insects at their botanical garden, and reviewed the meager scale insect collection at Templado's institute. Not having much more to do, I visited the Prado Museum with its large collection of Goya, Murillo, El Greco, and Velasquez paintings. I also signed up for a weekend bus tour to Toledo. It was really hot and dry in mid-July. Because of the weekend, I ran into a large crowd while visiting El Greco's house and museums with his paintings. This ancient city, bordered by the river Tajo, is unique and picturesque. In the shops the prices were 30–50% higher than in the United States, and these prices helped me avoid shopping and having to carry gift items with me around the world.

The sidewalk plantations were full of semi-tropical scale insects. I could not resist taking samples, since every scale insect species found here was new for our collection at Virgina Tech.

I compensated myself for not shopping with a dinner at the Monterey restaurant that introduced me for the first time to Sangria, the semi-sweet red wine with chunks of fruit in it. I liked it very much. After what I had seen in Spain, I made up my mind that I should return with my family for a longer stay, which we did two years later.

My next stop was in Rome, where I took the train to Naples. At the Naples railroad station I was greeted by Dr. Antonio Tranfaglia, who took me to the Institute of Agricultural Entomology at Portici. Here I was offered free housing, provided that I would take what they had in the Silkworm Research Institute (Fig. 75). It turned out to be a bed attached to the wall of their silkworm-rearing room. The bed could be released from the wall at night for sleeping. A nearby bathroom was also available. So, I took the offer. I don't think Tili would have slept there: one could listen all night to the chewing of mulberry leaves by the beautiful finger-sized caterpillars. I thought that for an entomologist it was perfect. For meals I was taken to a nearby small family restaurant where signed photographs of famous former Italian entomologists hung on the walls.

I consider the Institute of Agricultural Entomology in Portici the Mecca of Coc-

Figure 75. The Silkworm Research Institute, where the "rearing room" served as my hotel, in Portici, Italy,

cidologists. Several generations of Italian experts had worked there and had left behind a most precious collection of scale insect specimens and an old library. I was well taken care of by colleagues. Because of the large collection, I could not inventory their holdings in detail, especially with all the social engagements lined up for me by my hosts. I selected and borrowed specimens for study at home. One afternoon I was taken by car to Naples where I ate the original "Napolese pizza". I think ours in the U.S. is better, because it is tastier, more versatile, and has fewer calories. The Napolese pizza had a thick, soft, dough base, with only olive oil, cheese, and tomato sauce for topping. The local red wine was excellent to wash down the rich pizza. Another excursion was to the ancient city of Pompeii, and the romantic city of Sorrento, with lunch in Amalfi. One bottle of wine cost only US70¢. My Italian colleagues were very gracious; they put out their hearts for me.

On my return trip, I had 24 hours in Rome before catching my plane to Beirut, Lebanon. To take full advantage of my first and short visit to Rome, I signed up on three different sight-seeing bus tours. Because it was Sunday, one of the morning tours would have included the Pope's traditional Sunday blessing for visitors on St. Peter's Square. The other tour, somewhat shorter, was without the Pope's blessing, but allowed participants to catch the second city tour for the afternoon. So, I got out of Rome without the Pope's blessing in order not to miss my afternoon city tour. That evening, the third tour took me 9 to 12 kilometers to the beautiful Tivoli Gardens with the many colorful lighted water falls, fountains, and artificial grottoes, at night. As a garden lover, I will always remember the grandiose landscapes there. After midnight I started taking the bitter quinine tablets to immunize me against malaria in the tropics.

A.S. Talhouk, the famous agricultural entomologist, met me at the Beirut airport and took me to the Alumni Club House for lodging near the American University. The University was located in a unique wooded quarter of the city with an ocean front. The shopping area started around the corner from my Club house; it had many open Kebab shops that attracted customers, as the air was filled with the good smell of this spicy grilled meat. Graceful tall palms lined the main roads. It was a beautiful, busy city. I admired the Emir Mansour Assaft Mosque, as well as the hotel rows lining the seacoast. Unfortunately, many of these were ruined during the long street fights soon after I left. I was taken by Dr. Talhouk in a car to a fruit tree research station along the road north toward Baalbeck. We visited the ruins of the 2,000 year old Roman city of Baalbeck, founded by Julius Caesar. Dr. Talhouk and I enjoyed an 8-course Middle Eastern dinner in a resturaunt. I ate a lot of my favorite dish, stuffed grape leaves. Unfortunately, because of the long war in Lebanon, I have lost touch with my gracious host, Dr. Talhouk.

In Tehran, Dr. Mohamed Kaussari, a coccidologist, made the local arrangements and waited for me at the airport with a driver and a young scientist interpreter. This trio from there on were my constant companions while I visited in Iran. I was taken to a plush room at the Hotel Atlantic and greeted with traditional Middle Eastern hospitality, that also included a bouquet of Gladiolus flowers in a room covered with Persian rugs. I was told that, as a guest of the Government, all my local expenses would be paid in exchange for my consultation. The next day, I visited several institutions and administrative offices of plant protection and entomology. All the rooms were decorated with pictures of the Shah and his family. We discussed their scale insect problems. For some of their questions, I mailed the pertinent information after my return. I was fed much rice and kebab for the two days. One night I dined with three chiefs of the visited institutions and was taken to a show with Iranian folk dances.

We drove down the impressive double highway, the Elizabeth II Boulevard, divided by a neat canal with two rows of trees and lawn. Iran, just the previous year, had celebrated the 2,500th anniversary of the founding of the Persian Empire by Cyrus the Great. The administrators serving as my hosts made a special effort to impress me with the progress made recently. I was taken to the beautiful Sepahsalar mosque and other tourist attractions. They also took me to a giant mausoleum built in honor of the Shah's parents, but they "forgot" to take me to the famous covered bazaar that I wanted to see. I soon realized that I was artificially kept in a "greenhouse" environment. I was taken only where my hosts thought it best to impress me. It was unusual for me to see agricultural fields, gardens, and houses, all protected by mud or brick walls. All windows on the houses faced inward. Women only rarely had their faces covered. Open concrete ditches took all the water to the suburbs along the road beds.

Dr. Kaussary, my official host, must have been close to retirement age. After meals and a few glasses of vodka, which he washed down like water, he often fell asleep, so I continued my conversation with our interpreter, whom I identified as a Young Turk. When alone with me, he used every opportunity to tell me his people's disappointments with the Government. It was good that nobody understood English around us. I realized that despite the generally good picture painted for my benefit, there was something brewing against the Shah's regime.

On the night flight from Tehran to New Delhi, I was able to stretch out over several seats in the middle aisle and get 3–4 hours of badly needed sleep. By now, I had become a seasoned traveler and had learned how to cope better with traveler's fatigue.

Dr. M.G.R. Menon of the Indian Agricultural Research Institute greeted me at the airport and took me to the noisy hostel for visiting scientists. For US55¢ per night, I got a large, spartanly furnished room with a large ceiling fan and dozens of cute geckos for mosquito control on the walls. My adjoining bathroom had a tub that was large enough for swimming or group bathing. I was very thirsty, so I asked for an unopened coke. It came lukewarm, but I did not dare to let attendants open it and pour it out into a glass that had been washed in local water or put ice in it made from the tap water. I was careful and still naive, thinking that I could avoid the dreaded diarrhea that is a curse for Westerners in some tropical countries.

I was taken to universities and museums and the next day to the Indian Agricultural Research Institute. The scale insect collection was made up of mostly dried specimens on the host. I was amazed to see workers using machete-like tools to trim the lawn at the Institute. The grass clippings were taken immediately away in sacks, probably to feed animals, maybe, some sacred cows.

We visited the Muslim University at Aligarh, where I was scheduled to meet researchers working on parasites of scale insects, and Dr. S.M. Ali working on scale insects. En route I noticed many people sleeping on roofs and on the ground, where it was cooler than in their tiny mud huts. Many poor souls worked for US33¢ per day.

Dr. Menon, at my request, arranged a Sunday train excursion to Agra for me to see the famous Taj Mahal and to visit with Dr. M. Mani at St. Johns College. Dr. Mani took me out with his students to collect my first true lac insects. These scale insects produce an important export item that is made into varnish and other industrial products around the world. It was 104°F in the shade when I visited the Taj Mahal in a sweat-soaked shirt, but it was worth it and a dream come true. This is the most beautiful shrine that I have ever seen, the result of wealth and love for a woman.

I was much relieved that I survived for two days without getting diarrhea. On my last day I was invited by colleagues for a midday meal that included delicious mango and other fruits, and vegetarian food of a variety of green vegetables. I had no heart to decline eating and possibly offend my hosts. By evening the diarrhea had taken over, and I was not able to touch any of the delicious food served on my flight to Singapore. I really needed three days in Singapore to recover from my Indian adventures. Luckily, I had packed a supply of Lomotil just for such events.

At the Singapore airport a large billboard greeted me. The three male heads painted on it each had a different length haircut. Passengers arriving with "too long hair" were told to go to the airport barbershop to shorten their hair; otherwise they could not enter into Singapore. I was pleased that I qualified for entering Singapore. My local contact, Professor D. H. "Patty" Murphy at the University of Singapore, took me to the Hotel Premier and gave me a sightseeing tour. He also took me collecting scale insects in the Butik Timah Forest, where we found a number of new scale insect records for the area, and a species new to science that we named in his honor. He took me to the Tiger Balm Garden, a unique introduction to Chinese mythology and fairy tales illustrated in a funny, but often frightening, fashion. We also visited a rubber plantation just across the northern border in Malaya.

Murphy's wife was Chinese. They both worked, so when lunch time came, he stopped with me at a sidewalk stand and ordered take-out lunch for his children. The Chinese vendor had his wok under a large umbrella, with many plastic bags with chopped up ingredients hanging from the edge of the umbrella. He prepared the individualized meals in the wok in minutes, according to the tastes of Murphy's children. While they were still warm, Murphy delivered them to his home.

I learned that it is not safe, due to sea piracy, to take a small boat to a small island, Rempang, in the Straits of Singapore. I wanted to re-collect some scale insects that are known only on that island; the original samples were lost during World War II. But my free time was utilized instead by a bus tour of the city.

Singapore is an exemplary city in providing affordable housing for low-income taxpayers. They had no homeless people or beggars. I was much impressed with the cleanest city I have ever seen. There were no cigarette butts or any other refuse on the streets or sidewalks. Even spitting on the streets was forbidden, and it was required to cross the streets only at the designated places. Lawbreakers were punished on the spot with very steep fines.

To avoid the tourist crowds, I went to the botanical gardens very early in the morning. Instead of tourists, I found there hundreds of native Chinese, taking their traditional Tai-Chi exercises. I felt out of place, so I went to the orchid collection that is one of the largest and most beautiful in the world.

The unique Wallace's Line is well-known in zoogeography. This line crosses the Indian Ocean between the islands of Bali and Lombok of Indonesia. The composition of the animal life of the two islands is as different as it is between England and Japan, although the two islands are separated only by 60 kilometers. I thought, I have to see this phenomenon myself so I can lecture in the future on this topic from personal experience. This was my professional excuse for stopping for three days in Bali, but I also included in my plans a performance of the graceful Balinese dancers. I had no local contacts, so I had to pay the highest hotel price on this trip, $14 per night.

Art lovers should stop in Bali. The entire island is an art show. Most of the art I saw celebrated religious traditions. The Balinese are Hindus, while the rest of Indonesia is Muslim. Here I admired the beautifully carved and painted family shrines in each courtyard. They gave the impression to Westerners, that these are miniature toy houses built on four stilts. Fresh flowers were placed daily in each as part of the adoration ritual.

My small thatched-roof bungalow overlooked the beach at Kuta. It was an ideal place for recharging my batteries before more professional engagements. One day I joined other tourists; together we rented a taxi to see some unique parts of the island. Our taxi passed through a number of villages, each specializing in some traditional art. In one I found wood carvers; in another, stone carvers or bone carvers; in yet another, painters; etc. Small children were already learning the skills from their elders, who for generations had practiced the same art. I was sorry, being half a world away from home with my limited luggage space, that I was not able to purchase any souvenir artworks. But one insistent vendor ran after me with a small bone carving to sell, so to shake him off I offered a very low price. After two more blocks, he sold me the item for my original offer, and I am now the proud owner of a fine, delicate bone art piece. I used my clothes to protect it from breaking on the long trip back. The monthly salary of employees at our motel was US$10. One evening I went to see the famous native legong and barong dances performed by young artists, and brought back for souvenirs two silk paintings of these dances. The dancing girls expressed the happy-ending love story with graceful rhythmic movements of their shoulders, arms, fingers, and eyes. The music came from brass instruments.

One day, a young Italian at our motel and I rented Vespa mopeds and took off around the island for more discoveries. We tried to collect some unusual shells, including sand dollars, on the beach. While concentrating on the long sandy beach surface, we suddenly found ourselves surrounded by naked bathers. It turned out we had stumbled upon a nudist beach section without seeing the beach signs. We ran away before getting into trouble with some of the muscular sunbathers. My unprotected body parts, nose and knees, got red from the harsh tropical sun by late afternoon, so I realized it would have been worse if I had joined the nudist group that day.

That evening I was invited to a cock fight. It was a sickening sight with about 300 noisy, betting natives. Sharp blades were attached to the legs of the sacrificed cocks. They were coerced to fight until one was fatally wounded and fell to the ground. But I left without waiting for the final outcome...

While shopping for fresh fruits at the local farmers' market, I met a number of Australian University students also shopping with the help of native girls. It was good to chat with these seasoned tourists and learn more about life on Bali. I was told that Australian students come here in large numbers during school vacation. At one of the Australian universities there is a yearly publication on freight boats taking on student passengers for a low fare. Students may work on the same boats for their fare, but most

of them get off at Bali. Here they could get by on $1 or $2 per day. For 50¢ a day they rented a small thatched hut built in the backyards of natives at Kuta village. For another 50¢ daily they could get their meals when buying their staples at the market with the help of native girls. Many native girls wanted to learn English from the Australian students, so in exchange for lessons, they helped the students with their housekeeping chores. What I missed for not being an unmarried student again! I could have stayed longer, and avoided spending $20 per day for room and board, but probably only until the girls realized that I spoke English with a Hungarian accent.

On the night flight to Sydney, I was able to stretch out and sleep again in the middle aisle of the airplane. I was fortunate to have a former Hungarian entomologist friend, Dr. Joseph Szent-Ivány, in Adelaide, South Australia. He, with much care, organized my itinerary for the 40-day visit in Australia and Papua-New Guinea. He had formerly served as Chief Entomologist for Papua-New Guinea. While in that position he introduced laws for the protection of endangered species, including their highly prized giant, exotic butterflies. My "uncle Joe", as I called him in Hungarian, made ideal flight and hotel reservations.

My first stop was in Brisbane at the Division of Plant Industry of the Queensland Department of Agriculture, to work on the scale insect collections of this Institute and of two nearby museums. I was taken on a collecting trip by my host, A. R. Brimblecombe, and got my first introduction to the unique adaptations to the local climate by the scale insects of Australia. Many scale insects produce plant galls (Fig. 76), especially on *Acacia* and *Eucalyptus* trees, and, by living inside the galls in self-made "greenhouses", they survive the hostile dry and hot environment. Some other scale insects have developed a marsupium, like kangaroos, to protect their eggs and young from dessication and the heat. I was much excited by the unique fauna and took many samples for our collection at Virginia Tech.

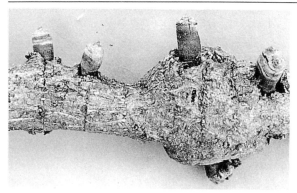

Figure 76. Plant galls and malformation produced by scale insects, Frenchia casuarinae, *on* Casuarina *trees in Australia.*

For the weekend, when the institution was closed, I flew north to Gladstone, and from there I was taken to Heron Island in a 4-passenger helicopter over the crystal clear, shallow waters with colorful coral formations. Here I stayed at the biological research station and collected some woodroaches and scale insects on the island that is located at the southern end of the Great Barrier Reef. It had for some time been my dream to see the Great Barrier Reef, do some snorkeling, and be introduced to the exciting sea life in the coral reef. I took advantage of snorkeling equipment at the station, but also took the glass-bottom boat tour.

I returned to Sydney and from there flew to Adelaide, South Australia, where at the airport, to my great surprise, three ladies waited for me. They were Mrs. Szent-Ivány, a biological artist; Helen Brookes, the scale insect specialist of the Waite Agricultural Research Institute; and her Hungarian-born technician, Vali Burnyowczky. I had met only Helen before. For dinner, I was taken by the Szent-Iványs to a Hungarian restaurant on top of Mount Lofty, with a great view of Adelaide. We had a Hungarian-style fish dinner that was washed down with excellent local wine.

One evening Helen Brookes' colleagues took me to the regular meeting of their Beef and Burgundy Club. I was surprised to find 10 wine glasses at my table setting, but for each drink we had to use a different glass. We started with an aperitif with the hors d'oeuvre, followed by fish with a variety of white wines, and steak with red wines. Some semi-sweet after-dinner wines ended the dining and closed the meeting. Each wine bottle was held in a numbered brown paper bag while serving. This was followed by evaluations by some volunteers and much guessing on the wine variety, vintage, and production site. After this, the brown bag was removed and the exposed bottle was passed around for further sampling. The club owned a vineyard with their own master vintner. It was a new experience for me "Down Under."

Helen took me on a field trip, where I was able to collect some soil-inhabiting scale insects with the marsupium, as well as others inhabiting plant galls. I also saw for the first time some cochineal scale insects that were introduced to Australia for the biological control of the prickly pear weed cactus. Vali's husband took me out to a waterfall, to the beach, and to their home where I had three different meat dishes and three different Hungarian pastries, besides a meat-vegetable soup. What a treat after not eating tasty Hungarian food for five weeks!

Helen arranged with her colleagues for me to travel in a car with them to Canberra so I could see more of the country. It was an educational trip that I much enjoyed. We passed along many large sheep ranches. My local colleagues complained that the cost of a half lamb had just gone up to $3.50, while in New Zealand you could get it for $2.00. Because I love lamb meat, I ate a lot while in Australia. In Australia's big cities, I often found the water bad-tasting and I realized why the common folks there preferred to drink beer.

In Canberra we were housed in the student dormitories of the Australian National University; thus housing was relatively inexpensive, as were the meals in the university cafeteria. This was the first time that the International Congress of Entomology had been held in Australia. Our Australian organizers did a great job. Helen Brookes and H. Jonathan Banks helped me with the organization of the first international meeting of scale insect specialists, attended by 20 persons, with 14 scale insect specialists. Each of us reported on our current research projects. After group photography, we all signed greeting cards and sent these to 48 colleagues unable to attend this meeting. We also decided to hold more formal meetings or symposia in the future, and the practice has continued to date.

Our local colleagues organized a joint field trip to the nearby parks to collect scale insect samples. My presentation at the formal meetings was well received, and I made a number of new professional contacts. During the meetings, in one of the hallways I ran into a table filled with gift items made from opal. I decided to buy some as gifts for my family. By then I had learned in the Middle East that I could usually get a better price if I bought 3 or more items in a package deal. So I asked what discount I would get if I purchased 3 gift items. The vendors, a man with his wife and son, looked to me and asked if I was Hungarian, because of my accent. So I proudly responded yes, because I started out from Hungary. They, too were refugees from the 1956 Hungarian uprising who had settled in Australia, where they purchased an old opal mine. They were not only mining, but processing and selling the opals themselves. So I got a 25% discount from them for my Hungarian accent and for purchasing several items.

After the meetings, I got back to Sydney to take my flight to Papua-New Guinea. At Port Moresby I stayed with my colleague from Hungary, Dr. L. Móczár, at the Papua Hotel near the seaport. We shared a room to reduce expenses. Several Hungarian biologists had built a reputation with the early exploration of the fauna and ethnography of Papua-New Guinea. Biró's book on his work in Papua was read by most high school students in Hungary. So, it was not a great surprise when we ran into some new researchers from Hungary.

We were taken to a social club and introduced to the uprooted European scientists and educators living in the area. Apparently most of these people were ending their work day in the German club. I was told they need companionship and alcoholic drinks to survive their working conditions in that developing coun-

try. We met only foreigners in the club. Although everyone can join, the natives can't afford the high cost of club membership. So, they have their own pub next door, where a police paddy wagon is constantly parked in front to take away those who had too many drinks and became dangerous to others. I was told that knifing is very common in that pub. Apparently, some natives can't hold alcoholic beverages well.

I did some collecting from the sidewalk trees and from plants in the botanical garden, consulted with the local plant protection experts, and gave an evening presentation on scale insects. There were six Hungarian names in the local telephone book. I was also invited to supper with two families, one from Germany, Heidy and Bob Pfeng, the other from Hungary, András Bálint. Such visits gave me insight into the lonely everyday life of these uprooted families in a developing tropical country. Most were on contract by the United Nations or the Australian Government. Both helped to bring to self-governing status this giant country.

Our second week with Móczár was spent in Wau at the Ecological Research Station donated to the Hawaiian Bishop Museum by Dr. J. Lin Gressitt. We lived a spartan life here. Gressitt's parents were medical missionaries in China, where he learned oriental cooking. He cooked a big pot of rice that lasted for one week for three of us. We just added to this basic staple whatever we could purchase from the farmer's market or pick from the trees on the research station grounds. I don't think my daily meals cost more than 50¢. We took turns in cooking and dishwashing, but we did shopping at the market together.

The research station was self-supporting, in part from the income of their coffee plantation. Young men were hired from the aborigine villages for maintenance work on the coffee plantation and botanical garden. According to their contracts, they were provided food and shelter, but were paid only at the end of the contract period. Most of these young men came to earn enough to be able to pay the parents

Figure 77. A native archer aiming for birds, in Papua–New Guinea.

isms that were carried on the backs of these beetles, including some mites and nematodes.

I was checking the moss forest with huge *Nothofagus carrii* trees and found many scale insects under the moss layer. These trees are considered the beech trees of the Southern Hemisphere. While on Mt. Kaindi, we had to sleep in sleeping bags in a 5 x 3 m metal sheet building that was too hot during the day and cold at night (10°C), but very noisy during the frequent rains. In addition, the many night creatures often woke me up with their screeching. It did not calm me to learn that the screeching was the "singing" of the bird of paradise. We devoured our left-over cold rice and hurried down the mountain, stopping only at some native bird hunters who used arrows (Fig. 77). I purchased from them three such bamboo arrows for souvenirs.

When a Hungarian television crew led by the soil mite specialist, Dr. J. Balogh, arrived at our station, I was coerced into preparing a Hungarian Gulyás for seven people. I needed potatoes, but no such staple was available at the farmer's market. I finally made some concoction out of taro roots, onions, chili peppers, and salted pork. None of us would recognize it to be even close to gulyás, but not having a choice, we finished the big pot. The TV crew wanted to demonstrate to the Hungarian TV viewers what happened in the tropics after the natives burned down the tropical rain forest on the hills and mountain sides to raise food crops. Their wish came true when such a fire was started on one of the mountain slopes surrounding Wau. The fire got out of hand, as usual, and for three days, because of heavy smoke, no airplanes could leave or land at the local airport. It became obvious from the yellow silt in the local river that a lot of soil erosion was precipitated by the fires. Finally the smoke was blown away, followed by rain that extinguished the forest fire, so the TV crew and we could return to "civilization".

I had to return to Sydney to take my return flight over the Pacific. My first two-day stop was at Fiji. I planned the two-day stops in Fiji, Tahiti, and Mexico City to gradually readjust

of a would-be wife for their daughter's hand. With the earnings they purchased pigs to be traded for their mates. Some girls were exchanged for only three, others for up to five pigs. After "obtaining a wife," the man in many aborigine villages could sit back because his mate did all the work around the house and in their garden. She also raised the children and pigs, collected fire wood, and cooked. After what I learned here, I was glad that my daughter married an American.

Gressitt had a research plot on the nearby 2,350 m high Mt. Kaindi and took Móczár and me to see the unusual biota. En route, we were looking for the famous bird of paradise. Gressitt's giant beetles were caged over their host shrubs. Because of the frequent rains, heat, and high humidity, his beetles were green from the algae and mosses growing over their bodies. He found about a dozen different organ-

my biological clock for the 12-hour difference between Sydney and Virginia.

I stayed in Fiji in a small hotel in Suva. While boarding a local bus, I asked the driver if I had gotten on the right bus line. He said yes, but one of the passengers who overheard me asked if I was a Hungarian native. I told him yes. Then he introduced himself as István Bor, another member of the Hungarian Diaspora. Five million Hungarians are living outside of their country.

While in Fiji, I visited some native thatch-roofed houses. I realized here that the hairstyle we call "Afro" is actually very close to that of the natives in Fiji. I was invited by the friendly natives into their houses where I was treated with a fermented drink from Kava and fruits. The natives complained to me about their fate in becoming mistreated second-rate citizens in their own native country. The government and commerce were kept in the Indian immigrants' hands. When I wanted to purchase some souveniers, I realized myself I could not find Fijian-owned shops, but only Indian shops.

I learned more about Polynesia in Papeete, Tahiti, but only after my luggage was fumigated for 90 minutes before release at the airport. I carefully calculated my remaining money to last for six more days. Then, I got a big surprise: the local calendar showed the same date as the day that I left Fiji. So, I had gained a day by crossing the International Date Line between Fiji and Tahiti, as Jules Verne's characters had.

But then I realized my leftover money wouldn't cover a seventh day! So, I would have to cash checks in Mexico. For the first time on this trip, I felt a real language barrier. The friendly folks in Tahiti spoke a local variety of French and I had no dictionary. To be able to sleep, I killed many mosquitoes from the walls of my room. I was disturbed during the first night by the noisy people on the streets, dogs, cats, and towards morning, by the many cocks. Ear plugs and/or beer will help the next time.

I found everything too expensive here, but I had a free entertainment that only an ento-

mologist could appreciate. The termites in a large fencepost were ready for "honeymoon" flight and just swarmed out at dusk, so I closed my windows and shut off the lights to avoid attracting them to my room. There were thousands flying in all directions; after mating, they shed their long wings and burrow into the ground to start their families. For me it was a most interesting event, but some of my neighbors who had their lighted windows open got hundreds of termites crawling into their rooms. I suggested the use of a vacuum cleaner instead of spraying. Many lizards, geckos, and birds filled themselves with the protein-rich termites. I could have also saved on the high price of meals by roasting the abundant termites for my dinner. During the day I collected some scale insects from bamboo and grasses, as well as some unusual and rare web-spinning insects (Embiidina).

It was a long flight from Tahiti to Mexico City, but I slept 4-5 hours on empty middle aisle seats of the plane. Professor Raul McGregor-Loueza, a coccidologist colleague, greeted me at the airport and took me in as his house guest. I was fortunate to have him as my host. The local banks would not cash my money orders made out in Swiss francs. So, he gave me cash and I signed my checks out to him, so he could cash those in his bank at a later date. Raul and his wife took me to the Mexican National Museum of Anthropology, and in the evening to a performance of folk music and native dances. The next day he took me to a square called Chapultepec, or grasshopper, with a large statue of a grasshopper. We also collected scale insects while visiting the nearby ancient Major Temple pyramids.

After drinking the local water and eating in restaurants, I got, for the second time on the trip, diarrhea, so it was time to return home on September 24th, my 72nd day since starting my journey.

Although I had a wonderfully educational trip, it was good to be back with my family in Virginia after ten weeks of gypsy life.

20 — Second Time Around (Sri Lanka, 1979)

My colleague at the Smithsonian Institution, Dr. Karl Krombein, provided me with an opportunity to study the scale insect fauna of Sri Lanka (Ceylon) and consult with local researchers. Karl was in charge of Smithsonian Research in Sri Lanka, financed through the PL-480 Program. This program uses local currency accumulated in the U.S. embassies as payment for American food (mostly grain) shipments. The money was to be used to finance joint research projects of mutual importance to both countries. In our case, American entomologists with local colleagues studied the fauna of Sri Lanka. We took insect samples together, processed the material locally and/or in the United States, and shared the "catch". Also, authentically identified specimens were deposited in the national museums of both countries for further studies by specialists around the world. Many research publications resulted from these studies.

All local expenses were paid from the PL-480 funds, except the cost of transportation to and from Sri Lanka. The participating American scientist had to come up with the air flight costs. I was lucky that I did not have to use my own funds. While I was organizing my research trip to Sri Lanka, Virginia Tech signed an agreement with the U.S. Agency for International Development (AID) to offer courses and consultation for the Postgraduate School of the Agricultural University at Peradeniya in Sri Lanka through the Academy of Educational Development (AED) Program. They needed two entomologists, so Dr. Robert (Bob) L. Pienkowski and I signed up. We were told that our wives could join us as long as they paid their own transportation. I encouraged Tili to come with me, and felt good that I was able to keep my 1972 promise to take her on my next, more extensive professional trip. Because PAN-AM was still offering the kind of ticket that I used in 1972, "Around the World in 80 Days", we decided to have stops in Greece and India and on the return in Singapore and Japan.

We left on September 15, ten days ahead of my official engagement in Sri Lanka, so that we could spend one week in Greece. Our friend in Athens, Eva Floridis, made room reservations. En route to Athens, we had to change flights in Belgrade, Serbia. Here the airport officials demanded transit visas from passengers who were changing planes at their airport. We lost time while waiting for visas and almost missed our connecting flight.

Also, one of our suitcases did not arrive. When I complained, I was taken out to a section of the open airport field, where hundreds of "lost" suitcases were stored. It gave me the impression of walking in a "suitcase cemetery". Some suitcases were already partly opened or badly deformed and damaged from the rain, snow, wind, and sun. But our suitcase was not among "the dead". I was told to look for it in Athens.

I soon realized how they could have accumulated so many "abandoned" suitcases. — Before the flights departed from Belgrade, the passengers had to walk toward their airplane along rows of suitcases to select their own. Only the selected-out suitcases were loaded into the plane. Because the suitcase attendants spoke only Serbian and often did not make an effort to find the suitcase owners, many uninformed passengers from the West, not knowing the local custom — and not being told of it — passed the suitcase line and entered the airplane. Apparently, the local air terminal officials did not care to find the owners of the left-behind suitcases. They believe that with such a system they could prevent the smuggling of bombs onto the airplanes.

Unexpectedly, we were taken only to Dubrovnik on the Dalmation Coast — and only after several hours of waiting did we board the flight to Athens. We got an uneasy feeling while waiting late into the evening in the Airport Hall in Dubrovnik. There were no English- or other foreign language-speaking airport personnel, or signs to tell us when the flights departed, and nobody whom we asked spoke any of the six languages we tried out to seek information. So we were kept in the dark until the last few minutes before our departure, when finally in broken English we heard the long-awaited words. Because of the delays, we arrived in Athens around 2:30 a.m.. I filed the forms for our lost luggage, and got to our hotel around 4:00 a.m. I made a pledge to myself to avoid taking flights through the Communist-run Balkans in the future.

Our Attica Palace Hotel was located in the center of the city with a good view of the Acropolis and the nearby National Gardens. Like most tourists, we visited the National Archeological Museum and the Acropolis. The beautiful collection of sculptures displayed in the Museum included the nude figures of Poseidon, the youths of Marathon, Antikythera, and Aphrodite. Splendid jewelry and vases were on display from the Hellenistic and Roman periods. At the Acropolis we also viewed the magnificent Parthenon and Erechtheion, and attended an artistic "Sound and Light" show in the evening when the excessive heat was gone. A one-day bus tour took us to Delphi, to see the ancient religious shrine, the Temple of Apollo, and the Theatre. Delphi is located in an impressive ravine overlooking a beautiful valley. The upright cypresses and the pine and olive trees on rocky outcrops provided a true Mediterranean landscape, which I enjoyed even more than the ruins. Not to mention that a few scale insects from these trees gave me my scientific souvenirs for the day.

We spent another full day on a 3-isles cruise to visit Agina, Poros, and Hydra. The ship took us on the blue waters of the Saronic Gulf with a beautiful view of the hillside towns that we visited. The many whitewashed square houses, often with flat or red-tile roofs, gave an idyllic view. Many hillside houses cannot be reached by automobiles, so donkeys are commonly used to carry needed goods to the houses. The local folks must walk a lot to reach their homes, probably one reason one doesn't see chubby or overweight people among the natives. Each community had a large building with a red-tiled, dome-shaped roof, identifying the local Eastern Orthodox church.

We had read about the ancient civilization that existed on Crete, so we decided to fly to Crete for a day-long tour. El Greco was born in Crete, near Heraklion in the village of Fodhele. In Heraklion, we visited the Archeological Museum, the Minoan plaster casts, and the ruins at Knossos, with colored murals and an impressive throne room. Knossos is located between two hills. The palace ruins have been reconstructed by the British archeologist Evans, starting from 1900.

The famous untamed beaches were a disappointment when we tried a swim there. No waste baskets were available, and no cleanup crews in sight. Motorcyclists were allowed to run freely on the beaches, dodging around us, as we walked bare-footed among the remains of many beach parties. In the local cafe, I had to try a Greek specialty: Souvlaki with chips.

Back in Athens our friend Eva and her relatives took us to a restaurant to sample Greek cuisine. I had many stuffed grapevine leaves (dolma), also stuffed tomatoes, omelets, and cheeses for hors d'oeuvres. For the main dish, we had moussaka, a spicy vegetable dish, grilled lamb, and a variety of seafood. I tasted the Greek pastry "baklava" and enjoyed it even though it is too sweet for some. Most Americans would not touch some of the other local specialties, that included beef tongue, brains, and grilled liver.

After three days, our lost suitcase arrived. I had a chance to consult with Dr. Loukia Argyriou at the Benaki Phytopathological Institute in Athens, and viewed their biological control experiments against scale insects.

We found Athens to be a nice historical city, but the many automobiles, overcrowding, heat, and air pollution were too much for me. Even the stones of the Acropolis showed some signs of the air pollution.

On the way to India, our connecting Pan Am flight was overbooked in Belgrade, and left us behind for one extra day in a hotel. There was no time for city sightseeing tours, but at least we had an evening pleasure-boat ride on the Danube to view the lighted streets and block houses on the two shores.

After a long flight, we arrived late at night in New Delhi, India, and slept in a "last-minute emergency hotel accommodation". Tili had made reservations ahead to visit the Taj Mahal and the Fort of Agra with a bus tour. Because of our one-day delay in Belgrade, I had no flight reservation for this day. I made desperate efforts to find transportation to Colombo, Sri Lanka. Luckily, I got on a late air flight, but without Tili, who followed me the next day.

Sri Lanka, with its pear shape, is located just 18 miles south of the Indian subcontinent; it became independent in 1948, after 130 years of British rule. It has one of the highest (85%) literacy rates in the developing world. Sri Lanka had almost 18 million people in 1993, on a land about 25,000 mi^2 (64,652 km^2), with 74% Sinhalese, 16% Tamils, and 8% Moors, a few Europeans, and even fewer Veddas. The latter are the natives, who were replaced by the first settlers from India, the Sinhalese, and later the Tamils. Unfortunately the latter two groups live in political, religious, and economic conflict that erupted into violence soon after we left Sri Lanka. The Hindu Tamils, who live mainly in the north and along the east coast, are demanding independence from the majority Buddhist Sinhalese.

I found it to be an expensive practice for their undergraduate higher education to offer the same courses twice in the two languages of the natives, for which there were no textbooks. Why not in English, which is the third official language of the country? Most graduate courses were taught in English. But students in these courses still had no textbooks,

and a terrible library. One reason there were no textbooks was that the cost of one text we used was as much as a middle class Sri Lankan would make in a month.

Most of the exports are in tea, rubber, coconut, and textiles; therefore, agriculture provides the main income for the country. This is where my university wanted to assist Sri Lanka. Sri Lanka, the "spice island", produces black peppers, cloves, and cinnamon as well as rice, sugar cane, coffee, and cocoa, mainly for local consumption. Their craftsmen are famous for carving furniture, especially from teak wood.

In Colombo, I got in touch with the National Museum officials who directed locally the joint PL-480 Project. Our accommodations were arranged; in Colombo we stayed in the large household of the former Museum Director's widow, Mrs. P.E.P. Deraniyagala. Here, we were treated like members of the "maharani's" extended family. Because she acted like a princess, I gave her that name for in-family use.

We learned to enjoy the large variety of tasty Sri Lankan food: the spicy chutney relish, the many rice and vegetarian dishes. We also drank a lot of tea and had lemonade made of fresh fruits. Our host's bungalow was close to downtown and to my museum office, so we often walked around the town. Snake charmers were common on the sidewalks, with their cobras in closed baskets, to be lured out with their long "necks" by the melody played on a flute.

The easy-going Sri Lankans kept the holidays — 54 days — of all major religions. In this country there are Buddhists (69%), Hindus (15%), Moslems (8%), and Christians (7%). Each month there was also a two-day celebration at the full moon (Poya days), often with a religious procession. Our native "house boy" and gardener was obviously affected psychologically on the full moon "Poya" days, because he became depressed and of little use around the household on those days.

I learned to ask permission first and offer some gratuity, each time I tried to photograph a snake charmer or elephant (Fig. 78) on the street. Some folks were performing to get gratuities, as was the case with a gardener in the Royal Botanical Garden in Peradeniya. Each day the young man had a large live scorpion on a thread, walking freely on his breast. After taking a picture, I purchased the performing scorpion, which ended up in an alcohol jar for our Virginia Tech Collection. Soon I learned that I could catch my own scorpions under the lights of our porch. The scorpions came for the insects attracted to the porch lights, only to be caught and eaten by the scorpions. I learned to use my readily available eating fork and spoon to catch them, when periodically inspecting the porch light area during our long supper. I just stuffed these in my waiting alcohol jars.

While visiting the "gem city" Ratnapura, where precious and semiprecious gems are mined, I admired the workmen while they dug in the bottom of dangerously deep pits. Only a bamboo stick frame provided some protection against burial under the wet soil forming the tall walls of the mining pit. They gathered mud to be washed by teams with baskets in water pools to collect the gemstones — ruby, garnet, amethyst, tourmaline, sapphire, topaz, and others. A number of street vendors tried to sell me "cut price" gemstones. I frightened them away by checking their "first class merchandise" with my own insect magnifying lens and pointing out the many faults in their stones.

While traveling to the Yala National Park in the southern dry land, I noticed mounds standing high on pastures. My closer observation revealed that these were termite mounds (Fig. 79). Because snakes hunt for them, I was discouraged from sticking my fingers into the openings on the sides of a termite "fortress".

Because of my experience during WWII in raising silkworms as a "patriotic" undertaking, I visited one of the sericultural plants in Sri Lanka to see how their mass production is organized. The Silk Authority, set up in 1976, provides silkworm eggs and mulberry cuttings, and needed facilities, and guarantees a fixed price for silk cocoons of best quality. The mulberries were planted as a hedge, making it easy

Figure 78. Elephant carrying its supper of palm leaves, in Sri Lanka.

to sheer off the new growth shoots to feed the worms. Large wooden trays layered on racks provide the rearing surface for the worms. Large paper sheets, each with a different sized round hole, provided the needed layers to easily separate the worms from their old, chewed up plant stems and droppings. Each cocoon is dropped in boiling water to separate the silk

Figure 79. Termite mound built over a tree trunk at Yala National Park, Sri Lanka.

strand that is between 800 to 1200 meters long. The strands of 10 cocoons are drawn together and reeled. The twisted yarn is then woven into cloth. The items still manufactured from silk are scarves, saris and dresses, and men's ties.

Nothing is wasted in this industry! The left-over silk waste or floss is used in carpets and rugs. The pupae are considered a delicacy in Japan and Korea, where those are eaten raw. But pupae could be used in fishmeal for its 51 % protein and 28 % oil content. It is also an ideal base for perfumes and soaps. I learned why many ladies' faces are "silky" smooth.

On the way to the highlands and Nuwara Eliya, I admired the waterfalls and the many tea plantations where Tamil women, dressed in saris, were picking the young tea leaves and shoots and throwing them into wicker baskets over their backs. They earned about US$1.00 per day in 1979 — now it's closer to $2.00. The English colonialists introduced to the highlands all the luxuries which they enjoyed at home: trout fishing, golf courses, and tennis courts as well as such vegetables as cabbage, potatoes, and beets. The local luxurious hotels, as their former clubhouses, attest to the lifestyle of the early rulers of Sri Lanka. A beautiful botanical garden with many tree-ferns at Haksala, near Nuwara Eliya, provided many scale insect samples for me.

In the lowlands black water buffaloes and many elephants are put to work. The buffaloes play a major role in paddy (rice) cultivation, irrigation, and even brick making. They also provide small quantities of a rich milk that is made into curd, a favorite food of the natives. Besides their hides, their manure is also well utilized. Farmers often give a head or two of Buffalo as part of the dowry, when children are married

After visiting in Sri Lanka, I realized that coconut trees are the most widely utilized tropical trees. The coconut juice is a good drink, and the nut meat is used in many ways and is exported. The thick nut shells are excellent fuel, but often are carved by local artists into art pieces or utensils. The large leaves of the co-

conut tree can not only be used for roofing material, but also as animal feed (Fig. 78). A strong rope is made from coconut husk. The trunk is used as lumber for construction. A milky nectar is collected from the flowers to ferment and prepare the local beverage, the "toddy". I admired the toddy tappers, who climbed the tall trees with the skill of a monkey. In some coconut groves two coconut husk ropes provided aerial bridges between the trees, to save the toddy tapper's energy by eliminating climbing up to each tree.

While visiting forested areas in the Wilpattu National Park, I found natives gathering firewood to be used not only in their households, but to make charcoal to be sold on the market. It is an unfortunate practice which, without close supervision, has resulted in mass deforestation of Sri Lanka. It started out, according to the local experts, when the price of kerosene, used in their small cooking stoves, went up manyfold, around 1982, and most people could not afford it any longer.

Because of frequent rains farmers often used sidewalks and roadsides to dry their rice and black pepper crops on canvases. For cultivation they neatly terraced hillsides and irrigated their crops as needed. Although two monsoons supply most of the annual rainfall (between 25 to 200 inches) in some areas, long drought periods are a regular occurrence and irrigation is essential.

My favorite garden that I frequented, even for eating my brown bag lunch there, was formerly called the "Royal Botanical Garden", located in Peradeniya next to our University. It was established in 1821, occupying 60 hectares with more than 4,000 plant species in 1979. Many of the giant, 150+ year old trees provided unique scale insects for my vials. I made repeated visits to the orchid house, to the cacti and other xerophytic plant collections, to the fernery and bamboo collection, and to the medicinal and spice gardens. The Royal Palm Avenue with its majestic Royal palm rows on both sides of the Avenue provided an unforgettable sight.

Because of my faculty status next door, I had a free pass from the Management. Except for Dr. E.E. Green, who had come 80+ years before, I was the first "bug man" interested in their scale insects. So I provided consultation to the Management about some scale insect infestations reaching a dangerous level.

In the botanical garden I found mealybug colonies under leaf shelters built by weaver ants, probably an *Oecophyla* species. These ants "milk" the mealybugs for their honeydew; in exchange, the ants protect the mealybugs from excessive sun, rain, and natural enemies with a shelter made from leaves. Because the working adult ants don't have the needed silk glands to produce adhesives for gluing the leaves together, they pick up their male larvae in their mouths (between mandibles). These small white maggots produce the needed "glue" to make silk strands, which, in the case of female larvae, are used in the making of a silk cocoon for pupation. So male larvae are used as a "tooth paste tube". The adult ants induce their larvae to release the "glue" to tie together the leaves in making the protective shelter for their "cows". The ant larvae are also fed with a mixture made of honeydew produced by the mealybugs. After such unique observations, no one can say to me that studying natural history is not an exciting endeavor!

A beautiful large scarab (dung beetle) provided entertainment for us as we walked across a cattle-grazing meadow one afternoon. The one-inch-long beetles were making balls from aged cow dung by working in teams of two (a male and female). The balls were rolled by the two insects (Fig. 80) to a spot soft enough to dig a hole for it. They then lowered the ball down to the bottom of the newly dug hole. The female laid an egg on it, and then they filled the hole back up with the freshly dug soil. What a job, involving both parents, to produce replacements for themselves! The eggs hatch and each dung ball provides enough nourishment for the full development of a larva, which pupates in the soil and, after transforming into a beetle, digs his/her way out from the soil, to

Figure 80. A ball of cow dung rolled away by two dung beetles, to be used as food for their progeny (Sri Lanka).

find a mate for life, copulate and "roll" their lifecycle farther.

Our beds in Sri Lanka always had a canopy to hold up the mosquito net that was a requirement for us to survive. Before getting into bed, we used a flashlight to inspect the inside of our enclosure for mosquitoes that often hid there, when careless housekeepers left it open during the day. On fieldtrips we often used a mosquito repellent. I also carried a vial of salt to dislodge leeches that attached themselves to our skin. To avoid drinking the local water while on trips, we usually had our driver purchase coconuts for us from the villagers, and he opened them when needed. This way a safe water supply was assured for us.

I could never get our driver or our technician to show up before 9 o'clock in the morning. They were easy-going fellows who had not had a steady job before that required starting on time. I wanted to avoid the mid-day heat combined with high humidity; thus I usually wanted an 8 o'clock start. Except for their tardiness, the two young men, who had assisted other U.S. scientists, did a good job for the project. Later, one of them, Lalith, came to the United States for graduate studies and contacted me.

We visited a number of areas, including two National Parks, Yala and Wilpattu, and collected scale insect samples along with some other insects. The catch was preserved dry or in alcohol and periodically sent for processing by specialists around the world, but mainly in the United States. Tili did the book-keeping for our crew, and on our return she received commendation from the Smithsonian officials for her most detailed professional accounting.

Our insect-collecting trips lasted about three weeks, and gave me a good cross section of the country. Because of the long dry season in some parts of Sri Lanka, large water reservoirs called "tanks", were built during the reigns of a number of old-time native kings. During our visit, five major projects were under way to divert and dam rivers, such as the Mahaweli, for new irrigation systems and to generate electricity. A lot of dynamiting was needed, so experts were sent from Sweden. Each major western country had sent some help to assist the newly elected Sri Lankan government and its people. The previous Marxist government was assisted by the Communist Block. The problem, we have realized, was that there was no central coordination for the many "do-gooder" groups from foreign countries. I ran into entomologists sent from three western countries, but none of us knew who was doing what. That could partly be explained by having the entomological work overseen by seven different ministries of the government. My early work resulted in about 300 samples of scale insects and hundreds of other small creatures.

After three weeks full time on the Smithsonian (PL - 480) Project, we took the train and moved from Colombo to Peradeniya near Kandy, to start my teaching through the AED (Academy of Educational Development) Program. To assist the entomology courses at the Agricultural University in Peradeniya, I duplicated 1,500 color slides and took them with me as a gift to their biology department. For their University library, I sent ahead several boxes of entomology books and bulletins, which on my arrival were still unsorted in a corner of their library.

Bob Pienkowski and I were jointly teaching a course in biological control of insects. We also consulted with faculty and students, and I had a few talks on how to organize their everyday work to be more successful in the profession, and on my experience at an agricultural university behind the Iron Curtain. I believe some Marxist students did not like my latter topic. I also made some professors unhappy when I introduced student evaluation of the course. Such a practice was unheard of at that time in Sri Lanka. But we were encouraged to introduce innovations in our teaching. So I did.

For field practice, we took our class in biological control to an Open Prison Farm where no chemicals were used against pest insects. Surely the convicts earned their keep plucking the insects from their field crops by hand. They were pleased to learn about our interest in non-chemical controls. So we exchanged notes, and our group was treated by the convicts with the juice of freshly harvested coconuts. Our smokers reciprocated with some cigarettes.

The American director of the AED Project in Sri Lanka called the old invited professors from the USA his "technicians"-. I believe that classification did not go well with most of us, who left behind our technician staff when accepting the work there.

The American faculty often visited the close-by city of Kandy, considered the cultural and spiritual center of this island country. Kandy attracts each year the largest crowds for the festival centered around the Temple of the Sacred Tooth (Buddha's) Relic. As a member of the Lions International, I was invited to the local Lions Club's monthly meeting with a variety dinner prepared by the wives of the members and served in a social club. Besides the usual sight-conservation efforts, the local club's programs included the free distribution of new tea plant varieties that were superior to the old cultivars.

On the roads leading to Kandy, I noted piles of big rocks along the roadside at every quarter mile distance, and a woman breaking the rocks with a hammer into gravel-sized chunks for road repair. Sometimes these women built a shelter from twigs for their small children as protection against the intense sun rays.

A long marriage proposal column in a Sunday Colombo newspaper caught my eye. Usually the parents or other relatives of young men and women make a real effort through the newspaper ads to find suitable matches for their "charges". Besides the age and physical description of the individual, it is almost standard to include records on ethnicity, caste, religion,

Figure 81. A rock painting from the Fifth Century (A.D.) at the Sigiriya religious shrine in Sri Lanka.

level of education, profession, employment, dowry (for girls), assets in real estate, cash, bank deposits, gold, jewelry, and cars. Often non-smoker and teetotalist habits are also listed. Almost all interested matchmakers required a copy of the individual's horoscope. With such a detailed and careful selection process, I am sure that their divorce rate is far below that of couples in western countries...

Close to the port city of Trincomalee our group spotted a local Tamil man carrying a giant (probably 6–7 lbs) lobster. I asked our driver to stop, so I could take a picture. He hesitated, but did so. After taking a photograph, I asked the young man where was he taking the lobster. He said to the hotel in town to sell it. So we gave him a ride, because we were going there also. I asked him how much he wanted for the lobster. He quoted a price. So after some bargaining with the help of my reluctant Sinhalese crew, who did not want me to purchase from a Tamil, I paid for the lobster, and the fisherman happily walked back to his village. The cook at the hotel fixed the lobster with some trimmings for the four of us that evening. I never in my life ate so much tasty lobster meat. It was a once-in-a-lifetime experience for us.

Our faculty group took field trips to assess the needs to improve agricultural production in Sri Lanka. On one of these trips we stopped at the famous giant rock at Sigiriya. Crowned with a fortress built during the Fifth Century, the square, mountain-sized rock has religious significance and is considered a shrine. On the path to the top we stopped at a beautiful rock painting of a bare-breasted princess with her maid (Fig. 81). We also visited Anuradhapura, a city that served as a capitol for 90 kings and has the oldest tree (documented 2,200 years old), the "Sacred Bo Tree". Here I admired the dome-shaped Buddhist shrines (Dagobas) that rival the Egyptian pyramids in size.

Tili, with the other "uprooted" spouses from the United States, had a leisurely life, because our rooms were cleaned and meals cooked by the personnel of the household and hotels we stayed in. She ironed our shirts, but obviously made our household personnel unhappy for doing "their" job. Her shopping and sightseeing walks had to be completed before lunch because in the Kandy area, as a rule, a heavy shower came down in the afternoon. We had no cars of our own, so we had to ask the Program Director one day in advance to provide the next day's transportation to the city or nearby areas. A lot of books were borrowed from the libraries and read by most of us. Also, some spouses found crocheting a good pastime activity, while artist Joni Pienkowski, Bob's wife, made free portraits for our hotel personnel and their family members. Frequent tea parties and other get-togethers made the time for foreigners easier to pass. Many visitors purchased batiks of brilliant colors and with most unusual designs. I brought home teak-wood carvings that have ornamented our living room ever since. Tili wrote many detailed Christmas letters to our relatives and friends while I collected and preserved insects wherever and whenever it was possible.

After my return to the United States, I concluded that our government's effort to assist Sri Lanka with its development and modernization of agriculture, to be able to provide enough food for its citizens, was only partially successful. After obtaining a graduate education with M.S. and Ph.D. degrees from the U.S., many Sri Lankan faculty and researchers did not return to their country to help achieve the goals set in the AED Program. Those who were Tamils were afraid to go back after the ethnic fighting erupted in Sri Lanka. Others found irresistible the salaries offered by UNESCO, FAO, or Saudi Arabia — often ten-fold what Sri Lanka could offer. So our AED Program provided assistance with the expertise of our trainees to many other developing countries, and only on a smaller scale to Sri Lanka.

After eight weeks in Sri Lanka, we left for Singapore. Here I took Tili to most of the places and tourist attractions I had visited in 1972. (I have described my visit to Singapore in Chapter 19.) Because our Pan-Am flight was again overbooked, we got free accommodations for a third day in Singapore. One of the unique, new places we visited was a wild tropical bird park, located in a large depression enclosed with a screen. We also enjoyed a Singapore Folklore Show, where different ethnic groups performed their national dances, ending in a live snake exhibit. Visitors could get pictures taken with select snakes around their body. We skipped the latter opportunity. We both enjoyed the clean city and the wide range of food specialties offered.

Our next three-day stop was in Japan, after changing flights in Hong Kong. While waiting in Hong Kong for our flight to Tokyo, we ran into a number of tired-out Vietnamese refugee families waiting for a flight to the United States.

My three Japanese colleagues — Drs. Kawai, Takagi, and Tamaki — took one-day turns to serve as our local guides. From Tokyo we were taken north by a fast train to the Research City of Tsukuba. There we moved into their hostel for visiting scientists, with very reasonable rates for a room with breakfast. This new city was landscaped by transplanting full-sized trees and shrubs, something I had never seen before but applauded. One of the 50 research institutes built in this city was the Tropical Fruit Research Institute, which I visited. After a colored slide show, we were given a guided tour, which introduced us to the research projects and facilities. Among other projects, they were working on a number of pest scale insect problems that interested me very much. Their laboratories, insectaries, and greenhouses were equipped with the most modern facilities. I could compare this complex with that of the Agricultural Research Service of the U.S. Department of Agriculture, in Beltsville, Maryland.

For the next two days we stayed in the Keio Plaza Hotel, considered medium priced at $82 per night for two with breakfast. I had never before paid such a high price for a hotel room. But the accommodations were excellent. Dr. Takagi took us to the major tourist attractions in Tokyo, which included the Imperial Palace Gardens and a Shinto Shrine. He also took us to a restaurant where we had to remove our shoes, sit on pillows on the floor, and drink sake while the delicious variety of Japanese cuisine including sukiyaki was prepared individually in front of us. For evening entertainment we signed up on our own for an all-night city tour that included dinner and entertainment with traditional Japanese shows. We were also taken to a Geisha House for a unique show where the Geishas wore fascinating kimonos.

From our high hotel window we had a great view of the picturesque Mt. Fuji and a wide section of the city. Just next to our hotel a new sky-scraper was under construction. I enjoyed observing the busy construction workers. It gave me the impression of an ant-colony at work. There were no breaks, no idle workers, and even the supervising foreman pitched in with the manual work of his crew. Their work ethic must be among the highest in the world. I have found similarity in work ethic with the free Chinese construction workers observed in Singapore. Now I compared those folks with the work ethic observed in Communist countries, where it was common to see 4-5 workers chatting and leaning on the shovels, while watching the 6th person taking a turn at working. I concluded that if the vast Chinese work forces were put to production with built-in incentives and the help of Japanese know-how and capital, the western countries would lose many of their export and home markets. Most of our textile and electronics industries, clothing and shoe-production, have shrunk to the lowest level ever. Some department stores I visited recently were filled with mass-produced,

poorer quality goods that are manufactured abroad, especially in Oriental countries; because they are cheaper, they sell well in the United States. Unfortunately, our import-export laws are out of balance and in favor of foreign nations. Often there are lopsided restrictions against our export products entering many countries. No other nation in the world, except the United States, would allow former government officials, with marketing know-how and government connections, to lobby for foreign companies and governments.

On our last day in Tokyo, Dr. Takagi took us to an elegant snack counter where raw fish was served. We had never had it before, so we tried it. The rolled-up thin fish slices (sushi) were dipped in Soya sauce and eaten with cooked rice. It was delicious and I ate several rolls. Tili was careful, and ate only one or two such rolls. Two days after our return to Blacksburg, Tili got sick, and her physician thought that it could have been from the raw fish. I, who ate much more, had no problems. Some experts think it might only have been due to psychological differences between us.

A long flight over Alaska brought us back to New York on December 3, before our 80-day tickets expired and the winter weather set in in the Virginia mountains.

21 — Our Mediterranean Experience (April–June 1986)

Because I received invitations for lecturing and consulting from institutions and colleagues in Israel, Egypt, and Italy, I saved my annual leaves for two years, and also received approval from our Provost for an additional five weeks educational leave with pay. Therefore, I could take off for 90 days as long as it did not interfere with my teaching duties at Virginia Tech. In each of these countries I had at least two or three professional engagements. In addition, the Fifth International Symposium on Scale Insect Studies was scheduled for June 24–28, 1986, in Portici, Italy. My official invitations from two countries included paying both my and Tili's local expenses, as long as we paid for the air fare.

We arrived in Tel Aviv on Monday morning, March 31, and were taken by Yair and Yehudith Ben-Dov to the San Martin Hotel, the guest house of the Weizmann Institute, in Rehovot. Along the road, the orange groves were in full bloom, and the wonderful fragrance of the orange blossoms gave a favorable impression of our new surroundings. After a badly needed short nap we went to explore the grounds of the Weizmann Institute, which is located 14 miles south of Tel Aviv on 250 acres. In the 35 buildings it had 20 departments, 5 faculties, with the Feinberg Graduate School training about 500 scientists for M.S. and Ph.D. degrees. It included a research staff of 1,850 scientists, engineers, and technicians and about 100 long-term visiting scientists. It would make a long list to try to describe all the areas of research. It was founded by Dr. Chaim Weizmann in 1934, who became Israel's first president.

While exploring on our own among the buildings of the Institute, we were impressed in this arid area to find well-maintained lawn and flower beds; it was like walking in a park. Listed on a plaque at the front entrance of each building were the donors from around the world who had contributed toward the cost of the building. I felt I was a beneficiary of such donations, because our room and buffet breakfast cost only $20 per day.

Our local professional connections, the Ben-Dovs — also David and Mazal Rosen — did their best to make us feel welcome in Israel. The Ben-Dovs had spent a year in our home town while Yair did his sabbatical research in my laboratory during 1982–83. I had known David Rosen since 1972. He became famous for his studies on scale insect parasites, and I tried to lure him to our department for a sabbatical year.

Yair prepared a detailed printed itinerary for our visit. The first evening was spent in the Ben-Dov's home where we enjoyed a delicious dinner and were introduced to the itinerary of our visit. The next day I was taken to the Biological Control Institute of the Citrus Marketing Board in Rehovot. Four entomologists gave me a guided tour of the institute. I had never before seen such a large "factory" of scale insect parasites, to be used for biological control of citrus pests in Israel. That afternoon I gave my scheduled talk on "Adaptations in Scale Insects" to the Faculty of Agriculture in Rehovot.

At the Volcani Center in Bet Dagan, I visited with each researcher working on scale insects or their natural enemies. Local colleagues and I reported on our research projects and exchanged reprints. Apparently, the Center has one of the largest groups in the world engaged in the study of scale insects and their control. The crops to be protected included avocados, citrus, grapes, olives, dates, and some others. During the late afternoon I was given a tour of the Department of Entomology at Tel Aviv University, from where we proceeded to dinner with the Ben-Dovs.

Thursday and Friday were reserved for our visits to Jerusalem and Bethlehem. We took on our own the local bus from Rehovot to Jerusalem, after making room reservations for the first night in the Windmill Hotel, a strictly kosher establishment that cost $40.00 for a couple per night. Because they could not assure accommodations for the second night, we asked the management to find us another place for Friday night. After a number of phone calls we were told that the only place still available was in the YMCA Building. They asked Tili if we realized that this was a Christian establishment, and asked if we minded that. So, she gave her assurance that we didn't. Apparently, we were taken for Jews.

During the first long and hot day, we visited most of the Christian sanctuaries in Jerusalem. Also the Quarters for Armenian Christians, for the Muslims, and for the Jews. Since 1948 the Jewish Quarter has been rebuilt in the old architectural style. Each time we entered museums or sanctuaries, Tili's purse and my side bag were searched by the security guards. About 3,000 Armenians still lived in fortress-like quarters, built for defense in the old times. We used both the Jaffa and Damascus gates to get a feel for the Old City, which was built on top of several layers of stone construction remains, the oldest being 2,600 years old. Each group — Jews, Romans, Muslims, Crusaders, and Turks — left behind some remains of their presence. The narrow passageways of the huge bazaar gave a real Middle Eastern touch to the Old City.

The Jewish, Muslim, and Christian holy places that we visited are well described in tourist brochures, so I am not going to treat them here. But I was disappointed to see the com-

mercialization of the holy places and that different religious groups were fighting for inches of space at the sanctuaries, including several Christian denominations. I have often questioned why the three major religious groups there — Jews, Christians, and Muslims — can't live in lasting peace with each other when they all recognize Abraham (Ibrahím) as their ancestoral holy prophet, worship one God, and accept the Ten Commandments.

The YMCA hotel is centrally located on 26 King David Street, with an excellent view of the Old City. It cost us about $20 per person per day, with a good breakfast, and they never asked us about our religious beliefs. After getting oriented on our own, we signed up for both a guided city tour by bus and a visit to Bethlehem and Hebron. On the hills along our route, many peach and almond trees were in full bloom, giving a beautiful view, and bringing the spirit of spring into our hearts.

On Saturday we went to the Dead Sea area in the Ben-Dovs' car. While passing through dry rocky landscapes, we noticed a number of nomad Bedouin shepherd tents, with grazing sheep and goats. Along the Dead Sea in the Judean Desert, we stopped at a Tamarisk shrub group, and I collected my first Manna scales from the branches. The evergreen shrubs were infested with a mealybug, *Trabutina mannipara*, that produces large quantities of honeydew. Scientists believe this was the source of the manna that helped the migrating Israelites to survive under the hot and dry desert conditions. I collected enough to taste this manna myself. Yes, it was sweet enough, but I don't believe I could survive on it as long as the Israelites did. —The "manna" is a sugar-coated insect (Fig.82). The mealybugs feed head down on the twigs. Their excessive sugar-rich liquid excrement (honeydew) is expelled and covers their body by flowing downward, but soon hardens in the desert heat. Thus many layers of the honeydew cover their bodies, providing a rich source of carbohydrates, while their bodies are full of fat and proteins. If water is available, one may survive on this unique diet. I don't find conflict between the scientific fact and the

Figure 82. The "manna scale" in the Judean Desert on Tamarix *trees. Scientists believe this was the source of the manna that helped the migrating Israelites to survive in the desert. Photo courtesy of N. Borchsenius.*

Bible story, as long as believers accept the idea that God created all creatures, including the "manna scales".

Our hosts took us to the historical fortress of Masada; later, to cool off in the mid-day heat, we swam in the Dead Sea. It was a new experience to float in the 25% salt content brine, in a lake that is 300 meters below sea-level at the Ein Gedi Spa. On the way back, we were taken to Jericho, but since it was getting dark, the Ben-Dovs decided, for our safety, to leave the Palestinian town early.Our unique dinner was served at David Rosen's house. David's wife, Mazal, is from Yemen, and she prepared some specialties from that country.

Sunday we toured in Yair's car the Jordan Valley and the Sea of Galilee area in northern Israel. After visiting at Capernaum, we ate some fried St. Peter's Fish in a restaurant, run by a local Kibbutz, on the eastern shores of the Sea of Galilee.

I visited with a Jewish scientist, Dr. F.D. Por, who came from Transylvania and was directing the efforts for a biological survey of Israel (Fauna Palestina) at the Israel Collection of Natural History. Because of my similar interest and work in the U.S., we exchanged ideas in Hungarian. Apparently there are many Jews in Israel from Hungary and Transylvania who speak Hungarian. We were taken to a Hungarian Pastry and Expresso Shop in Tel Aviv, where we learned more about these folks who transplanted some Hungarian cuisine and customs to Israel.

That afternoon at the Volcani Center, I gave a status report with color slides on the U.S. Biological Survey effort.

Tuesday evening we flew to Cairo. Dr. Samia Nada with her husband and Professor Yahia M. Ezzat and five others greeted us on our arrival at the Cairo Airport. Tili received a beautiful flower bouquet. I was told that our meals and lodging were provided free by the government.

In our room at the Raja Hotel we found a large welcome fruit basket. Tili and I enjoyed eating all the fruits from the welcome basket that we could peel. But we also received many large and beautiful strawberries. We had been told ahead not to touch fresh fruits or other uncooked food on this trip. Now, we were faced with the dilemma of how to handle the strawberries that looked very inviting. Washing them under the faucet in local water would not solve our problem. So, Tili and I carefully peeled and then ate most of the strawberries. Our precaution paid off, because we never got diarrhea on this trip.

Our local hosts, the scientists from the Plant Protection Research Institute, took turns in consulting with me and entertaining both of us. The daily routine included taking Tili to some tourist attractions in the morning hours while I was visiting offices and laboratories and consulting with scientists and administrators. One main reason for inviting me was to assist two

Ph.D. candidates with their dissertation problems on scale insects. They needed some rare literature not available in Egypt, and also advice and verification of their species determinations.

Wednesday (April 9) was spent with courtesy visits to two Chiefs, visiting the Agricultural Museum, and consulting with the Ph.D. candidates. We were taken for a fancy lunch to the Police Club, followed by a short boat trip on the Nile.

Thursday morning I gave a talk and consulted on the scale insect research in their and my laboratory. Unfortunately, I found much duplication between research projects conducted simultaneously in Israel and in Egypt, due to the failure to exchange scientific information between workers of the two bordering countries. Apparently, scientists in Egypt were discouraged from corresponding with Israeli colleagues. My consultation was followed by visits to the Citadel and the Cairo Tower.

Friday Sherif Afifi, my former Postdoctoral Fellow, came over from Athens, Greece, to spend some time with us. Sherif was the Area Director for an American Chemical Company. He generously provided guided tours and entertainment. Sherif took us in his car from the Giza Pyramids on a desert road to Alexandria. Here we visited with his uncle's family, who had a home like a private museum and presented me with a Fez as a gift to go into my hat collection from around the world.

Sherif drove us to see the old and modern Alexandria. He took us to a Sport Club along the Mediterranean Coast, where his family had membership and a cabin. Tili and I were determined to have a swim in the Eastern Mediterranean, something we had missed while in Israel. We got into the water but found it too cold on the breeze coast. After warming up, we visited the Al Montazah Palace, the summer residence of the former royal family. It is situated on high dunes overlooking the beach. One of the main buildings housed a museum and a casino. The dinner with Sherif's relatives and local friends was served at Tikka Grill

with a beautiful view of the seacoast. We slept in the Landmark Hotel.

On Saturday, Sherif took us back to Cairo on another road, close to the Nile, along many irrigated agricultural parcels. It was an interesting sight to see donkeys walking in a circle to turn a water wheel, drawing water from a ditch to a higher irrigation channel. I admired the white-washed pigeon towers or dovecotes made from Nile mud. They stood like sugar cones near the farmhouses (Fig. 83). We spent the evening in Samia's house, where a reception was held for us and many Egyptian delicacies were served. Samia was the Director of the Scale Insect Research Laboratory.

Sunday we were taken to a Coptic Catholic mass by Mona Ghabour, one of the two Ph.D. candidates I consulted with, and her family. Mona visited my laboratory in 1992. The mass was followed by visits to the Coptic Museum and some ancient Christian sanctuaries in Cairo. For evening dinner and entertainment Sherif took us to the Gezira Sporting Club. He, as a former National Champion of Egypt in

Figure 83. Pigeon towers built from Nile mud in Egypt.

Squash, was warmly received in the Sport Clubs.

I consulted Monday morning with colleagues working on local pest problems — many of these pests being scale insects. I was also taken to the Botanical Gardens where we collected many scale insect samples. Sherif took us to the Cairo bazaar in the afternoon, and during the dark evening hours we were entertained with the show "Sound and Light" at the base of the Sphinx and the Pyramids of Giza. "The nocturnal magic of the pyramids" as it was called, was an enjoyable new experience. We learned about the ancient history of Egypt with music and sound effects while colored floodlight beams, from 850 projectors, pointed to the historical sites surrounding us. The show was nearing an end, when a sudden sandstorm forced us to leave. It was lucky that we had our sunglasses with us to provide some protection against the fine sand that settled all over us.

Tuesday I gave my second talk with color slides at the Plant Protection Research Institute, this time on "Adaptations in Scale Insects". There were many black African students in my audience. They had been taking agricultural courses in Cairo. During the afternoon we visited the Saqqara Pyramids and Memphis, followed by a chicken barbecue in a garden restaurant at the edge of the desert.

Wednesday I gave a slide-illustrated talk at the Plant Protection Research Institute on "Why Would a National Biological Survey Benefit Egypt?" For entertainment we were taken to the Egyptian Folklore Theatre, and had an Egyptian cuisine dinner provided by Professor Ezzat. Dr. Ezzat had received his Ph.D. degree from the University of Maryland, and our friendship started in the 1960s.

Thursday I assisted the two Ph.D. candidates with their scale insect projects. En route to some museums, we were shocked to see our driver taking a narrow passageway on a four-lane highway, and leading the fifth or sixth automobile column on this four-lane street. The city was over-crowded because many families moved to Cairo from the rural areas. Two of the several beautiful mosques that I still remem-

ber included the Mohamed Aly and Azhar Mosques.

For the evening, we invited colleagues, administrators, and their families to our hotel restaurant for a good-bye dinner. Tili and I wanted to express our thanks for their wonderful hospitality and to present our gifts brought from the United States.

Friday, being our last full day in Egypt, we did our last-minute shopping and visited the famous Cairo Museum where, besides many other antiquities, the fabulous Tutankhamen tomb treasures are on display. Professors Ezzat, also Samia and Mona, along with their husbands, arranged for us an evening good-by dinner on a small pleasure boat on the Nile. After dining, the beat of the music changed, to my surprise, but soon a shapely belly dancer appeared and performed for our group. She made a special effort to charm me and to induce me to dance with her. She must have been instructed to try to make me dance with her. So, after some encouragements from my dinner companions, I danced with her, "just to satisfy the expectations" of my colleagues.

Later in the evening, while in our hotel room, we learned from television that American military airplanes had bombed targets next door in Libya. That really frightened us, especially since our air flight the next day was routed close to the Libyan coast. Saturday we departed from Cairo around 3:00 p.m. and reached Rome by 9:00 p.m.

From Rome we flew to Naples. Dr. Gennaro Viggiani, the head of the Institute of Agricultural Entomology of the University of Naples, was waiting for us. He took us by car to Torre del Greco, to the Santa Teresa Hotel, located close to Pompeii. During the first few nights, we had to use every cover available, because the rooms were not heated and it was still chilly at night in mid-April.

After a few days, we moved to Ercolano, just under the Vesuvius Volcano (Fig. 84), into a furnished apartment on the fourth floor with a balcony toward the courtyard. It was a blue-collar, lower-middle-class neighborhood that gave us a chance to learn more about the ev-

Figure 84. Part of Ercolano, our town of residence under the Vesuvius Volcano.

eryday life of the Italians. It was a most densely populated neighborhood, and I was wondering how long it would last. The volcano has erupted about 50 times since Roman times, the last eruption having been in 1944.

I had a contract with Gennaro to teach a 20-lecture course on "Scale Insects of Quarantine Importance in the Mediterranean Area". He promised to pay half of my stipend on arrival and the other half after I completed teaching the course. It took five weeks for the Italian State Accounting to release the first half of my honorarium and a whole year to pay the rest. So we lived on small weekly advances from the department's slush funds. I took the bus to my working place in Portici, and usually had a free ride home, provided by Rita Marullo. Rita was one of my lab partners, with Doni Battaglia and Salvatore Marotta, while I was in Portici.

I sent, in six boxes, about 132 lbs of research bulletins from our university — the latest literature — to give to the 20 students and young faculty persons taking my course. In addition, I printed ahead of time the course outlines and handouts to complement my lectures. I realized that a number of seniors and graduate students taking my course did not know enough English to follow my lectures closely; therefore, I illustrated my topics with an overhead projector, and also had the able assistance

of Dr. Donatella Battaglia. She translated most of my English text for the benefit of the class.

I ran into problems with the departmental Xerox machine operator, who had a note on his office door that he was available for photocopying only between 10 and 12 during the five workdays. Because of my handouts-based teaching, I needed to copy more material than his limited time would allow. He claimed that his Union-approved contract made him responsible only for the two-hours work daily. Like most of the other staff members, except the telephone operator, he never returned after the long siesta. So I was caught in the middle of these restrictions, and finally asked to be able to do the copying myself. With some intervention from the chief, I was allowed to use the copier, but made the Xerox-operator unhappy.

Gennaro talked me into offering a second, intensive four-day course on scale insects just for Italian administrators and other researchers. So I went along, since he was very helpful to me. Because of the new course, I had to print even more handouts, but the course was a success. One course participant came from Spain and one late-comer was from Greece. Later, the first one, Miss Gema Perez, completed Ph.D. work on scales in our laboratory at Virginia Tech.

For two months, I was also available for consultation and advice to graduate students and faculty in Portici. In preparation for the Fifth International Symposium on Scale Insect Studies, I was asked to review and correct for English, as needed, several articles and abstracts prepared by my Italian colleagues for the Symposium in June.

The time for the symposium was approaching, and I, the initiator of the symposium series, felt uncomfortable because I wasn't seeing any pre-preparations for this special event. I quietly offered my help to the organizers, but was assured that things "will fall in place in time". I was "sitting on pins and needles" for the delays that could result in stress and last-minute chaotic haste. To avoid such stress, I always work months ahead of deadlines.

Two weeks before the meeting, a "miracle" happened in front of my eyes! The Director of the Institute, Dr. Viggiani, acted like an orchestra conductor. At his Department meeting, he told each person his/her responsibility. The building got new life, like an ant colony before rain. The hallways and stairways in our 200-year-old building were swept clean. The old dirty walls with missing plaster were covered up with tall potted plants, including palms. The posters were prepared, guiding signs for visitors were put up, the lecture rooms were spruced up. The program was finally printed. Phone calls were made to banks, civic organizations, and town halls, for sponsorships and for donations, etc. Reservations were made for buses, and for meals at restaurants and at the University cafeteria.

I was amazed! I would have never thought that there was so much hidden energy around me. I also pitched in, especially with their English texts and signs. The international meeting was a success, and the proceedings were published for free by the Department. By soliciting financial aid from a number of sponsoring businesses and organizations, Gennaro was able to reduce to a minimum the cost of the meeting for the participants, and for the group excursions. This was especially important for the symposium participants from behind the Iron Curtain: China, Hungary, Poland, and Russia.

During our free time—in the late afternoons — Tili and I explored on foot our surroundings. Because we were situated about one-third up the slopes of the volcano Vesuvius, everyday we took a different route on the roads leading down or up these slopes. So gradually we covered most of the streets and alleys surrounding Vesuvius. Later, we expanded the distance by taking a bus uphill and returning on foot, downhill.

En route we admired the many well-maintained home gardens. Every inch of the garden plots was fully utilized by growing fruits, vegetables, and flowers. Because of the long growth season, often up to four crops were harvested from the same plots. It bothered us that on the sidewalks we ran into plastic shopping bags filled with garbage. Instead of depositing garbage in cans, the "City Fathers", as I was told, disapproved the use of "unsightly" garbage cans which might ruin the outlook of this historical city; instead, they sent daily the garbage collectors to shovel up the garbage into open trucks. But overnight the wandering dogs, cats, and rats opened the bags and spilled their contents all over the walkways and roadsides, creating unsanitary conditions and breeding cockroaches, flies, and rats. I hope they have changed this practice since 1986.

The "Figaro" in the house next door used only two long scissors when cutting my hair. It took him twice as long than with regular clippers, but he got his money, because he charged twice the usual fee. So the next time I went to a regular barber to save time and money.

Tili also had some new experiences when shopping for our household. Each work day a different kind of shop was closed. The butchers, the dairy product and pastry shops, the vegetable and fruit shops, and groceries — each had a different day for keeping closed. She was looking in vain for days for sour cream for our Hungarian dishes, until an English-speaking neighbor told her that Italians don't use sour cream. Also there were bunches of last year's tomatoes hanging on the walls at the vegetable stand in May; this was a local thick-skinned variety that stores for many months. Saturday mornings diving fisherman were selling their catch from the sea bottom in large pots and pans on the sidewalks. The "catch" included all kinds of sea creatures that we have never seen on the American market. Because of the high pollution level in the nearby Bay of Naples, I abstained from trying out seafood. Our caution with the locally-caught sea creatures was justified when Tili, in a local restaurant had small mussels for topping over her pizza, instead of the usual tomato sauce. She soon got sick from eating the only partly-cooked mussels.

In Naples the Archeological Museum displayed many of the beautiful frescos, wall paintings, and ceramic and other art pieces salvaged from excavations of Pompeii and Herculeanum. This ancient city is in a beautiful location but because of overcrowding of narrow streets with too many automobiles, the air is really polluted. I was told that some cats were found dead from auto exhaust pollution in low-lying areas of downtown Naples.

Italians pay much attention to the quality of bread they eat. In our block, within 500 yards, we had three small family bakeries. The local folks will get in queue in the early morning in front of their favorite bakery to get the still warm, freshly baked, hard-crusted bread. The variety in cheeses, in fresh fruits and vegetables, the Milanese salami that tasted like the Hungarian one, and the freshly roasted chicken that provided four servings for us, made the bulk of our meals here. We "suffered" only for a few days, when many of the fresh fruits, vegetables, and dairy products were taken off the market due to the Chernobyl nuclear accident, which affected most of Europe.

I don't know how we did survive for 60 days without a telephone or TV in our small apartment! Soon we purchased a small radio so we could listen to the English language news from the American Airforce Base in Naples. In addition, the balcony gave a cross section of the everyday life in our neighborhood. Each balcony in our building was fully utilized. It was a general storage place, also a sunning area for babies and the elderly; an area to keep small pets in cages, or even rabbits for food. One

enterprising neighbor had his 20-liter (5 gallon) glass bottles lined up for his wine-making. He usually had a tasting session each evening to make sure his wine was aging in the right direction instead of becoming wine vinegar, as often happens. Each balcony had 3-4 plastic cord lines for drying the laundry and also had some flower pots or boxes over-hanging the rails. So on laundry days or when the flowers in boxes were watered, we did not dare stick our head out from our balcony, or walk on the walkway under the balconies, unless we were prepared for another "baptizing". Housewives used the balconies to transmit messages or grocery orders in small baskets lowered on a long string. Sometimes street vendors filled the baskets with the orders lowered to them in those baskets. Practical people! Because of local customs and overcrowding in apartments, some housewives on the ground level often had their gossip hours in front of their doors, while their husbands and grown-up sons stayed in sidewalk cafes and clubrooms that must have formerly been stores. Here they played games while exchanging stories. Often a cross on the wall identified them as a church-affiliated organization.

We found Italian people easy-going and warm-hearted, with much patience and helpfulness to strangers like us, who often needed guidance. We both carried pocket-sized dictionaries while in the towns. I found many similarities between the Italian and Romanian languages. I liked their phonetic, musical sounding language, and I had no problem with the pronunciation.

Our local acquaintances, the Tranfaglias and Viggianies, each invited us twice to typical Italian home dinners. These included 8 to 10 courses and lasted 3–4 hours. Antonio Tranfaglia, his wife Rosanna, and their little daughter Elena, visited us in Blacksburg during the winter of 1977. Antonio consulted in our laboratory and in Beltsville, Maryland. They enjoyed our snow-covered environment, which was new to the Neapolitan family.

Each time I was taken by car to Naples, I was frightened by the local drivers. Besides the

Figure 85. The square sign on the Island of Capri, honoring the martyrs of the 1956 Hungarian uprising.

excessive speed and frequent lane changes, the drivers normally did not stop at red lights, but after checking the cross-traffic conditions, drove through at the stop signs and red lights.

The Italians, including our neighbors, were much excited during the days of the World Soccer Championship games. Televisions were loudly broadcasting the games, and the whole town came to a stand-still close to the final matches. No taxis were available; the bus drivers had their pocket radios on. Everyone was glued to the TV at the final rounds and, when finally Italy won the "World Cup", our town folks hit the streets like a swarm of bees, singing and shouting. Groups got into open trucks and with waving Italian flags demonstrated their happiness across the city.

Tili organized for us weekend excursions to romantic and historical sites. We took boat trips to the Islands of Ischia and Capri. Both are about 80 minutes by ferryboat from the mainland. Ischia was the first Greek colony in the west. It is a health resort, due to its volcanic hot mineral springs. Its vineyards and chestnut and citrus orchards make it a green island, rare in the Mediterranean. The fascinating landscapes with rock settlements, the unique mushroom-shaped rock — Il Fungo at Lacco Ameno — the historical Aragon Castle, and the foreign artist colony were just a few of the many attractions awaiting us.

We stayed two nights in Capri at a small family hotel close to the Marina Grande, and took the local bus for excursions. We wanted to visit the famous Villa San Michele of the Swedish physician and author Axel Munthe in Anacapri, whose biography I had read and found inspirational. I can't describe his villa better than he did: "I want my house open to sun and wind and the voice of the sea, like a Greek temple, and light, light, light everywhere". A panoramic road led to the villa from the Marina Grande. We took the bus, but had to stop halfway to enjoy the unforgettable view of the Gulf of Naples and Sorrentine Peninsula. The villa is under Swedish care and is well preserved with beautiful marble columns, old Greek statues, plants, and great landscaping. Munthe's autobiography was translated into 49 languages, including Hungarian, and Tili owned a copy of it.

Every tourist has to visit the Blue Grotto, a favorite place for lovers. Visitors are taken by boat into this natural wonder, a large cave with dark blue water. We took long walks on Capri to enjoy the natural beauties and views that this island has to offer. We walked the path down to Marina Picolla to see the legendary Rocks of the Sirens, the beautiful sugarcone-shaped rocks that stick out of the azure blue sea. It's hard to imagine that wild boars had once inhabited the island when the ancient

Greeks arrived and named it after the boars (Kapros). I was really impressed when I found a small square named in honor of the 1956 Hungarian Freedom Fighters (Fig. 85).

Our favorite excursion place was Sorrento. We used the inexpensive train coming from Naples to reach this and many other attractions en route to the Sorrentine Peninsula. We found Sorrento a great place to walk, with its narrow streets to the marina areas, to enjoy the beautiful view from the Via del Capo, to do window shopping in the commercial district, and to eat an Italian meal washed down with excellent local wines. To reach some other attractions on the Peninsula, we took the bus from Sorrento to Positano and Amalfi. Each offered some distinct and memorable sights, such as the Catholic Cathedral built in the Moorish style in Amalfi (Fig. 86). A number of women bathers from Western Europe were topless on the beaches, so I closed my eyes halfway when Tili was looking at me.

Pompeii was just a few kilometers from our home, so we visited it by train, as we did several times the ancient ruins of Herculeanum. The latter was a 15-minute walk from our apartment. While inspecting the 2,000-year-old lead water pipes, I started wondering about the effect of the lead, when dissolved by a slightly acidic water, on the brains of the Roman upper-class and their rulers. Could the decline of the Roman Empire be explained by the lead pollution? If scientists have not checked the remains of the inhabitants of Pompeii (many well preserved) for lead content, it may be worth looking into, to find a scientific explanation for the strange behavior of many Roman rulers.

We visited by bus Pozzuoli and the closeby Solfatara, west of Naples. In Pozzuoli the partly submerged Temple of Serapis was a unique site with the reflection of the temple columns in the shallow sea pool (Fig. 87). There were a number of underwater archeological remains from Greek and Roman times. At Solfatara we visited the Phlegraean (Burning) Fields, with numerous extinct small craters and connected hot springs, some of them still spewing hot

Figure 86. A Roman Catholic shrine, built in the Moorish style, in Amalfi, Italy.

steam and covering the area with fine sulfur deposits.

I had to see the famous fish market at Pozzuoli. Because of the market smell, Tili declined to join me, so I did my walk with Gema Perez, who joined us for the trip. Again the variety of sea creatures the natives consumed amazed me.

After five weeks of living on meager loans, we suddenly became millionaires, at least in Liras! The first half of my stipend was finally released on a Friday afternoon, and included about three million liras (U.S. $2,000). All this in cash! There was no way to deposit it in the bank, so I had to take it all to our apartment. We were just preparing for a three-day weekend in Rome, but had been cautioned not to leave money or other valuables in the apartment. So we paid our rent for the past five

Figure 87. Columns of the Temple of Serapis in Pozzuoli, near Naples, submerged in a sea pool.

weeks, but still had to carry most of the bundles of money with us to Rome. A few bundles I packed in plastic bags and placed in the center of our large sugar or salt jars and covered with the sugar and salt. We looked like well-fed foreigners after most of the money was stuffed in our large money belts.

As it turned out, our precaution paid off in Rome. We ran into groups of small children who had been trained to empty the pockets of tourists. Inside the entry hall of the church on top of the Spanish Steps, I ran into a young American couple surrounded by these 8–10-year-old gypsy children. The children held up large pieces of cardboard, giving the impression that they were begging for money to be placed on the boards, but actually they covered their fine hands while checking the pockets of tourists.

I realized from the strange behavior of the children that they were actually cornering the couple. I asked the Americans if they still had their money. The man checked his inside coat pocket and, with a white face, confided that his billfold was missing. I demanded that the children hand it over, but they showed their empty hands and pockets. So, after repeating my command in vain, I picked up each child, turned him upside down and shook him until the billfold fell out from under the loose shirt of one of them.

After returning the billfold to the grateful couple, I asked them if we should take their case to the police on the square. They declined, happy that they got back the stolen money, and feeling no need to go further. So the children were released to continue their stealing. I noticed on the square that a tall man with typical gypsy features and mustache was keeping an eye on the children from a safe distance. Later, I was told by the Italian police that the children were brought from Yugoslavia by such unscrupulous adults, trained for stealing, and used as slaves. Because the minors have no documents on them, have no home address, and speak no Italian, they are released from the police soon after they are caught.

Before this experience, I had already become aware of some gypsy children's thievery in Naples. A group of such children were dancing on the sidewalks around me, intentionally bumping into me and trying with their small fingers to feel out the contents of my two hip pockets. So I chased them away. But in the large Naples railroad station hall, I was approached by a begging gypsy woman with a cute baby in her arms. She was asking for money to feed her baby. Basically, she wanted to find out where the tourist's billfold was kept, to alert her closeby husband or friend, where to find the money on the warm-hearted tourist. Probably many tourists, especially foreign-

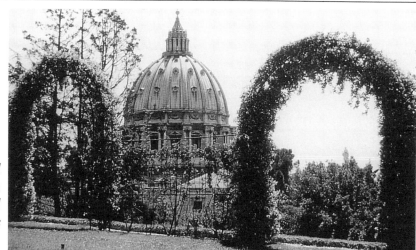

Figure 88. Trees and shrubs in the Vatican garden that provided scale insects as free souvenirs for the author.

ers, fell for her trick. After these experiences in two cities, I placed my bundles of liras under my hotel pillow each night.

There was so much to see in Rome that we took advantage of our long weekend. We visited many of the tourist attractions, especially those we had not seen before. These included the Catacombs, the Vatican Art Exhibits, and the Vatican gardens. As souvenirs from Rome, I returned to the U.S. with some unique alcohol-preserved scale insects from the trees and shrubs in the Vatican Gardens (Fig. 88). I don't think that the Pope, whose walking paths we followed, minded me depleting his scale insect colonies.

After my two courses and the Symposium ended, we took the long train ride to Budapest to visit my mother and other relatives, before returning to the United States..

Participants in my intensive (second) course on scale insects in Portici, Italy, in 1986. Photograph by Dr. Gennaro Viggiani.

22 — Transylvania Revisited (1956–96)

I had been unable to visit my relatives in Romania for 12 years (1944–56). So, when the border finally opened in 1956, I rushed there. I wanted to see my many cousins, aunts, and uncles living in Bucharest, Braşov, and Tărlungeni and at Cehețel in the County of Odorhei. The last time I had seen those in Bucharest was in 1940.

I combined my trip with two professional engagements, by arranging to visit with Dr. Aurel Săvescu, the scale insect specialist in Bucharest, with whom I developed an excellent professional cooperation. I also contacted Frederic König, a lepidopterist in Timişoara, and arranged to join him and his brother for a few days on an insect-collecting trip in the remote Retezat Mountains.

I went by train to Bucharest, where I stayed with Aunt Anna, my father's sister. I found their surroundings much changed; the close-by empty agricultural fields were now filled with tall apartment buildings. Their water came from a municipal source now, not from their own well. After 16 years apart, it was a joyful reunion with her and her two daughters, Vilma and Anna. I still treasure and use the paring knife she gave me as a gift.

They took me in a neighbor's car to see the much changed city. We went to the former Royal Palace Square (Fig. 89). We drove by some of the places I had lived, including the four-story building at 17 Maria Rosetti Street. Here, I must have shocked the mother of my childhood Romanian friend Fănel with my sudden appearance. Fănel was not there, and his mother must have been afraid to have contact with a foreigner because she would not give me her son's address.

I took the train to Constanța to enjoy a weekend at the Black Sea shore, where I rented a room in a private home. At noon, I stopped at a seashore restaurant for a drink and ordered a mug of beer that cost 3 leis; the server, "not having change" kept my 5 lei coin. I waited at a bus stop to take the bus to Mamaia. After half an hour of waiting in vain, a large truck loaded with logs stopped at the bus station. The driver offered us a ride to Mamaia. I said to myself, "What a great guy!"

We all hopped in back and sat on top of the logs. Soon the driver's assistant crawled over to us and collected the same fare that the bus ride would have cost. I was later told that this type of enterprise is common now in Romania. Because of the low salaries, drivers of state-owned vehicles, if asked, will take passengers on their route, but expect a payment for it.

I was surprised to find my first nudist beach at Mamaia. The next surprise waited for me in Braşov. Here, I was attracted, by its smell, to a shish kebab meal in a restaurant. The meat was impaled on a vertically-rotating metal skewer, while it was roasted over hot flames. I asked the person roasting the meat how much a plate would cost. He said, "It's 5 leis, but don't go to the cashier for a ticket; I'll serve you a special plate for the same price if you pay me directly." So, to avoid poor service, I paid him, and got a special plate of my favorite dish.

On the local buses, my fare was often collected without my being given a ticket. Apparently, this was how the poorly paid employees made up the difference in their income. I had lived through a baksheesh system as a young boy in Bucharest; the conditions had gotten worse under the socialist system.

My relatives treated me well in each place. We exchanged gifts, but I felt bad for not having local currency; I was not able to take them

Figure 89. Part of the former Royal Palace, now a museum, in Bucharest, 1974.

to a restaurant because I was not allowed to bring Hungarian currency into Romania, nor could I exchange money in Budapest for Romanian currency. Therefore, I was forced to improvise. I had learned ahead of time that, because of the government-imposed austerity program, no bijou items were manufactured or imported into Romania. So, in Budapest I purchased a lot of costume jewelry, cheap necklaces, bracelets, brooches, etc., to exchange for Romanian currency. I felt like an early explorer in Africa, loaded with glass beads for the natives. I spread out my wares on a dining table in a school cafeteria where teachers were attending a conference. I was overwhelmed by a happy crowd of female teachers. I sold in a few minutes my entire stock and finally had some spending money.

I met the Königs in Timişoara, and we travelled by train until we were close to the Retezat Mountains, then continued on foot, each of us with a backpack containing food and insect

collecting gear. Luckily, we found an empty tourist shelter. Although primitive, it was useful for the few nights we spent there. Being the youngest, I volunteered to find the nearby shepherd family and ask them to sell us two liters of cow milk each morning while we were in the area. I found them and made the deal, and bought some milk and fresh sheep cheese for our next meal. One morning I went for the milk and found the shepherdess in the act of straining our fresh milk before pouring it into our milk jug. I was shocked to discover that she used the pulled-out front of her undershirt for straining our milk. The Königs just laughed when I told them about the straining process. They told me we were safer this way than without it, because we avoided floating manure pellets in our milk. So I insisted on boiling the milk from then on, because I was not sure how often our shepherdess changed her undershirts while up on the mountain for several months in the summer.

Second Trip, 1974

My second trip back to Transylvania was in a rented Renault 5 car with Tili and Eva in 1974. We started with a visit to Bucharest to see my relatives, who gave us a city tour, with some picture taking (Fig. 90).

My "girls" had a hard time adjusting to the Romanian toilets on this trip. Eva had not seen a toilet before where there was only a hole in

the floor, even at the famous former Royal Castle in Sinaia. The two such toilets for the tourists were "filled to the brim", stank badly, and were unusable.

The castle, located in the mountains, just before entering Transylvania, with its artistic wood carvings is a unique tourist attraction (Fig. 91), and it is a shame not to clean and upgrade

Figure 90. The Museum Atheneul Roman in Bucharest with my family and three relatives in the foreground. From left: niece Anna, her son Ion, Eva, Tili, and Uncle János Nagy.

the toilets, even if it meant charging for their use, like in other close-by countries. We lost our appetites after the foul-smelling toilets of restaurants in the Romanian lowlands at Turnu Severin and Craiova.

Eva was shocked to find in Odorheiul Secuiesc, where most of the people are ethnic Hungarians, that the menu of the Main Square Hotel Restaurant was written only in Romanian, German, and French. It was the same way in Cluj, where the waiters were not even allowed to speak with us in Hungarian, their native tongue.

While in the Odorheiul Secuiesc restaurant, we were seated at a table close to the entrance door. Soon, a well-dressed Gypsy family arrived inside the entrance and waited patiently to be seated. The waiters, after discovering them, immediately placed "Reserved" signs on all the empty tables, and told the Gypsy family, "All the tables are taken or reserved." Although the tables stayed empty for over one hour, the family was not seated.

Eva witnessed the event and was shocked by the treatment given to the Gypsy family. So, when we were close to leaving, Eva cleared one half of our table and invited the Gypsies to be seated, because we would be leaving soon. I was proud of my "Americanized" daughter.

Unfortunately, besides the ethnic Hungarians, the Gypsies of Romania, who make up the largest ethnic population (2.5 to 4 million), are also badly discriminated against.

In Braşov we wanted to rent a room in the Postavaru Hotel, which was rated first class. After seeing the poorly equipped rooms, we just gave up on checking in. So we showed up one day earlier than expected at Uncle Zsiga's house in Tărlungeni. The family, in our honor, had just finished repainting the house. My relatives in Tărlungeni had never seen my family before, so there were many joyous family gatherings. To be able to satisfy the invitations from each family, we accepted from each only one meal: breakfast, lunch, or dinner. It turned out that each meal was a 4–5 course dinner that did not help our shape. The Changos have an ancient custom of almost forcing on guests more and more food.

Next-door to Uncle Zsiga's house, lived my cousin Gyula (Foris), still a bachelor at age 53. We had not seen each other for 18 years. It was a joyous reunion, but I had to remind him of how he had treated me as a child, when I spent my summer vacation in the town. Gyula — six years my elder — played jokes on me, the 12- year-old city boy from Bucharest, whenever he had the chance. One of these jokes I

Figure 91. Castle Peleş at Sinaia, Romania.

never forgot. He offered to show me the afternoon moon through his home-made "telescope". I was still in my swimming trunks after a good swim in the river. Gyula had his "telescope" put together from old stovepipes, tied to a tall step ladder. At the low end, he had attached a black cloth that covered my head while I was looking through his "telescope" and complaining that I could not see the moon, only a small section of the blue sky.

But he insisted that I need to have patience and had to look longer and harder while he was re-directing his "telescope". So, while my head was under the black cloth, he climbed to the top of the stovepipe and poured down over my face a bucketful of water. It stained my face and body with the soot accumulated in the old stovepipes. I got angry for the unexpected black shower and shook my laughing cousin off the ladder. I had to return to the river to wash off the black soot before my grandfather discovered me.

I made a hit with my Polaroid camera in the towns I visited. Many of the young children were lined up to have their first color portraits taken. I was told that I could have made a bundle of money if I had brought a suitcase full of in-

stant-film for Polaroid shots. I found it practical to take Polaroid pictures, so I could present the pictures right away to each family instead of mailing them later.

While in Cluj, I had admired the beautiful statue of the Hungarian King Matthias. This statue is a rare exception that was still standing from Hungarian times but kept by the Romanian authorities because Matthias was considered to have had, in part, Romanian ancestry. Close to the Main Square is located a statue depicting the ancient story of the babies Romulus and Remus being fed by the mother wolf. Our local Hungarian guide told us that this statue actually symbolizes the truth about the "Romanian-Hungarian fraternity" in Transylvania. The baby in front, Romulus, that is shown having reached the nipple and is suckling is the Romanian brother, while the other, Remus, who is depicted as struggling, but never reaching nourishment, is the Hungarian brother.

Romulus killed his twin brother Remus and founded Rome in 753 BC. I just hope that while building the Great Romania, the ethnic Hungarians will be spared from extinction.

Third Trip, 1977

My third trip back to Transylvania was during the summer of 1977. This time I visited alone the Sekler's region: Odorhei, Lupeni (Farkaslaka), Corund (Korond), Sovata(Szováta), Cehețel, Harghita Mountain, Lacul Rosu (Gyilkos-Tó), and Tusnad. At one of the cabin rental places I ran into a young ethnic Hungarian, who had received his Seminary education to become a Roman-Catholic priest, but because of his political views, the government refused to give permission for his ordination into the priesthood. Apparently, Ceaușescu's regime had the last word on the ordination of priests in Romania.

There were obvious shortages in meat products and industrial goods. Most of the shelves in the stores were empty. The bread from the state bakeries was inexpensive, but of such inferior quality that my relatives used it to feed their chickens and pigs. This is what socialization of farming brought to this rich agrarian country.

I took the ancient bus from Odorhei to Cehețel, where I found only one distantly related person still living: Uncle Áron Kovács. His deceased wife Ilona was my mother's half sister. His children were all away in the cities. He was pleasantly surprised to see me after 26 years. He insisted on coming with me around the town, wherever I visited old-time friends and neighbors.

I was also surprised that all the persons I visited, although very pleased to see me, never invited me inside (Fig. 92), but instead talked to me from their doorsteps. Uncle Áron later told me the reason for the strange behavior of the villagers. If a foreigner entered a private home, the visited person had to report immediately in person to the Police Station where they would be interrogated about the talk with the foreigner. This was why Áron insisted on staying with me throughout my visit, so that only he, and none of the persons I visited who talked to me only in their yard in his presence, would need to report to the Police. Also, it was a regulation that foreign visitors could not be housed in private dwellings, even if they were relatives. So, I made sure to leave town before dark to avoid sleeping in Áron's home.

In 1977, my Transylvanian relatives were still lacking the opportunities to travel, even to the other Socialist countries like Hungary. Romania had become more and more a closed country under Ceaușescu. I felt sorry for the entire population. Some escapes from the "Worker's Paradise" made headlines in the West. One of these was about a crop-dusting plane loaded with 2 or 3 dozen escapees that flew so close to the ground that neither the Romanian nor the Hungarian military radar systems could detect its presence until it landed in Austria.

My cousin Zoltán worked for 14 years under the Ceaușescu System as director of the area's consumers cooperative, in Tărlungeni. He told me how the slogan and orders received from Bucharest were acted on. It reminded me of the same system we had in Hungary for a shorter period. The idea was that the peasants and the industrial proletariat work together in

Figure 92. A Sekler farmer's general use room.

Figure 93a. View of Tărlungeni, with the Romanian Eastern Orthodox Church.

Figure 93b. The Hungarian Lutheran Church, and part of the town of Tărlungeni. At the upper right corner is the river where my grandfather lost two children by drowning.

close cooperation to build the glorious Socialist Communist future. The factory workers produce the industrial goods needed by the farming peasants, while the peasants produce the food and fiber needed by the factory workers. Farming peasants had to turn in for every sack of cement, every 100 bricks, and other industrial merchandise some eggs, chicken, etc. Because most of the peasants were not producing chicken or eggs, etc., they went to the close-by city and purchased these to be turned in to their village depot in order to qualify to purchase needed industrial goods. Cousin Zoltán packed the thousands of eggs, and hundreds of chicken and rabbits, and carried them to the nearby city, Brașov, and distributed these to the state stores, as the faithful contribution of the peasantry to the feeding of the city dwelling industrial workers. Next week the entire circle started over again.

Ceaușescu liked to visit the factories and the state-owned and cooperative farms. These visits were anounced several months in advance. For his visits and talks, large crowds were herded together to loudly cheer and clap during his stay. Although only 10 to 20% of the crowd cheered and clapped, many microphones were set to high volume and close together to produce soaring cheers when the events were televised the following evening.

In advance of his arrival, beautiful and fat livestock would be shipped in railroad cars from special state farms, to be displayed when Ceauşescu visited the local farms, so he could get a good impression about the prosperity of the visited farm, instead of displaying the poor quality livestock actually produced in the local state or cooperative farm. As soon as the visit was over, the borrowed livestock was returned to the lender or shipped directly to the town to be visited next by Ceauşescu. Villagers told me that when Ceauşescu's train was to pass their village, the local Party boss ordered the people to place rows of already harvested cabbage heads in the nearby fields, so that Ceauşescu could witness the prosperity of that farming town. Some folks think that Ceauşescu knew

about the manipulations behind his back, but this way he could play the innocent who was misguided by the people around him. He wanted to look like the friend of the common people.

I don't think that the people of Romania suffered more, even during World War II, than they did under Ceauşescu's brutal dictatorship. The sufferings were even worse for the ethnic minorities. When Ceauşescu and his wife were executed during the 1989 popular uprising, few people in Romania shed tears for them. The overthrow of the government started in the multi-ethnic city of Timişoara (Temesvár) in the southwest corner of Transylvania (Banat). It was started with the passive resistance of an ethnic Hungarian Calvinist minister, László Tökés, now Bishop of the Oradea (Nagyvárad) Diocese.

Fourth Trip, 1995

My fourth trip was only for one week during November, 1995, to visit relatives in Braşov and in Tărlungeni. My cousin Stephen Csere's son, András, provided free transportation. But, because of the poor road conditions, his car broke down and I had to return by train to Budapest.

I visited the Chango Lutheran Cemetery in Tărlungeni, located on a hill overlooking the town. The Romanian population is concentrated on the upper end (Fig. 93a) with their colorful church, while the Chango-Hungarians live in the lower end, close to the river (Fig. 93b).

I was pleasantly surprised to see the quantity of food, fruits, and vegetables available at the Central Market in Braşov, although the prices were high for the natives. The University students were just demonstrating on the Main Square, demanding tuition-free education, as they were doing in Hungary at that time. I enjoyed visiting the beautiful Lake St. Anna. This time I even found some wastebaskets on the shores, the lack of which I had regretted on my last visit. Still, there were no toilets around the lake for visitors, so tourists, when the need arose, had to visit the bushes.

My experience in the two restaurants we visited was a disaster. I wanted to take my niece Lencsi and her family to a fancy restaurant patronized mainly by tourists. So, we stopped at the Hotel Carpaţia, near Lake St. Anna, and all of us ordered fried chicken liver. The liver apparently was never inspected by the kitchen personnel, or they did not care. It was bitter from the bile of the gall bladder which must have been allowed to spill over the liver.

The next time I thought, we cannot go wrong with pizza, which Lencsi's family had never tried before. So we found a pizzeria under a hotel on the Main Square in Braşov. Our pizza was fresh-made in an oven. I had never before seen a pizza where the dough was folded over the top to make a closed pocket with the ingredients inside, so I was anxious to try it. Unfortunately, after opening the "pocket pizza", we found the dough cover to be underbaked and raw inside. When I pointed this out to the pizza maker, he just shrugged his shoulders. Apparently, he had never mastered the art of pizza-making or did not care to prepare an edible pizza. From then on, we avoided eating in fancy restaurants.

Figure 93c. Unitarian minister in Cehețel cutting hay for his milking cow.

It was close to All Saints' Day, so all my relatives in Tărlungeni were busy cleaning and weeding cemetery plots of dead relatives. A lot of *Chrysanthemum* flowers were transplanted to these plots. On the evening of All Saint's Day, thousands of candles are lit by the villagers in commemoration and honor of deceased relatives. The villagers spend most of the evening in the cemetery praying for the souls of their relatives and for their resurrection.

November usually brings frost to the mountain communities of Transylvania, so I helped to take from the yard to the root cellar the houseplants, such as Oleanders and Geraniums, that needed to overwinter indoors. I found, already stored in the root cellar, the potato crop to last for nine months, root vegetables layered in sand, cabbage heads, onions and garlic, a large crock with sauerkraut, and Batul apples mixed with straw on a shelf. On the outdoor walls string bags filled with freshly harvested walnuts were hanging to dry.

When I was taken by car to Brașov, I saw many Gypsy families digging for leftover potatoes in the large potato fields already harvested by the local cooperative farm. The town's Gypsy community still lived in the same area as they had 60 years before, on the outskirts of the village near the riverbank. These people took seasonal farm jobs, served as musicians

for the community, and some used to trade horses — now it's used automobiles. A number of the families made a living for generations by crafting household items such as large pails, spoons, etc. from wood, while others became expert tinsmiths; they patched holes in pots and pans for housewives when I lived there. Some of the women are expert fortune-tellers and use a special deck of long cards, the Tarot, for this purpose. Some are just "palmists."

They love their children and usually have large families. Many of them still live in shack-like houses, but a number built spacious brick houses — as in Tărlungeni (Fig. 94) — at the end of the villages; those in cities live in apartment houses. They are known to have their own close-knit community, often governed by a chosen elder, the Vajda. They came to Europe many centuries ago from Northern India in horse-drawn wagons. They wandered for the first time to Transylvania during the Turkish wars. They call themselves Romas, and besides the language spoken by the country they live in, many also speak their own Romani language.

When I was a child, it was common to see Gypsy caravans on the country roads. They normally had a horse-drawn wagon with a semi-circular woven wicker roof that kept travellers

Figure 94. Masonry houses owned by Gypsies in Tărlungeni, Transylvania.

cool in the summer; in case of rain, a tarpaulin over it provided protection from a downpour. The horse was often so slim that its ribcage showed. A dog on a rope was usually attached to the rear of the wagon, while the family with all their belongings was jammed into the wagon.

The women walked barefooted until the first frost. Their heads were normally covered with a red scarf; they had large metal earrings and a necklace full of silver coins; their long, shiny black hair was braided. They wore a colorful blouse, a reddish pleated skirt, and usually several aprons, each with large pockets; for shopping or begging for food, they had a side bag.

To make sure who was "wearing the hat in the family", or was the boss, their men always wore a black felt hat that had a dome-shaped top and a bent, broad rim. They wore a white shirt with the sleeves rolled up in the summer, a vest with shiny metal buttons, and black trousers with the legs tucked inside their tall black boots. They had long mustaches, usually pointed at the tips. Their leader, or Vajda, usually carried a silver-handled walking stick. Their children, until about 5 years old, were kept naked in the summer (a practical solution, so no diapers were needed), or they just wore a large old shirt.

They usually set up camp for the night just outside the villages and prepared their meals at an open fire. I was told as a child about their recipe for roasted chicken. It started: "First you steal two chickens..." Surely the villagers had

their prejudice against the Gypsys; unfortunately it is still there. It reminds me of the prejudice instilled in us as youngsters, so beautifully expressed in the song, starting: "You have to be taught..." by Rogers and Hammerstein in the film *South Pacific*.

Some of the former Socialist Governments in Central and Eastern Europe tried to permanently settle Gypsies in city apartments and provide jobs and educational opportunities for their children, with some success. Now, because of the chauvinistic campaign against the 2.5 to 4 million Gypsy minority in Romania, many tried to leave the country, and the government welcomed such moves.

Unfortunately, the future of ethnic Hungarians is not much better. The only Hungarian university, Bolyai at Cluj, was combined a long time ago into Babeş-Bolyai, with only some departments providing instruction in Hungarian. The church-affiliated High Schools that provided training in Hungarian were nationalized and converted into Romanian schools, with no hope during the recent privatization campaign to be returned to the Hungarian-speaking ethnic community. There were Hungarian language schools in Bucharest in the 1930s — I attended one — but I could not find any the last time I visited there. Why can't the Romanian government follow the Swiss example in the treatment of their ethnic minority, the Rhaetiens, as given in the Addendum here?

Fifth Trip, 1996

On October 2, 1996, at 10:15 a.m. I took the Rapid Romanian train ALUTUS from Budapest and arrived in Braşov by 9:30 p.m. I had no company in my 1st class compartment. I had always traveled 2nd class before and had plenty of company, but I'd been told by locals that it would be safer for me to stay in a 1st class coach. The toilet had no toilet paper or soap powder. But I got used to such conditions in the Balkans, so I carry my toilet supplies on such trips. My coach was marked for non-smokers, but smoking was allowed in the walkway. On my return trip, the wastebaskets were overflowing and empty beer bottles were rolling on the floor with leftover food hidden behind the seat cushions. I was disappointed because this train came only from Bucharest. Apparently the coaches are not cleaned after each route. My compartment windows were dirty on both rides. I had to pull down the windows each time I took photographs. In Braşov, I had to queue up for an hour to purchase an advance seating reservation, although only one-third of the seats were occupied both ways in the first-class coach.

My cousin Lencsi and her son Csaba picked me up at the railroad station and took me by car to Tărlungeni. After a good sleep, I walked through their narrow but long orchard and sinfully, like Adam, tasted the fruits from each tree. The ripe Batul apples, local pears, and plums reminded me of the most delicious fruit taste that I had missed since my childhood. I just could not stop tasting and eating more and more until I was full.

Lencsi showed me the root cellar that was filled with the excess fruits, after 200 liters of apple wine had been fermented for the family. I admired her resourcefulness: how she manages the household for three men, three cats, one dog, and a number of chickens. She usually fattens some pigs, for which she needs potatoes for feed. Therefore, she takes some share-cropping work with the local cooperative farm. She also makes ladies' dresses for herself and others.

During my first afternoon in Tărlungeni, Lencsi and I visited the cemetery and did some weeding on neglected plots. We also picked up ready-made mititei meat so we could grill that evening the well-seasoned Romanian sausages and eat these with mustard and bread, washing it down with beer or wine. The butcher, Endre Bálint, dictated down the mititei recipe so that I might be able to prepare it in the USA.

Later that day I visited the priest Levente Székely, of the local Lutheran congregation. He let me browse through some birth and baptismal records of my ancestors to complete the search for my Transylvanian roots. Most of my ancestors came from large families. 100 to 150 years ago it was common to have 8–10 children, but only about half of these reached adulthood. The Lutheran church in Tărlungeni was 175 years old the year of this visit, but they had already built their first church in 1513, followed in 1759–1761 by their second church. The latter church, because of earthquake damage, had to be replaced in 1821 by the present one.

In the evening, my Uncle Sándor Albert's family came over from Braşov for a visit. With the help of a few drinks we recalled the events of the old days, some worse, some better, than those of today. We also made plans to visit Cehetel, the Alberts' ancestral town, on Saturday.

The next day I was taken by cousin Lencsi's family to the Bran castle to follow Dracula's footsteps. I described my findings in Chapter Five. On the way back, we stopped at a restaurant in Braşov for dinner and then shopped for food in the local market. We also visited my cousin Zoli's daughter Kristina and her family, where we ate some pastry and drank sour cherry liquor, called vişinata — one of my favorite drinks.

While on the road close to Tărlungeni, I observed the potato harvest. The rows of potatoes were turned over by a plow and the potatoes were hand-picked with the aid of special pitchforks, where the individual fork fingers are fairly close together to allow the sift-

Figure 95. The Unitarian minister's home in Cehețel, with beehives at the lower right and two satellite dishes on the roof to provide television program transmissions to about 70 homes.

ing out of the soil and the separation of the tubers. To avoid stabbing the tubers, the fork fingers end in small balls. The cooperative farm that planted and cultivated the potato fields gives 20% of the crop to the harvesters. We have seen many city folks, especially pensioners and gypsies, checking the already harvested fields for overlooked tubers. Some had already filled their sacks and were headed home or to the market with their wheelbarrows.

The next day, Saturday, was reserved for potato harvesting by Lencsi's family. So I was taken by Uncle Sándor's family to Cehețel, my early childhood residence which I had not seen for many years. Our car and its passengers suffered on the last 11 kilometers of the unpaved road that had obviously been neglected for some time. — I was pleasantly impressed to find the road signs and town name signs bilingual in the area inhabited by Seklers, now called Harghita and Covasna Counties. But the poverty that my brother Seklers had to live with was obvious. It was apparent that the Government neglected the area inhabited almost exclusively by the Hungarian-speaking ethnic minority. The condition of the roads and the lack of public transportation (buses or trains) reflected my assumption. By keeping the ethnic minority under substandard conditions, the Government achieves the goal set by the Ceaușescu regime: force the ethnic minorities to leave the country, or assimilate them into the Romanian population. So, many people left these villages to find livelihood in the cities, where with inter-marriages to Romanians they lose their ethnic identities. For example, the population of the town of Cehețel, where I was raised to age 6, shrank from 340 citizens to 170 in 21 years. Almost all the young people left, while the elderly stayed to cultivate the land. Although natural gas occurs in the outskirts of this town, it is not allowed to be used in the local villages; instead it is pumped far away to be used elsewhere.

We only visited with a few old-time friends; all my other relatives had died or left the area. My grandmother's orchard and garden stayed in Uncle Sándor's family, so we picked some plums and apples from the trees and ate these on the grass with our sandwiches. What a joy it was for me to sit on the grass in my childhood backyard.

The local Unitarian communitiy had just celebrated the 1,100th anniversary of the Hungarians settling in the area. During the all-day festivities, they installed a new church wall and a beautifully carved gate to the churchyard. The minister (Szombatfalvi)(Fig. 93c) himself is a talented wood carver, and gave me some of his carvings as souvenirs. I was impressed with how

Figure 96. Potato harvest in Pădureni (Besenyö). Potatoes are the most important staple for both humans and some of their domestic animals.

he is serving the small community by showing a good example in modern agrotechniques, vegetable cultivation, and beekeeping (Fig. 95). On our return trip, we stopped near Tîrgu Secuiesc (Székelykeresztur) and purchased two wicker baskets from local gypsy craftsmen. — My day ended with an excellent dinner at József Albert's house in Braşov.

Sunday was reserved for visiting in Pădureni (Besenyö), the small village hidden behind the mountain, close to Sfăntu Gheorghe (Sepsiszentgyörgy). The last time I had seen it I was a teenager. I suspected that I might find more relatives with my last name here. I was glad to have Aunt Anna (Demeter) joining us. She served as my best still-living source of information on these relatives. Her Romanian husband had died a long time ago. She enjoyed the task of assisting me.

Again, the last few kilometers were driven over unpaved roads. Our relatives were harvesting the potato crop (Fig. 96), their most important staple food. Only my retired Uncle Gábor (Koszta Rab), about 80 years old, was not in the fields. He and his wife were visiting from Bucharest. We had a lot to catch up on because I had not seen him since 1940.

My suspicion paid off when I discovered six men and two unmarried women, whose last names were Koszta Rab, and all were related to me. So my family tree chart was about completed at the end of my visit there. The branch of our family that settled in Pădureni kept the original spelling of the family name.

On our return trip, we stopped in Sfăntu Gheorghe and visited with the 84-year-old Aunt Lujza and her daughter's (Ibolya Rodé) family. Aunt Lujza was the only Communist Party member in our extended family and had been such since the late 1930s. Most relatives just smiled on her Marxist preachings and gave up on arguing with her. Because of her past as a member of the illegal Party, I was told that she now enjoys a "padded" pension from the Government.

That evening I packed my belongings, all the many gifts received from relatives, and my purchases. In the early morning I made my sandwiches for the long train ride back to Budapest. Lencsi and her son Attila took me by car to the Braşov railroad station.

It was a long ride back to Budapest, but I had the compartment all to myself for 10 hours and thus had enough time for a recollection of my short trip packed with pleasant happenings. The view from my train window gave me a cross-section of southern Transylvania, as I am trying to recollect it here.

In the Braşov and Sibiu area along the southern Transylvanian Alps, I observed a number of communities built by the Hungarian or the Saxon population. The Saxons built well-planned towns with paved streets and sidewalks. Their Lutheran church was often built into a church/fortress (Fig. 39) located in the middle of the town and usually on a hill for better defense against invading armies. Even their individual houses were built for easy defense. The front housewall faced the sidewalk, with tall masonry walls for gate support and with high well-closed heavy wooden or iron gates that could accommodate the hay-filled wagons. Originally these towns were inhabited exclusively by Saxons who had their own school system, often run by their Parish. Today, most of the formerly vacated Saxon villages are inhabited by Gypsies and Romanians transplanted from the Provinces of Moldova or Oltenia, with very few elderly Saxons still living there.

The typical Transylvanian-Hungarian (including Sekler) villages include one or two white-washed churches with high steeples, some built for defense as a fortress church (Fig. 40), normally located on the highest point of the village, surrounded by the cemetery. On the hilly sides of the village are apple and plum orchards, and occasionally vineyards, and farther back on steeper hills are the hayfields and pastures surrounded by forests. The houses are normally lined up in the valley along a main road that parallels a creek. Most of the houses are made of red brick, with red-tile roofs. The property is fenced in by wood boards. Normally there are small flower gardens in front and larger fruit and vegetable gardens in the back. In the valley we find fields planted with corn, potatoes, beets, alfalfa, and clover. The corn fields often are bordered by tall stems of sunflower, and yellow pumpkins are raised between the corn stalks. The latter are used to feed the cattle and pigs. Behind the houses are the vegetable gardens and further back are some grapes, walnut trees, raspberries, and red currents.

Beautiful sunflower fields are common where a seed press is available to produce cooking oil. Sugar beet fields are abundant where a sugar refinery is close-by.

Where the creek is large enough or ponds and lakes are available, a lot of geese are raised, especially for their pricey liver. The Sekler folks at Odorheiul Secuiesc are well-known for their special skills in making wood-framed flour sifters with the screen made of horse-tail hair. Almost all the men-folk do some wood processing, and often carving, especially in the winter months. Many families keep bees to obtain honey and wax for home use and for extra income.

The Transylvanian-Romanians, when living in a mixed-ethnic population village, usually have their houses located on the higher parts of the town, with their colorful church surrounded by their cemetery. This is how I found it to be in Tărlungeni, where the two native groups — Hungarians and Romanians — always lived in peace with each other. Their school system allows education in both languages, and their public school has bilingual signs — an example that should be followed by many other communities in Transylvania. Inter-ethnic marriages between Romanians and Hungarians are common. I found among my own relatives that, from among those who found jobs only in the Romanian cities, outside Transylvania, about 50% married Romanians, and in the Transylvanian mixed-population communities, about 25% to 30% married Romanians. Most of the children from such inter-ethnic marriages spoke only Romanian.

Some historians believe that the fact that the Romanian community, in a village with a mixed-ethnic population, is located on the higher ground, and the Hungarians in the lower parts of the valley, along the creeks or rivers (Figs. 93a and 93b), is a proof of the later arrival of the Romanians, after the best parts of the valley had already been inhabited by the Hungarians.

23 — Mixing Useful Chores With Fun

My philosophy on how to be successful in life can be expressed in a 4-word slogan: "Do it, but now." This slogan was painted on a batik banner for my office wall by my daughter Eva after she completed High School. Because I used this slogan on her whenever she tried to postpone needed work as a teenager, she gave me the banner as a reminder of those times.

I had a number of schoolmates and, later, colleagues who were more talented than I, and could have been really successful in life, but they never learned to get organized in their everyday life and never prepared long-range plans which they stuck to. They often jumped from one chore to another before completing the first one. The Germans have a good term for these folks: they say such a person does not have the sitzfleisch ("sitting flesh") to finish a task. I often used this expression with my students, as well as the phrase I learned while working in Costa Rica: "No Mañana Please!" (=Don't wait until tomorrow.) Procrastination kills progress!

Those persons are fortunate, who are able to consider their professional work as part of their hobbies, as I am. Throughout my teaching career I tried to instill in my students this philosophy: "Try to live for your profession, not only to make a living from it."

My everyday routine for a typical day may give insight on how I utilize my precious minutes and hours both at home and in my office. I usually get up only at 6:30 because I need my 7 hours of sleep to manage my daily chores with only 2 half-mugs of coffee. One half-mug regular instant is ready in 2 minutes in the microwave and is cooled and improved with one half-mug of low fat milk and one packet of sweetener. I mix my own "sugar- and fat-free" breakfast cereal in a one-gallon plastic jar that lasts me for about a month. After adding one packet of sweetener, I drench it with milk and heat it for about 20 seconds in the microwave. For the cereal I often substitute two waffles, spread with some margarine and jelly or maple syrup, or with any of the breakfast rolls or croissants that are in reach. For a better morning start, I often drink some orange juice.

Because I already have taken my shower in the evening, I just have to wash and shave in the morning. The latter is done with an electric shaver that needs recharging once a week and is also good on European 220 volt current. Because, usually, I am not satisfied with having left part of my whiskers, I moisten my face with a bar of soap and keep the soap layer on while brushing my teeth. After washing off the soap, I finish the details, especially around my mustache, with a disposable razor. I like the smell of clove oil, which I had used for many years in my entomological practice. So, with a few drops of clove oil, some distilled water, and alcohol, I make my own aftershave lotion. The ladies around me never objected to the odor of my aftershave. The sweet spice smell might have made them hungry.

During my shaving routine, I have time to think about my chores for the day ahead. So I scribble notes on my most important tasks for the day. I normally also check my home engagement calendar to complement my chore list. To find parking, I get to my office around 7:50. If weather permits, I may walk in (10 minutes each way) around 7:30 or 8:30 to avoid the exhaust fumes from the ever-increasing 8:00 a.m. traffic. After unloading my briefcase that always has some folders with manuscripts and other jobs that I completed at home the previous evening or during the weekend, I display my work list near my telephone and check it against my office engagement calendar. Next, I respond to the messages left on my voice mail, prepare my mail for the morning pick-up, and complete some of the tasks on my work list. Even after retirement, I often receive requests to review articles and to write reference letters for former students who are seeking jobs or are being considered for promotion. After 30 years of teaching numerous courses and actively pursuing research at my university, I still have extensive files on the students who formerly took my courses and/or completed research in our laboratory.

I drive or walk home for a lunch that is made of left-overs or sandwiches with salads and fruits. I envy Tili, who can "afford" to have a small glass of wine after lunch. I can't, because I need to go back to work, and alcohol will make me sleepy and slow me down. So, instead, I have my second mug of the same milk-coffee as at breakfast. The afternoon in my office is spent finishing up the left-over chores from my list, but I am often interrupted by persons who need my advice or help, some from across the country.

What I am not able to finish in the office, I do at home. I have found a pleasant system for completion of many of my routine professional chores. I do these at the end of our dining table. This is a strategic location because I can work while listening to popular music on the radio or on records, or even watch TV with "half an eye" from the same seat. I also have a good view of both our front and back yards. Actually, I planned the location of the dining room and living room picture windows with these conveniences in mind.

I like to grow vegetables and flowers. I also prepare certain Transylvanian dishes for special occasions. Tili, who already has had 43 years to learn these from me, insists that she, as a native of Budapest, can't do as good a job on these dishes as I, "the boy from Transylvania", can. One of these dishes is an "Eggplant Spread", the other is my "Improved Transylvanian Cheese and Cornmush Casserole". The latter recipe is given in the Addendum.

On the days when I don't walk to my office, I do my physical exercise with some garden chores or during the winter in my greenhouse, and with such routine work as bringing firewood into the boiler room for further drying and the dry wood upstairs to the fireplace. I am the fire tender, the ash cleaner, the garbage sorter, and in general the disposal person for all materials to be taken outside. Tili, the city girl, runs the inside of the house. I, the farmer's grandson, do most of the outside chores. My early training in horticulture must have predestined me for such a work-division. We collect all the organic materials from the kitchen in a 5-gallon plastic can with a top. This is kept outside in the garage next to the kitchen door. Before Tili starts smelling the decomposing greens and complains, I empty the can on the "fresh" compost pile and cover it up so the neighbors will not object to the acrid smell of decomposing grass clippings mixed with kitchen residues. The fireplace ash also ends up on the compost pile. My "old" compost pile is layered inside shipping pallets to be used the following year for improvement of the soil in our flower and vegetable beds.

Every Saturday morning it takes about an hour to water my greenhouse plants and to refill my 8–10 one-gallon plastic bottles with tap water. The water is to be used one week later, after most of the chlorine has evaporated and the water has stabilized at the temperature of the greenhouse. I enjoy, both for recreation and for practical use, propagating plants. So I divide my stock plants, root shoots in water and in pots, repot, and seed as needed. I raise around 150 to 200 plants, many to flowering stage for decorating our rooms, to provide for friends, and for the flower beds in front of the house or for the vegetable garden. These are some of my "useful" recreational activities.

During the summer I water twice weekly the plants in the four plant boxes, as well as the several potted plants kept hanging or sitting on our deck. During drought, I also water the flower and vegetable beds, the lawn, the shrubs, and the smaller trees in our yard. I stopped spraying my grapes with insecticide, but catch the Japanese beetles with a baited trap. Normally I have to mow the grass with my 8 HP riding mower every 10 to 14 days. This is a 45-minute to one-hour job. The clippings are dumped from the grass catcher directly into the "fresh" compost pile. The flower, rock, and vegetable gardens need periodic weeding, but I often end up with more weeds than I like, especially when I return from extended out-of-town trips. While on such trips, I depend on student help for lawn care and watering.

The trees in our back yard need more attention than I like. I kept almost all the trees that were originally on the empty lot in the backyard, except the ones that were on the site for house building and the ones in the front yard which had to be back-filled with a thick layer of soil. The original trees in the back yard included some wild cherries that died from black knot fungus, and I inherited 8 black walnut trees which provided some shelter from the sun for our house, but I had half of those removed.

Although old walnut trees are valuable for the wood-processing industry, they are a nuisance in the yard. They are the last to leaf out in late spring and the first to start shedding leaves, starting in mid-summer. The nuts (because of their strong taste) are not valued for eating by most people, but they mess up the yard for over one month in the fall and get in the way of lawn mowers. The husks, besides staining the picker's fingers, are filled with huskfly maggots that most people, except entomologists, do not appreciate. The worst is a toxic substance released by the far-reaching roots of the walnut trees that kills tomato plants, apples, and other trees in the yard.

All the broken-off and cut-down tree branches and trunks end up in two piles in my back yard — one for kindling, the other for firewood. After drying for a year or so, the kindling is broken up, packed in cardboard boxes, and carried into the boiler room before the fall rains arrive. To start my fireplace fire, I place the kindling over newspaper rolls made by Tili. The firewood usually comes from my back yard,

before from my farm. We truly enjoy having a fire in the fireplace on cold nights; it supplements our central gas-heating.

I also enjoy raising vegetables that are not normally available in the local stores. One of these is the Jerusalem artichoke. This plant would be better called sunchoke because it has nothing to do with Jerusalem and is not related to the artichoke. It is actually related to the sunflower, and I consider it a much underutilized miracle plant. It is ideal for elderly and/or lazy people because it does not require weeding, hoeing, replanting, or storing. It grows from 6 to 8 feet high and will not allow weeds to compete with it. For six years it has come back in the spring, no matter how careful I am to pick the last tubers from the ground. I can go out in the middle of the winter and dig some fresh tubers from the frozen ground. The fleshy tubers taste like water chestnuts and can be eaten raw in salads after only brushing them under water, or boiled, baked, cooked in soups or stews, etc. The sweet tuber of the "sunchoke" contains inulin and can be eaten by diabetics. In the fall I make a number of women happy, including Tili, with bouquets of "sunchoke" flowers. I also use the stout woody stems for kindling in my fireplace.

Other unique plants in my vegetable garden are the acid-flavored French sorrels, kohlrabies, Hungarian pumpkins, yellow peppers, and celeriac. The latter is considered an aphrodisiac by some European wives, who often prepare soup or fresh salad from it for their "aging" husbands. I tried its potency on my giant Belgian meat rabbits during World War II when the borrowed male rabbit repeatedly was not accepted by my females. So, at the suggestion of a farmer's wife, I fed celeriac leaves to the reluctant crew. After that, I enjoyed having many baby rabbits. Most Americans are not familiar with this unique plant.

I have been asked a few times throughout my life if I ride a horse, ski, or play tennis or golf. I have to say no to each of these. "How come?" was often the next question. So, here is my response. When I was about 5 years old, some teenagers in the village wanted to play a trick on me, and put me on the bare back of a working farm horse. I did not want to ride, but I was their captive. They told me that this was my chance to learn horseback riding and I should just hang on to the mane of the horse. They whacked the poor horse, and he started galloping with me in the fields until I was shaken off. A big loud laugh followed my "performance". This drastic introduction to horseback riding turned me off from future experimenting with horses.

As for skiing, I owned an old pair of skis for only a few weeks, as described in Chapter 8. I never tried those out. So later, I had no chance to be introduced to skiing. One reason was economical. The cost of the equipment and facilities and the travel to mountainous parts of Hungary was too high for my budget. My other reason was that I was too busy while holding a job and attending the University after World War II.

A few times I tried to play tennis with other beginners, but I have never practiced long enough, for lack of time. I thought if I have to sweat, why not do something useful in the yard or around the house, *e.g.* chopping wood? Golfing was out of the question for my generation in Communist Hungary. We were told that every inch of land had to be put to the cultivation of food crops, not to be wasted for a golf course. Later, in the United States, I found a good book, or my gardening hobby, more exciting than golf.

My friends call me a "born optimist". But I had such a fortunate life that it made me an optimist. I learned early in life to appreciate things as they come. Almost every major bad event in my life, as it turned out later, was for my own good. For example, when the Principal of the Romanian High School in Bucharest, in 1939, declined to register me in the school because of my Hungarian ethnic background, at first I felt bad. But it turned out that his refusal opened up new and better opportunities for me. After this event, my family left Roma-

nia, and my chances for a better life increased with our immigration to Hungary. Also, when the auto repair shop owner in Budapest during the winter of 1941 declined to accept me for apprenticeship in auto mechanics, because I had only a 6-year elementary school education from Bucharest, I was disappointed and sad, but it turned out to be for my own good. After that, I enrolled for more schooling in Hungary, that benefited my entire life, for I was able to combine my professional work with my hobby.

I was arrested and jailed by the Nazis in December 1944. Surely I felt bad. But as it turned out, the jail was the safest place for me, as it enabled me to avoid being drafted and taken out of the country, to be used in the final defense of Nazi Germany.

When, in the fall of 1956, before our escape to Austria, Tili and I had to leave our five-month-old daughter, Eva, with Tili's parents for an uncertain time, we both felt very bad. As it turned out, that was the best choice we could have made for our baby's sake. Her life would have been endangered by our risky escape from Hungary, as described in Chapter 1.

In the Camp Kilmer refugee camp, near New Brunswick, New Jersey, in February 1957, we received the disappointing news that my Aunt Julishka's relatives in Connecticut had declined to sponsor my family's immigration to the United States. We were much discouraged and sad. Yet it was for our own good, because after that, the U.S. National Research Council signed our sponsorship papers. They gave me an opportunity to take my first intensive English language courses while they searched for a suitable job for me, for which I am eternally grateful.

In conclusion, I learned that every disappointing event could be to our benefit. So, now I have a philosophy to try to look at both sides of the coin and cheer up, knowing that the present bad event could turn out well for me in the long run.

Addenda

Follow-up on some of the main characters

Tili, after working part-time 16 years for the U.S. Department of Agriculture, retired and is running our household full-time, except when swimming or attending aerobics, computer, or other classes. Both of us like to travel, and we take trips whenever opportunities come up that do not interfere with my gardening hobby.

Eva (Kosztarab)(Fig. 97), has her own law office in Fairfax, Virginia. Her husband, Kenneth M. Kastner, is an environmental attorney in D.C. They live in Falls Church and are raising our two grandsons, the 12-year-old Gregory Michael and 10-year-old Matthew Joseph.

Attila Bessko, Eva's smuggler, also escaped to Austria in 1957. After studying in Vienna for two years, he came to the U.S. with Washington Bishop Hannan's sponsorship, who also obtained for him a scholarship to the Catholic University. But after six months with us, he took a job in his profession in Baltimore, rather than pursuing University studies. He was soon drafted and served in France. After service, he took a job in electronics in Montreal, Canada, but after 10 years he withdrew his pension fund and purchased a sailboat in England, that he operates for tourists out of Antigua during the Winter and Spring. He resides in Sao Paulo, Brazil, where he married and has one daughter. He visits with us occasionally. On his invitation we spent a week on his boat in 1993. As a "free-spirited" man, he prefers a variety of freelance work rather than a regular job. Only a "free-spirited" person like Attila would have taken the risky adventure to help smuggle our Eva out to the Free World.

I visited with the **Dékáns** in 1978 while they both were still in good health and photographed them. Both have since passed away.

Figure 97. Author with daughter Eva, reminiscing after 40 years at the Sopron Railroad Station, site of her escape from behind the Iron Curtain in 1957. (See Chapter 2.)

Figure 98. Baby Eva's caretaker in 1957, Grete Schalling, with Eva during our visit to Salzburg, Austria, in 1974.

The forest ranger, **Hedl**, and his wife were glad to meet me in person for the first time in 1994. They were pensioners when I visited with them in Brennerberg and photographed the couple. By the late 1970s, when I was able to visit Helenenschacht, Austria, both **Stubnas** were deceased.

We were able to visit a few times with the **Shallings** in Salzburg, express our thanks, and spend some time with them. Both died in the 1970s. Eva was happy to get to know the woman who was her caretaker when she was a baby in Austria in 1957 (Fig. 98).

Both **Uncle Zsiga** and his wife **Vilma** lived in the old Kosztarab house in Tărlungeni. They passed away in 1985. Their daughter **Lencsi** and her family live in the remodeled old house now. **Zoltán**, their son, and his Saxon wife, **Liane**, emigrated to Germany and live in Regensburg. Lencsi and Zoltán are my cousins related to me through both of their parents.

Uncle Sándor and his four sons, two with families, live in Braşov. Sándor, my mother's brother, is the oldest surviving and closest relative at present. His youngest son, Zoltán, prepared the ethnographic illustrations for this book.

I have been corresponding with **Iby Braun** (Mrs. Lewin) who is widowed, and who now lives in Tel Aviv. She brought me up to date on the fate of the Braun family, as included at the end of Chapter 8.

Seklers' (Székelys') Anthem
(Free-form translation from Hungarian)

Who knows what fate has in store for us
Taking the rough road in the darkness of the night.
Oh Csaba, our Prince, lead us your people
Again to victory astride the milky way.

Midst the struggle of the nations
The tiny band of rocklike Székelys
Seem doomed to crumble into dust...

Our heads withstand the endless
Inundations of the roaring seas...
For pity's sake, oh my God
Do not abandon Transylvania!

The "Transylvanian Spirit"

I have found the native Transylvanians, no matter to which ethnic group they belong, to be different from their own ethnic brothers living in the lowlands. The Hungarians (including Seklers and Changos) are psychologically different from their relatives in Hungary. This became obvious when my family moved out from Transylvania and settled in the Budapest area. The native Transylvanian Romanians are different in their philosophy, their attitude, and their everyday life, from those in the Bucharest area or in Moldova. I heard from my cousin Zoltán in Regensburg, that the Transylvanian Saxons were much different in their character from their brothers in Germany.

It appears to me that the centuries of isolation in the mountains or highlands of Transylvania from the main body of their major ethnic group made them different. Their dependence on each other, and the several barbarian and other foreign incursions into Transylvania, produced a different type of people, with what I like to call the "Transylvanian Spirit". We got closer to each other in our characters, much closer than to our ethnic brothers living outside Transylvania. Our common past and destiny brought out of us the "Transylvanian human race" that learned to survive all kinds of political and economic upheavals. It introduced the spirit of helping each other, that is probably best expressed in the custom of "Kaláka": where the community gets together in voluntary co-operative work to help a family in need (*e.g.*, rebuilding a fire-destroyed home; harvesting the crops of a family left without menfolk, *etc.*). The common fate taught us to appreciate each other, respect the other's religions, and when needed, unite against our common enemies invading Transylvania. We lived in peace with each other for a long time until outside political forces tried to place our fatherland under their domination and attempted to force a wedge between us.

Even during my trip in 1996, I did not find problems between native Transylvanian Hungarians and Romanians. They lived peacefully together, as in Tărlungeni, where the population is about 50-50 Romanian and Chango-Hungarian. There are ethnic problems only in the large cities, such as Cluj and Tîrgu Mureş, because of the large numbers of recently transplanted Romanian settlers. The latter somewhat still rootless people look down on the native Transylvanian ethnic Hungarians. They probably do not feel secure enough in their new homes and jobs.

This is the reason that the pogrom could have happened against the native Hungarian population in Tîrgu Mureş during 1990, when the famous Hungarian writer, András Sütö, was almost blinded by the incited and misled Romanian mob (Marosi 1990). The local police's arrival to control the Romanian crowd was intentionally delayed, probably on orders from Bucharest, and when finally present, the police still allowed the beating and maiming of many Hungarian intellectuals. Only Hungarians and Gypsies were prosecuted and jailed after the attrocities of the Romanians. It was apparent that the Bucharest government was looking for an outlet for the frustration of the crowds, because of the political and economic crisis that followed the toppling of Ceauşescu's government. Again, the ethnic minorities were blamed, as so often in the past, for the problems. It is time for all native Transylvanians to stand up and protect themselves from outside interference into their affairs.

A Kosztarab Family Tree, somewhat "pruned"

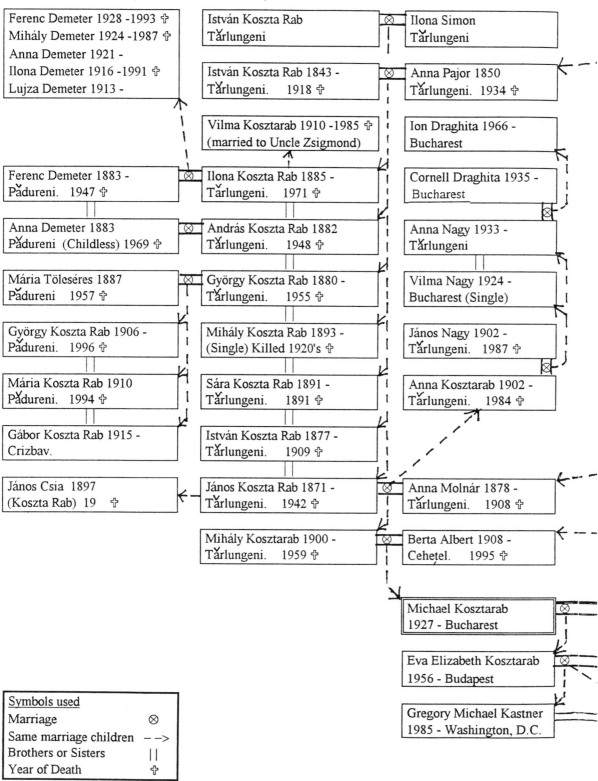

Ferenc Demeter 1928 -1993 ✚
Mihály Demeter 1924 -1987 ✚
Anna Demeter 1921 -
Ilona Demeter 1916 -1991 ✚
Lujza Demeter 1913 -

István Koszta Rab
Tărlungeni

Ilona Simon
Tărlungeni

István Koszta Rab 1843 -
Tărlungeni.   1918 ✚

Anna Pajor 1850
Tărlungeni. 1934 ✚

Vilma Kosztarab 1910 -1985 ✚
(married to Uncle Zsigmond)

Ion Draghita 1966 -
Bucharest

Ferenc Demeter 1883 -
Pădureni.   1947 ✚

Ilona Koszta Rab 1885 -
Tărlungeni.   1971 ✚

Cornell Draghita 1935 -
Bucharest

Anna Demeter 1883
Pădureni (Childless) 1969 ✚

András Koszta Rab 1882
Tărlungeni.   1948 ✚

Anna Nagy 1933 -
Tărlungeni

Mária Töleséres 1887
Pădureni   1957 ✚

György Koszta Rab 1880 -
Tărlungeni.   1955 ✚

Vilma Nagy 1924 -
Bucharest (Single)

György Koszta Rab 1906 -
Pădureni.   1996 ✚

Mihály Koszta Rab 1893 -
(Single) Killed 1920's ✚

János Nagy 1902 -
Tărlungeni.   1987 ✚

Mária Koszta Rab 1910
Pădureni.   1994 ✚

Sára Koszta Rab 1891 -
Tărlungeni.   1891 ✚

Anna Kosztarab 1902 -
Tărlungeni.   1984 ✚

Gábor Koszta Rab 1915 -
Crizbav.

István Koszta Rab 1877 -
Tărlungeni.   1909 ✚

János Csia 1897
(Koszta Rab) 19   ✚

János Koszta Rab 1871 -
Tărlungeni.   1942 ✚

Anna Molnár 1878 -
Tărlungeni.   1908 ✚

Mihály Kosztarab 1900 -
Tărlungeni.   1959 ✚

Berta Albert 1908 -
Cehetel.   1995 ✚

Michael Kosztarab
1927 - Bucharest

Eva Elizabeth Kosztarab
1956 - Budapest

Gregory Michael Kastner
1985 - Washington, D.C.

Symbols used
Marriage   ⊗
Same marriage children   – –>
Brothers or Sisters | |
Year of Death   ✚

A Kosztarab Family Tree, continued

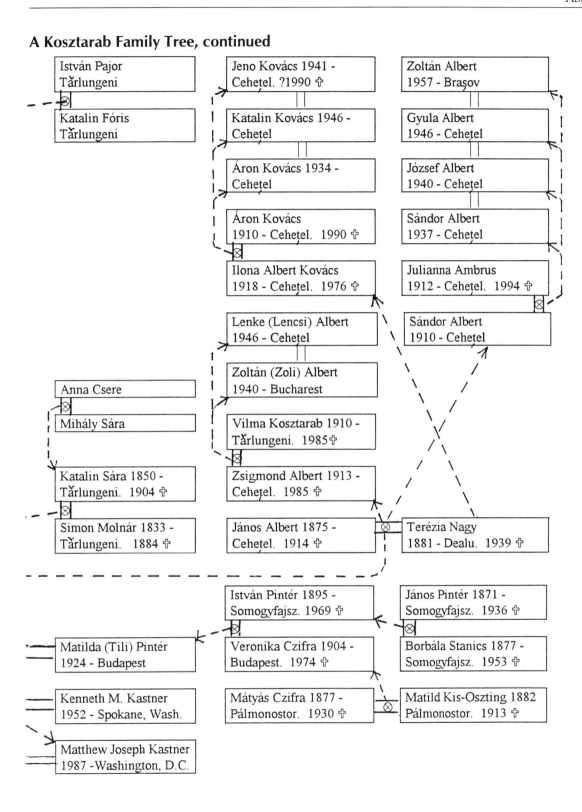

Transylvanian "Soul Food" Recipe
(CORN MUSH-CHEESE CASSEROLE - Serves 12)

Ingredients:
20 oz. corn meal, not self-rising. I use yellow Quaker's corn meal.
12 cups water
2 tbs. salt
12 oz. grated sharp cheddar cheese
12 oz. grated Mozzarella cheese
8 oz. light sour cream
8 oz. bacon, fried, drained, and diced
2 medium onions, finely chopped and sautéed (light brown)
16 oz. Polish sausage, sliced
2 tsp. sweet paprika (Hungarian)

Directions:
1. Bring water and salt to a boil in a 7 quart, or larger, pot.
2. Gradually sprinkle corn meal into boiling water while stirring vigorously with a whisk.
3. Cook corn meal 30 minutes, stirring often with a wooden spoon or spatula to avoid sticking. Add boiling water from a teapot if mush becomes too thick while cooking; ready when mush sticks to spoon turned upside down.
4. Preheat oven to 350 degrees. Grease two 12 x 8 x 2 pans.
5. Spread mush into half-inch layer in bottom of pans with two large spoons. Dip spoons in sour cream to avoid sticking.
6. Spread small amount of sour cream on top of mush, layer half of sautéed onion, half of cooked bacon pieces, and half of grated cheeses.
7. Spread another layer of corn mush and repeat the other layers.
8. Top with a thin layer of mush, sprinkle top with paprika, garnish with sausage slices.
9. Place on middle shelf of oven.
10. Bake for 20 minutes at 350 degrees.

Serve with a bowl of tossed green salad, beer, or wine.

Leftover casserole can be refrigerated or frozen. The unused corn mush can be served hot with cold milk or cold with hot milk for breakfast or snack. This is often the breakfast food for Transylvanians.
(Copyedited by Donna and Avas B. Hamon.)

NOTE: In Transylvania the corn mush is layered with sheep cheese only. Due to customs and economic conditions no other ingredients or sausage are used.

Romania — Why not follow the Swiss example?

The Romanian government is striving toward integration into the European Community (EC). But there are stipulations in the EC Charter for a member nation, such as living in peace with its neighbors and providing equal rights for its ethnic minorities. According to the latest (1977) official Romanian census, there were more than 1.6 million ethnic Hungarians (actually close to 2.5 million) living in Romania; thus they are one of the largest ethnic minority populations in Europe. These people, who are my brothers and sisters, were treated as second-rate citizens in their place of birth for almost 80 years. Romania, to become worthy of EC membership, will have to abide by the EC Charter and improve on the treatment of the ethnic minorities forced to live there since 1918.

A good example for the Romanian government, in treating their ethnic minorities, is provided by Switzerland with regard to the Rhaetian ethnic minority (Stephens, 1976). These people, less than 1% of the Swiss population, speak Romansch, an ancient language derived from vernacular Latin. Most of the Rhaetians live in the mountainous Canton of Graubünden. The Census of 1970 listed only 50,339 people who spoke the Romansch language in all of Switzerland. But already by 1938, the Swiss Federal Constitution had been amended to include Romansch as one of the four national languages, and in the Canton of Graubünden, where 23.4% of the population spoke Romansch in 1970, it is one of the three official languages. In Graubünden, the civil servants are required to master at least two of the official languages of Switzerland plus Romansch. In the districts where Romansch is the principal language, it is also the medium of instruction in the primary schools. Romansch is taught at four Swiss universities and their teachers are trained at the College in Chur.

Laws and regulations are published in Romansch at Federal expense. Official business can be transacted in Romansch, and defendants have the right to be tried in their own language. Communities with bi-national populations have the right to use Romansch, together with German, on place-names and street signs. The 1990 pogrom in Tîrgu Mureş against the Hungarian ethnics (Marosi 1990) started because a local pharmacy put up a bilingual sign "Farmacie-Patika" in Romanian and Hungarian. The city until recent times was inhabited by a Hungarian-speaking majority.

The Romansch language benefits from Federal subsidies, including publication of textbooks and other cultural means. Radio programs of Studio Zürich since 1972 include daily news bulletins and weekly features broadcast in Romansch, and The Romansch Radio Corporation has its own program. Since 1963, Swiss television has been broadcasting in Romansch and in 1976 began the inclusion of a thrice-weekly current affairs program, with other weekly features.

The Rhaetian people of Graubünden are respected by their Federal Government, and are allowed to develop and strengthen their culture as they choose. A proverb much quoted in Graubünden is: "An ounce of Goodwill outweighs a ton of Good Reason" (Stephens, 1976).

Does Romania have the one ounce of Goodwill to change its policy toward the ethnic Hungarians? Let's hope so, now that the former Communist Iliescu's government has been replaced.

Cited References

Ara-Kovács, A. 1990. *Antiszemitizmus és a romániai holocaust.* (=Antisemitism and the Romanian holocaust) Erdélyi Magyarság. 1(2): 56–57.

Bako, L. and W. Solyóm-Fekete. 1969. Hungarians in Rumania and Transylvania. Washington, D.C.: U. S. Government Printing Office. 192p.

Beke, Gy. 1980. *Fölöttünk a havasok.* Dacia, Napoca: Családi Kronika. 244p.

Binder, P. 1994. *Az erdélyi magyar evangélikus egyházközségek és iskolák története és névtára (1542–1860).* D & H Soft Kft. Brassó 184p.

Cadzow, J.F., A. Ludanyi, and L.J. Elteto. 1983. *Transylvania — The roots of ethnic conflict.* Kent, Ohio: Kent State University Press. 368p.

Coşbuc, G. 1974. *Poezii.* Ion Creanga. Ed. Bucureşti. 176p.

de Kruif, P. 1926. *Microbe Hunters.* New York: Harcourt, Brace & Co. 363p. (In Hungarian).

Du Nay, A. 1977. *The Early History of the Rumanian Language.* Lake Bluff, Illinois: Jupiter Press. 275p.

Florescu, R. & R.T. McNally. 1973. *Dracula — A Biography of Vlad the Impaler* (1431–1476) (New York.) xiv+242p.

Gellérd, J. (ed.) 1996. *Ending the Storm.* Chico, California: Uniquest & Center for Free Religion. 222p.

Halmos, M. 1982. *The Truth About Transylvania.* Youngstown, Ohio: Authors Publ. 16p.

Illyés, E. 1982. *National Minorities in Romania — Change in Transylvania.* East European Monographs No. 112. Boulder Colorado. 355p.

Kazár, L. 1993. *Facts Against Fiction: Transylvania — Wallachian/Rumanian Homeland Since 70 BC?* Sydney, Australia: Forum of History Publ. 247p.

Kiss, K. 1988. *Tudományos tanácskozás az Akadémián — A moldvai csángó-magyarokrol.* Budapest: Magyar Nemzet. January 30: 1 p.

Kosztarab, M. 1984. Editorial: *A biological survey of the United States.* Science 223: 443.

Kosztarab, M. 1988. *Biological Diversity:* National Biological Survey. Proc. First Annual Symposium on the Natural History of Lower Tennessee & Cumberland River Valleys. The Center for Field Biol. of Land Between the Lakes.•Clarksville, Tenn.: Austin Peay State Univ., pp. 1–25.

Kosztarab, M. 1991. *Concluding remarks for the Symposium on Virginia's Endangered Species.* Pp. 631–633. In Virginia's Endangered Species. Blacksburg, Virginia: McDonald & Woodward Publ. Co.

Kosztarab, M. 1992. *Virginia's largest insect collection — A rich resource for biodiversity information.* Banisteria 1: 20–23.

Kosztarab, M. 1993a. *The Center for Systematics Collections at Virginia Polytechnic Institute and State University (1973–1991).* Virginia Journal of Science 44(1): 27–36.

Kosztarab, M. 1993b. *Our Virginia state insect: the tiger swallowtail butterfly.* The Virginia Butterfly Bull. 1(1): 3.

Kosztarab, M. 1996. *Scale Insects of Northeastern North America: identification, biology, and distribution.* Martinsville: Virginia Museum of Natural History. Spec. Publ. No. 3: 650p.

Kosztarab, M. and F. Kozár. 1978. *Scale Insects — Coccoidea.* In Fauna Hungariae (In Hungarian; English Summary). No. 131, Vol. 17, Part 22: 1–192.

Kosztarab, M. and F. Kozár. 1988. *Scale Insects of Central Europe.* Acad. Publ. (Hungary) and Junk Co. (Holland). 456p. Two editions.

Kosztarab, M. and C. W. Schaefer, eds. 1990. *Systematics of the North American Insects and Arachnids: Status and Needs.* Virginia Agricultural Experiment Station, Information Series 90–1: 247p.

Kövári, A. 1979. *The contemporary Rumanian National Myth. I - Introduction — Accident and Necessity in Romanian Nationalism.* Crossroads No. 1: 216–233. *II — The Rumanian National Mystery: Myth-Makers Under the Microscope.* Crossroads No. 3: 201–241. *III — The Rumanian National Mystery: Myth-Making in Everyday Life.* Crossroads No. 5: 18 pp.

Löte, L.L. (ed.) 1980. *Transylvania and the Theory of Daco-Roman — Rumanian Continuity.* Carpathian Observer 8(1): 112p.

McNally, R.T. and R. Florescu. 1972. *In Search of Dracula: A True History of Dracula and Vampire Legends.* Greenwich, Connecticut: New York Graphic Society. 224p.

Makkai, L. and A. Mócsí. 1987. *Erdély története* (History of Transylvania), *Vol. 1.* Budapest: Akad. Kiadó. 611p.

Makkai, L. and Z. Szász. 1987. *Erdély története* (History of Transylvania), *Vol. 2.— 1606 -tól 1830 -ig.* Budapest: Akad. Kiadó. pp. 617–1185.

Marosi, B. 1990. *Március 19: A terror napja Marosvásárhelyen.* (=March 19: The Day of Terror at Tîrgu Mureş) Romániai Magyar Szó, March 21.

Montgomery, J.F. 1947. *Hungary, the unwilling satellite.* New York: Devin-Adair Co. 281p.

Orbán, B. 1863-1873. *A Székelyföld Leirása - Történelmi, régészeti, természetrajzi s népismei szempontból.* (= The Description of the Land of the Seklers, History, Archeology, Natural History, and Ethnography.) Vol. I (1863), 240p.; Vol. II (1869), 163p.; Vol III (1869), 212+73p.; Vol. IV (1870), 226+63p.; Vol. V (1871), 248p; Vol. VI (1873), 448p. Pesti Könyvnyomda Rt. Budapest. Reprinted in 1981 by Bibliofilo Press, Firenze-München (with notes and additions by E. Illyés).

Panaitescu, P.P. 1991. *The German Stories About Vlad Tepes.* Pp. 185–196 In *Dracula:*

Essays on the Life and Times of Vlad Tepes, ed. K.W. Treptow. East European Monographs No. 323. New York: Columbia University Press. 336p.

Pascu, S. (ed). 1974. *Istoria Clujului.* Consiliul Popular al Municipiului Cluj. I. P. Cluj. 576p.

Rosetti, A. 1968. *Istoria limbii române de la origin pîna in secolul al XVII-lea.* Bucuresti: Editura Pentru Literatura.

Seton-Watson, R.W. 1963. *A History of the Roumanians — From Roman times to the completion of unity.* Reprinted by Archon Books Co. USA. 596p. First Edition by Cambridge University Press, 1934.

Sisa, S. 1990. *The Spirit of Hungary — Part III. The Turkish Era,* pp. 77–104. Part V. *A Nation Without Boundaries.* pp. 183–296. Cleveland, Ohio: Central Committee for Books and Education. Second Edition. Fifth Printing. 374p.

Sisa, I. 1993. *Nemzet Határok Nélkül.* Cleveland, Ohio: Árpád Könyvkiado Co. 256p.

Stadtmüller, G. 1980. *Die albanisch — rumänische Wanderungsbewegung (11–13 Jahrhundert).* Carpathian Observer 8(1): 74–85.

Stephens, M. 1976. *Linguistic Minorities in Western Europe.* Llandysul, Wales: Gomer Press. xxxv+796p.

Stoker, B. 1897. *Dracula.* London. With numerous new editions up to the present day.

Stroup, E.W. 1983. *From Horea-Cloşca to 1867: Some observations.* Pp. 128–147. SEE at Cadzov et al. 1983.

Szász, Z. 1987. *Erdély Története* (History of Transylvania) *Vol. 3. 1830 – tól napjainking* (from 1830 to date). Budapest: Akadémiai Kiadó. Pp. 1193–1945.

Tautu, L. 1967. *Catholics of the Rumanian Rite.* Pp. 720–721 In *New Catholic Encyclopedia, Vol. XII.* Washington, D.C.: Catholic University of America. 1255p.

Zathureczky, G. 1967. *Transylvania Citadel of the West.* Gainesville, Florida: AHLG Research Center Publ. 61p.

Index
Page numbers in italics indicate illustrations.

- E -

- H -

- M -

- T -

Wooden grave markers (Kopjafa) in a Sekler village.